SHAKESPEARE'S DRAMATIC LANGUAGE

SHAKESPEARE'S DRAMATIC LANGUAGE

ESSAYS BY *Madeleine Doran*

THE UNIVERSITY OF WISCONSIN PRESS

Published 1976

THE UNIVERSITY OF WISCONSIN PRESS
Box 1379, Madison, Wisconsin 53701

THE UNIVERSITY OF WISCONSIN PRESS, LTD.
70 Great Russell Street, London

First printing

Printed in the United States of America

For LC CIP information see the colophon
ISBN 0-299-07010-7

To the memory of HARDIN CRAIG

Contents

Acknowledgments

FOR THEIR kind permission to reprint, in whole or in part, essays in this volume, I wish to thank the following: for the essay on *Hamlet*, the Editor of the *Huntington Library Quarterly*; for the one on *Othello*, the Director of the Brown University Press; for the one on *King Lear*, the Director of the University of Chicago Press and Professor Milton Crane of the George Washington University; for the one on *Antony and Cleopatra*, the Editor of the *Queen's Quarterly*; for the Appendix on *Richard II* and *1 Henry IV*, the General Editor of the *Modern Language Review*. Full acknowledgment of copyright is made in a note to each of the five essays.

I wish to thank Professor Maurice Charney and a reader who asked to remain anonymous for their thoughtful criticism of the four essays in print and of the new essay on *Julius Caesar*. Their suggestions were very helpful to me in my revision of these five essays. So also have been those of Elizabeth Steinberg in her sensitive and meticulous editing of the copy for the University of Wisconsin Press.

For a Guggenheim Fellowship in 1967-68, for the generous allowances of time the University of Wisconsin has given me, and for the equally generous encouragement of my colleagues in the English Department and in the Institute for Research in the Humanities I am deeply grateful. I owe a special debt to the many young people in my classes who have been sharers with me in the never-ending discovery of Shakespeare.

Madeleine Doran

Madison, Wisconsin
13 April 1976

SHAKESPEARE'S DRAMATIC LANGUAGE

Shakespeare's
Dramatic Language

THOSE OF US who make our roomy home in Shakespeare never cease to wonder at his artistry. And each of us, in his own presumptuous way, is endlessly challenged to describe, analyze, and explain how Shakespeare does what he does. As if we could! Why not just let him do it? His plays, alive on the stage and in the hand for all these centuries, continue to demonstrate, over and over, the efficacy of his dramatic art. Still, our investigative and critical minds persist in asking, "How?" There is no simple answer, for the art is a complex one in which many special arts—theatrical, psychological, rhetorical, and poetic—co-operate. Moreover, criticism has its own artistic shape, depending on the times, the point of view it starts from, the temper of the critic. But we should not for these reasons hesitate to ask questions and to propose answers, with the intent of enlivening our perceptions and enlarging our understanding of Shakespeare's art.

My own special questioning was prompted by my growing sense, during years of reading and teaching Shakespeare and of seeing him played, that each of the plays, with the exception of the apprentice and collaborative few, has a distinctive quality, something peculiar to that play alone—a quality that is not altogether attributable to differences in plot,

3

theme, character, and setting, but something that feels different, or that sounds different to our ears, something as peculiar to the play as the music of any of Beethoven's mature symphonies or quartets is to that particular composition. Such a quality would seem to be in the style.

But of course language is the primary means in the theater, and the only means in reading, by which we apprehend plot, theme, characters, and even setting. It may be that the difference we feel from play to play is simply a demonstration of the truism that the whole is more than the sum of its parts. Yet in the great tragedies, at least, one feels that there is something not so accounted for, something common to the style of each play that transcends or underlies, as overtone or undertone—whichever way one chooses to put it—all the differences from situation to situation, theme to theme, character to character. Everything in *Lear*, no matter what character is speaking, sounds different from everything in *Antony and Cleopatra*, no matter the character. So I began looking for what in the language of any one of the great tragedies might be responsible for such harmony of effect, making it different from the harmony of any other.

I shall return to this special problem later. I wish first to examine some simple ways in which Shakespeare quite early makes style serve dramatic purposes, such as by enhancing a special quality of the story, and how he very soon learned to use style as a unifying device. Analyses of Shakespeare's style in a given play tend to be focussed on its characterizing function. I shall put more attention on something often neglected—that is, on its relation to situation and, especially, to the fable as a whole, not just on its local function of sharpening a particular situation.

Very early in his career Shakespeare showed skill in plotting, and great sensitivity to the particular qualities or possibilities—one might say "the genius"—of the stories he chose to dramatize. It is not surprising, therefore, that he soon learned to use language not merely to serve the plot but also to enhance the spirit of the story, that is, to bring out and emphasize something essential in it.

An early example is the treatment of the third play in the Yorkist-Lancastrian series, *3 Henry VI*. The rather loose structure of the play is imposed by the chronicles: a sequence of alternating military victories and defeats until the decisive Yorkist victories at Barnet and Tewkesbury remove all effective opposition and leave Edward IV in clear possession of the crown. The successive interchanges of power between the two factions suggest the cyclic Falls of Princes theme; and Baldwin's *Mirror for Magistrates* (1559) had already included the "tragedies" of many of the participants in these wars, among them Richard Duke of York, Clarence, Warwick, Clifford, and Henry VI. Shakespeare exploits in speeches as well as in situations the familiar commonplaces of the theme: pride, ambition, the sudden turns of fortune, "ubi sunt," the blessings of the mean estate. He does so principally in the two "molehill" scenes.

In the first (I. iv), after the Duke of York is captured at the Battle of Wakefield, his fall is symbolically acted out. Early in the scene, at his capture, Clifford compares him to Phaëton, the standard symbol of misplaced ambition: "Now Phaëton hath tumbled from his car,/ And made an evening at the noontide prick" (ll. 33-34). Then he is forced by Clifford and Northumberland to stand upon a molehill and listen to Queen Margaret's taunts (ll. 66 ff.). In heavily underlined irony she mocks his vaulting ambition, degrades "Fortune's hill" from mountain to molehill, evokes the "ubi sunt" theme:

> Come, make him stand upon this molehill here,
> That raught at mountains with outstretched arms,
> Yet parted but the shadow with his hand.
> What, was it you that would be England's king?
> Was't you that revell'd in our parliament,
> And made a preachment of your high descent?
> Where are your mess of sons to back you now,
> The wanton Edward, and the lusty George?
> And where's that valiant crook-back prodigy,
> Dicky, your boy, that with his grumbling voice
> Was wont to cheer his dad in mutinies?
> Or with the rest, where is your darling, Rutland?

She gives him to wipe his tears the napkin she had stained in Rutland's blood, mocks his patience to make him mad, and sets a paper crown upon his head:

> York cannot speak unless he wear a crown.
> A crown for York! and, lords, bow low to him;
> Hold you his hands, whilst I do set it on.
> Ay, marry, sir, now looks he like a king!

But "Off with the crown; and, with the crown, his head." York, after his own bitter diatribe against Margaret, yields the paper crown with a retributive curse:

> There, take the crown, and with the crown, my curse,
> And in thy need such comfort come to thee
> As now I reap at thy too cruel hand!

When she and Clifford have stabbed him to death, Margaret rounds off the theme of "pride must have a fall" with pointed, ironic wit:

> Off with his head, and set it on York gates,
> So York may overlook the town of York.

As a complement to the theme of dangerous ambition, which subjects a man to the uncertainties of fortune, there is found in Senecan tragedy the theme of content with the much safer mean estate.[1] In the second molehill scene (II. v), complementary to the first, it is King Henry who is on the molehill, not involuntarily or as a mockery of ambition, but by choice, to signify his humble desires. He would prefer, like the homely swain, "to sit upon a hill, . . ./ To carve out dials quaintly, point by point," and live out his life to its end in a quiet grave. The shepherd's homely curds and cold thin drink are better than a prince's "delicates" and "viands sparkling in a golden cup," the one's hawthorn shade than the other's embroidered canopy, the one's untroubled sleep under a fresh tree than the other's wakefulness in a "curious bed,/ When care, mistrust, and treason waits on him." Henry's meditation has in it all the familiar terms. But trite as these sound, the meditation provides a moment of stillness in the play. His sad, quiet reflection counterpoints the noisy voices, continually impelling to restless action, to attack and counterattack—a repetitive push and pull, back and forth, over and over again. Shakespeare has made this choric speech a preface to an episode suggested by a sentence in Hall: "This conflict [the Battle of Towton] was in maner unnaturall, for in it the sonne fought against the father, the brother against the brother, the nephew against the uncle, and the tenaunt against his Lord."[2] Shakespeare, by having Henry witness a son kill his father, a father kill his son, and their grieving discoveries, gives a moving demonstration of the horrors of civil war to the pawns in the dynastic struggle. As the King moralizes: "O piteous spectacle! . . ./ The red rose and the white are on his face [the dead son's],/ The fatal colors of our striving houses; . . . / Was ever king so griev'd for subjects' woe?" (ll. 73, 97-98, 111).

The point should be made that the character of York in the molehill scene is less important than the situation. Note that he is arrogant enough when he is on top, as when he is bullying King Henry with his claim to the throne (in I. i. 76, 85, 102-3). But when he is brought down, the pathos of his situation is amplified. He is now the woodcock striving with the gin, the cony struggling in the net (I. iv. 61-62), he is patient for a long time under Margaret's goading, and he surrenders his life with a prayer to God for mercy. In a similar way, important as is King Henry's timid and indecisive character to the plot, in the molehill scene what matters chiefly is less his character than the contrast in situation to the other scene— there the proud man brought low and mocked, here the humble man meditating on the low and enviable station his position does not allow him to occupy. The various "princes" or lords—Edward of York, Warwick, even Clifford and Margaret in part—are handled as York is, more or less unsympathetically when they are pressing for power or exercising it, sympathetically when they have lost it and are helpless. This kind of treatment puts heavy emphasis on the cyclic theme.

For *Richard III*, Shakespeare had ready-made in More's lively narrative, available to him in the chronicles, a more limited story, centered on the swift rise and fall of one domi-

nant, vividly realized figure, and told from a mirror-for-magistrates point of view. More begins his history of the reign with
a sketch of Richard's appearance and character, and an account of the unnatural circumstances of his birth (feet first,
with teeth, his mother cut), which may have been predictive
of his unnatural life: "whether that menne of hatred reported
above the truthe, or that nature chaunged his course in his
beginnynge, whiche in his life many thynges unnaturally committed, this I leve to God his judgemente."[3] After his account
of the murder of the princes, just before he breaks off his history, More anticipates Richard's end:

> . . . whiche thynges on every parte well pondered, God gave
> this world never a more notable example, either in what
> unsurety standeth this worldes weale, or what mischiefe work-
> ethe the proude enterprise of an highe harte, or finally, what
> wretched ende ensueth suche dispiteous crueltie. . . . kynge
> Richarde him selfe was slaine in felde[,] hacked and hewen of
> his enemies handes, haried on a horsbacke naked beynge
> dead, his heere in dispite torne and tugged, lyke a curre dogge.
> And the mischiefe that he toke within lesse then thre yeres, of
> the mischiefe that he dyd in thre monethes be not comparable,
> and yet al the meane tyme spente in muche trouble and payne
> outwarde, and much feare, dread and anguishe within.[4]

The same theme was heavily exploited in the *Mirror for Magistrates* itself in Richard's narrative, which is introduced as
spoken from "the diepe pit of Hell, . . . howlinge."[5] It was an
addition to the 1563 edition together with the tragedies of
Rivers, Hastings, Buckingham, and Mistress Shore.

In repeated, amplifying references and images Shakespeare
keeps from his sources the unnaturalness of Richard's birth, the
satanic implications of his deformity, and the linkage in his
character with the boar of his heraldic crest:

> Thou elvish-mark'd, abortive, rooting hog!
> Thou that wast seal'd in thy nativity
> The slave of nature and the son of hell!
>   (I. iii. 227-29)

To his victims and enemies Richard is as well a hedgehog, a
foul or bunchbacked toad, a bottled spider, and worse—a hell-

hound. Far from turning Richard into a psychological case study of a man compensating for his ugliness, Shakespeare has emphasized the essential, devilish evil in the man he found portrayed in the histories he read.

But without at all mitigating the evil of Richard's nature, Shakespeare has turned this creature into the most fascinating and enjoyable of theatrical villains by means of his vigorous speech—confident or impatient, innocent or threatening, witty, blunt, or indirect, at need. More's Richard has all the intelligence—the wit in that primary sense, the dissimulation, the changes of mood. But Shakespeare's Richard exhibits a much greater versatility. Besides, the verbal wit of his cat-and-mouse games and the self-satisfaction of the cat with the canary inside are alone his. He takes sheer pleasure in doing in "simple plain Clarence," or in winning Anne to be his bride, "All the world to nothing!" And it would be hard to say that the audience does not, morality suspended, delight in the artist-Richard's triumph:

> Shine out, fair sun, till I have bought a glass,
> That I may see my shadow as I pass.
> (I. ii. 262-63)

At the same time, Shakespeare has not lost the serious intent of his story. He does not, however, achieve the seriousness within so narrowly personal or so moralizing a frame as the mirror-for-magistrates formula. The rhetorical framework of revenge was Shakespeare's way of transcending the melodramatic character of Richard by giving the play a larger tragic significance, Senecan rather than Christian in conception. The old Queen Margaret, who speaks in the mood of a Senecan Fury, or of a ghost seeking revenge, provides a larger tragic motivation and a firm structural framework—that is, the working out of a retribution on the Yorkists for their crimes against the Lancastrians. In her view Richard is "a hell-hound that doth hunt us all to death," Yorkist and Lancastrian alike. As the evil genius of his family, he becomes an agent of retribution against it, hence its nemesis.

Although Margaret, now powerless, takes no action, she yet marks the stages of the plot with her curses and predictions

early in the play (I. iii. 187-239) and with her return later to
gloat over her successor Elizabeth, the poor "queen in jest":
"Where is thy husband now? Where be thy brothers?/ Where
be thy children⁶? . . ." and so on (IV. iv. 92 ff.). She, the other
women (the Duchess of York, Elizabeth, Anne), and the children of Clarence provide a changing chorus, at once lament-
ing, reminding, and commenting (in II. ii. 34-100, IV. i. 31-
103, IV. iv. 9-135). The style throughout these parts is formally
rhetorical, depending heavily on schemes of repetition and
balance; the dialogue is frequently antiphonal. For example,

> Q. Eliz. Ah for my husband, for my dear lord Edward!
> Chil. Ah for our father, for our dear lord Clarence!
> Duch. Alas for both, both mine, Edward and Clarence!
> Q. Eliz. What stay had I but Edward? and he's gone.
> Chil. What stay had we but Clarence? and he's gone.
> Duch. What stays had I but they? and they are gone.
> (II. ii. 71-76)

> Q. Mar. I had an Edward, till a Richard kill'd him;
> I had a Harry, till a Richard kill'd him: . . .
> Duch. I had a Richard too, and thou didst kill him;
> I had a Rutland too, thou holp'st to kill him.
> (IV. iv. 40-41, 44-45)

Clearly these choric speeches are not as poetically interesting
as are Richard's speeches at their best, and they are tediously
long. Nevertheless, they give the play balance and meaning.
They cannot be wholly omitted, as they were in the Olivier
film, without great damage to the serious sense of tragedy the
play is meant to convey. Margaret returns as witness to "a dire
induction," "bitter, black, and tragical" (IV. iv. 1-7).

For all its dramatic success, however, and its brilliance,
Richard III is overlong, evidencing too little pruning of long
speeches, dialogues, and repetitive scenes, and too little resistance to the temptation to write poetry which goes beyond dramatic needs, as, for example, in Clarence's dream. Three plays
following it will serve to illustrate Shakespeare's increasing
mastery of dramatic style. These three—*Romeo and Juliet, A*

Midsummer Night's Dream, and *Richard II*—belong close together in time of composition, perhaps all in the one year of
1595; if so it might well be called Shakespeare's first "wonderful year." Such precision in dating, alas, is hardly possible, but
even a range of dating from 1594 to 1596 is still good enough
for the essential point to be made about the three: together
they make a high point of achievement, a climax and a period
to Shakespeare's early years of experiment. For they are similar
in the markedly successful adaptation of style to dramatic
conception. All are small masterpieces in which plot, theme,
character, setting, and style co-operate to give each play a distinctive character. Two (*Romeo and Juliet* and *A Midsummer
Night's Dream*) are alike in a combination of formality and
informality in style to achieve contrasts in tone; all three are
alike in a good deal of lyricism, in the verbal creation of setting, and in the close appropriateness of style to fable. Yet
each one is distinct from the others in this very appropriateness
of its style to its story.

To take *Romeo and Juliet* first, since it shows traces of apprentice work, perhaps remnants of an earlier version of the
play. The Romeo and Juliet story was old and popular when
Shakespeare tried his hand at it,[7] and everything he did with it
served to heighten its essential character—the pitiable love of
two very young people doomed from the start to a tragic end
by the feud between their families. Shakespeare intensified the
action itself and its inherent irony by reducing the age of the
lovers, by drastically shortening the elapsed time from nine
months to four-and-a-half days, by introducing Paris and
Tybalt almost at the start, and, above all, by placing the killing
of Tybalt and the Prince's sentence on Romeo between the
wedding and the wedding night. And with the intrusion of his
brilliant invention, Mercutio, into the crisis of the action, he
started a new and widening circle of irony.

Shakespeare used setting structurally in the assembly of the
Capulets and the Montagues and their feuding followers in a
public place to mark the beginning, the middle or high point,
and the end of the action. He enhanced the irony of the action

in the staging itself—the public place (streets or square), ominous for the feuding factions to meet and fight in and for the appearance of the Prince to give warning or sentence; Juliet's window above the Capulet garden for wooing and separation; and, finally, the Capulet monument and the churchyard, for the deaths of the lovers and the tardy reconciliation of the parents. But one cannot separate the physical setting from the language; for Shakespeare's daylight stage, without painted scenery, illusion had to be created in the spoken lines. In *Romeo and Juliet* it is in the frequent references and images that the setting is most intimately apprehended and made to symbolize the ironies in the tragic story. The hot bright daylight of the streets always means danger, "for now, these hot days, is the mad blood stirring"; Mercutio's blood stirs to challenge Tybalt, and Romeo becomes "Fortune's fool." In the still dangerous, yet safer, darkness of Capulet's garden the moon, which "tips with silver all these fruit-tree tops," shines on love and Juliet is the sun. At Juliet's window, "jocund day" standing "tiptoe on the misty mountain tops" and the morning lark's "sweet division" end the night of love and bring the full daylight of separation:

More light and light, more dark and dark our woes!

Finally, in the blackness of the monument Juliet's beauty makes for Romeo "this vault a feasting presence full of light"; the paradoxical contraries of light and dark running in scene and imagery throughout the play are reconciled in death and the lasting darkness of the tomb.

The verse, likewise, is at the service of the story. For the wooing verse is bejeweled and sometimes very formal, as in the sonnet of meeting at the Capulet party (I. v. 93-110); the love poetry is not the "natural" language of lovers but the heightened language which speaks to the idealizing spirit of young love. Romeo's rapt monologue in the garden when he sees Juliet at her window (II. ii. 2 ff.), his eloquent apostrophe to Juliet in the Capulet tomb (V. iii. 91 ff.), Juliet's "arias" of excited longing for the wedding night (III. ii. 1 ff.) and of fearful anticipation of awakening too early in the sepulcher

(IV. iii. 14 ff.) are all in the rich poetry of passionate imagination, amplified with tropes, formal figures, and copious varying.

The artifice of the lovers' verse is balanced not only by the Nurse's gabby coarseness and old Capulet's fussiness and low humor—both in verse—but also by Mercutio's witty scoffing and lively, bawdy prose. Mercutio introduces a skeptical realism which seasons the romantic richness with salt, yet in no way destroys the truth of the lovers' experience. He knows only about Romeo's lover-like posing for the sake of the cruel Rosaline, never anything about his new intense love of Juliet. The older man's jesting, therefore, actually serves to intensify the pathos of Romeo's isolation in his dangerous love of Juliet.

In *A Midsummer Night's Dream*, Shakespeare again tried a story of love crossed by circumstance, this time in comic mood, and this time of his own fabrication, put together with hints from various places. The Hermia-Lysander-Egeus story has affinities to the same ancestral plot behind *Romeo and Juliet*, that is, to the Pyramus and Thisbe story, one he actually brings into the comedy under its own name to mishandle in an outrageous parody of Ovid's pathetic tale. But he complicates his love plot with a second pair of lovers, thus introducing the motive of rivalry in love, something he had experimented with in *The Two Gentlemen of Verona;* now he further exploits the theme of infidelity and manipulates the confusions more expertly in a series of cross-wooings. From Chaucer's *Knight's Tale*, in which the wise and humorous Duke Theseus acts as moderator of the rivalry in love of two young men for the hand of the same lady, he took suggestions for the framework of his comedy, some of its complications, many details of its setting, and much in its point of view. From there and elsewhere in Chaucer he perhaps took some hints for his fairies. But the fairies, the prime agents in complicating and untangling the love plot, interfering as they do, like the great gods, in the affairs of mortals, come from everywhere and nowhere except Shakespeare's imagination.

As in *Romeo and Juliet*, the setting in *A Midsummer Night's Dream* is experienced verbally as well as visually, and primarily so. No staging can do what the words do. Indeed the

fairies who are part of the setting, the minuscule attendants on
Titania who gather dewdrops as pearls for cowslips' ears, can
be fully apprehended only in the language, for they cannot be
faithfully represented on the stage and must appeal to the
imagination for the credibility of their lines. I need not review
here by what poetic subtleties Shakespeare creates the fairy-
haunted wood,[8] with its moonlight and starlight, its faint prim-
rose beds to lie on, its bank fragrant with thyme and musk-
roses for Titania, its delicacies for the palate—apricots and
dewberries, honey-bags from the humble-bees; but also its dark
bewildering fog and its shuddery night creatures—blind-
worms, bats, crawling serpents, a clamorous owl. The wood is
the domain of Phoebe, beholding "her silver visage in the wat'ry
glass"; but for an instant before dawn the shadow of triple
Hecate, the moon in her aspect as a goddess of the underworld,
of crossways, and of dark mysteries, passes over the wood.

I need not review, either, how in the poetry Shakespeare
creates for Theseus and Hippolyta an allusive home in heroic
Greece; or how he creates other landscapes for us to glimpse
in the greater world beyond the wood—the inhabited land of
farms and villages where Robin Goodfellow is at home and
where the seasons of bad weather have drowned the fields,
rotted the corn, killed the sheep with the murrain; the promontory where Oberon heard a mermaid on a dophin's back
calming the rude sea with her song; "the spiced Indian air" in
which Titania and her votaress, big with child, sat side by side
on "Neptune's yellow sands" watching the trading ships, as the
wind filled their sails, move out on the flood-tide.

It is not alone through word and image, however, that all the
changes of tone are subtly conveyed; just as important a means
of suggestion is the form of the verse and the prose. The verse
is modulated throughout the play in varying meters, with rime
and without it, to suit scene, situation, mood, sometimes class
of character. Blank verse and rimed pentameter distinguish
fine differences of tone, for in the context of the play the one
carries more weight and seriousness, the other more lightness
and comedy. The blank verse of the adults in the relatively
stable court world is set off against the rimed couplets of the

young lovers in their impulsive decisions and in their shifting
infatuations and infidelities under the fairy spells. The artifice
of the rime in this context gives brittleness, making for our ears
a subtle polyphony with the desperately earnest words of the
lovers. In the moments of deeper perception or idealism, however, the lovers speak eloquently in blank verse. Such moments
come in Lysander's lines on the enemies of love—war, death,
sickness—which make it "momentany as a sound,/ Swift as a
shadow, short as any dream,/ Brief as the lightning in the
collied night, . . ." (I. i. 141-49); in Helena's recollection of her
"school-days friendship" with Hermia, when they sat on one
cushion embroidering one flower, warbling one song, "as if our
hands, our sides, voices, and minds/ Had been incorporate,"
"with two seeming bodies, but one heart" (III. ii. 201 ff.); or
in Demetrius' awakening to his better self, when the night's
strange fancies recede and he returns "as in health" to his
"natural taste" and his faith to Helena (IV. i. 164-76).

There is much rime, too, in the fairy parts, and also varying
meters. The blank verse of the King and Queen of Faery at
their meeting in Act II, scene i, matches that in the human
world of the Athenian court, not just because Oberon and
Titania are rulers, but because they, like Theseus and Hippolyta, have the responsibility that goes with their power.
Their quarrel is not just a comic interlude, a passing squall like
the lovers' quarrels, but a serious disturbance of the natural
order. Elsewhere, whether their verse is blank or rimed de-
pends on the situation. Titania in love, for instance, speaks in
rimed pentameter couplets as the human lovers do. The spells
pronounced by Oberon and Puck and Puck's choric comments
on the stages of the love plot are set off by shorter lines,
usually four-stress and in couplets:

Night and silence—Who is here?
Weeds of Athens he doth wear: . . .
Churl, upon thy eyes I throw
All the power this charm doth owe.
When thou wak'st, let love forbid
Sleep his seat on thy eyelid.

(II. ii. 70-81)

But the rime patterns for the spells vary and the lines may be
shorter (as in Puck's at III. ii. 448-63). The rime in all such
speeches functions quite differently from that in the lovers'
dialogue; here it makes for emphasis and ease of memory, just
as it does in the pentameter couplets of Oberon's set piece of
description: "I know a bank where the wild thyme blows,/
Where oxlips and the nodding violet grows, . . ." (II. i. 249 ff.).
Short meters in varying patterns of rime please the ear in the
lyrics of the attendant fairies (e.g., II. i. 2-17; II. ii. 9-26).
There is no need to expatiate on the intrusion into the poetic
and magical fairy world of Bottom's and his friends' limited
eloquence and downright prose or of Bottom's country lyrics:
"The woosel cock so black of hue,/ With orange-tawny bill,
. . ." The burlesque of the state of Blind Cupid's victims in the
scenes in which the enraptured Titania woos the complaisant
and unmoved Bottom (III. i. 129 ff.; IV. i. 1-45) are a triumph
of orchestration in diction, image, verse, and prose: Titania's
fairy music to Bottom's tongs and bones.

As for "The most lamentable comedy and most cruel death
of Pyramus and Thisby," it is burlesque in another key, echoing
the parental thwarting of love, the elopement of Hermia and
Helena, their fears and desperate impulsiveness. Its actual
literary parody is, in general, of a long line of standard conven-
tions in love poetry and, in particular, of poetasters' inept versions of Ovid's well-known tale in the *Metamorphoses*.[9] The
topsy-turvy treatment of this tragic story of true love makes a
suitable antimasque for the wedding ceremony, because the
"real" story with a similar beginning is to end in marriage instead of suicide. The antimasque is appropriate in a deeper
sense. A true solemnity should have in it its hour of misrule, its
cleansing irreverence, as well as its ordered and holy pomp.

With all its movements from midsummer-night madness to
daylight sobriety, from the fairy world to everyday, from
dream to waking, and with all the varieties of texture in style
which this sleight-of-hand requires, *A Midsummer Night's
Dream* is nevertheless seamless. It is everywhere informed by
the play of that creative imagination which Theseus, so deli-
ciously for us, is scornful of.

In comparison with A *Midsummer Night's Dream* and perhaps even *Romeo and Juliet* the style of *Richard II* may strike us as less varied, the tone as more uniform. The web seems to have less variety in pattern and in hue. The seriousness is nearly unrelieved, the rhetorical formality of the verse is seldom relaxed, there is no prose. Richard's monologues are long, the interchanges between him and his companions or enemies relatively brief. The studied speeches are not, however, confined to Richard's part or to monologue. Think of Gaunt's fatherly advice, filled with "wise saws and modern instances," to his son Bolingbroke, and Bolingbroke's reply (I. iii. 275 ff.), Gaunt's prophetic vision of the troubles about to befall England (II. i. 31 ff.), his stern admonitions to Richard (II. i. 93 ff.), his earnest conversation with his sister-in-law on leaving the avenging of Gloucester's death to heaven (I. ii), the Queen's "conceited" premonitions of bad news, when Bolingbroke is her "sorrow's dismal heir" (II. ii. 1-72), the Gardener's parable of the garden as a model of England (III. iv. 24 ff.), the antiphonal pleading of York and his Duchess to King Henry against and for their son, Aumerle (V. iii. 76 ff.). The great variations in mood are centered in Richard himself, and he thinks chiefly in poetic images and in precise conceits.

For Richard, in the character Shakespeare has given him, is abundantly endowed with poetic imagination and from it creates the world he lives in, one quite at odds with actuality. The pictured situations which he builds with words and with which he enchants himself are *his* realities, always more convincing to him than political, or even physical, actualities:

> Feed not thy sovereign's foe, my gentle earth,
> Nor with thy sweets comfort his ravenous sense,
> But let thy spiders, that suck up thy venom,
> And heavy-gaited toads lie in their way,
> Doing annoyance to the treacherous feet,
> Which with usurping steps do trample thee.
>   (III. ii. 12-17)

What Shakespeare does with Richard's imagination makes an interesting variation from what he does in A *Midsummer*

Night's Dream. In both plays Shakespeare has created two
worlds, a simulated real one and a fanciful one. In the comedy
the fantasy in the wood, complete with "fairy toys" and "airy
nothings," may be taken as a demonstration of one aspect of
the creative imagination at work. The characters are not themselves aware of the fantasy in which they are taking part, except in the sensation of awakening from something like a dream.
When Shakespeare makes Theseus, in doubting the reality of
the experience the lovers recount, ally the poet with the madman and the lover in their "seething brains" and "shaping
fantasies," he tosses us, as if by the way, a question about the
whole nature of poetic creation (V. i. 2-22). The Duke's mistrust of poets is double-edged, for he and his sane world are
also the products of one of those suspect poets. In *Richard II*
Shakespeare turns his light on the poetic imagination in the
act of creating its own world, which he sets side by side with
the "real" one. The questions raised in this form are less aes-
thetic than psychological and moral. For Richard lives by the
forms his imagination "bodies forth."

This conception of Richard's character is Shakespeare's brilliant invention, to give life and absorbing interest to the outline
of the ambitious, but weak, capricious, and sensual Richard
of the chronicles. Since Shakespeare was always alert to verbal
suggestion, perhaps *his* Richard, with his tendency to depres-
sion and his sensitivity to words, opens out from a single phrase
in Holinshed's statement that Richard, "being now in the hands
of his enemies [in the Tower], and utterlie despairing of all
comfort, was easilie persuaded to renounce his crowne and
princelie preheminence."[10] "Despairing of all comfort": on
"comfort" and "discomfort" Shakespeare builds a whole scene
(III. ii) of theme and counter-theme on Richard's ups and
downs between false confidence and despair as, newly landed
on the Welsh coast, he hears piece by piece the news of Bolingbroke's swift advance and the rapidly worsening military situation. Richard sees himself in the rôles suggested to him in turn
by his alternating moods—as the rising sun with the searching
eye that will frighten the thief and murderer, Bolingbroke; as a
king whose name is twenty thousand names; as the king who

has lost care with the loss of his kingdom and will serve God in his loyalty to a new king; as the king betrayed, he thinks, by his friends, three Judases; as the king within whose crown Death the antic keeps his court. For the first time his eloquence is fully displayed, with its imagined pictures of himself in his different, sometimes antithetical, rôles, its extended metaphors or allegories, its lyric repetitions and echoes ("discomfortable cousin," "of comfort no man speak," "Where is Bagot?/ What is become of Bushy? Where is Green?"). The scene is composed musically, with theme and counter-theme, reiterated and developed, and closing with an almost paradoxical resolution in a strange composition of contraries:

> Beshrew thee, cousin, which didst lead me forth
> Of that sweet way I was in to despair!
> What say you now? What comfort have we now?
> By heaven, I'll hate him everlastingly
> That bids me be of comfort any more.
> Go to Flint Castle; there I'll pine away—
> A king, woe's slave, shall kingly woe obey.

The scene is a foretaste of Richard's moods to come, and of the rhetoric in which he savors them, for the pathos is always controlled by his precise wit.

Again, as with the reigns of Henry VI and Richard III, Shakespeare had a Falls of Princes theme to work with, but this time he used it more intimately, and with more complexity, for the King is in himself a tragic figure, deeply sympathetic as he stands at bay before his betrayers, yet initially, in his weakness, the maker of his own doom. Throughout the play the familiar symbols of royal power (especially the sun) and of its instability (e.g., the alternating buckets in the well) reappear. York's vivid description to his wife of the triumphal entry of Bolingbroke into London and of the now despised Richard's following after, with dust "thrown upon his sacred head," marks chorically the pitiable fall of Richard's fortunes (V. ii. 1-40).

It is primarily Richard himself who is made to interpret his own story as an exemplum of this pattern of history, this *de*

casibus virorum illustrium. In the "comfort" scene, giving in to
the succession of bad news, he acts as his own chorus:

> For God's sake, let us sit upon the ground
> And tell sad stories of the death of kings:
> How some have been depos'd, some slain in war, . . .
> All murther'd—for within the hollow crown
> That rounds the mortal temples of a king
> Keeps Death his court, . . .
>   (III. ii. 155-62)

The speech does more than provide psychological insight into
Richard. In its allusions to both the *de casibus* and the Dance
of Death themes, it puts his fall into a universal framework of
transitory and illusive human pretensions.

The uniqueness of Shakespeare's treatment of the Falls of
Princes theme in this play is in Richard's way of verbalizing his
every action or inaction in appropriate symbols, or, to put it the
other way around, in Richard's acting out of his own metaphors. When he lands on the Welsh coast after his absence in
Ireland, he must salute his "dear earth" with his hand, greet-
ing it with tears and smiles as does "a long-parted mother" her
child (III. ii. 8-11). In his visible descent from the battlements
at Flint Castle to the base court, he acts out the fall of
"glist'ring Phaëton," "wanting the manage of unruly jades":

> In the base court? Base court, where kings grow base,
> To come at traitors' calls and do them grace.
> In the base court, come down? Down court! down king!
> For night-owls shriek where mounting larks should sing.
>   (III. iii. 180-83)

In Richard's surrender of the crown to Bolingbroke, done so
that Bolingbroke must "seize" it, physically—"On this side my
hand, and on that side thine"—he moralizes the cyclic interchange of power with the image of the rising and descending
buckets in a well:

> The emptier ever dancing in the air,
> The other down, unseen, and full of water:
> That bucket down and full of tears am I,
> Drinking my griefs, whilst you mount up on high.
>   (IV. i. 186-89)

Alone at the end, in prison, he must people "this little world" with "still-breeding thoughts," "in humors like the people of this world:/ For no thought is contented" (V. v. 1 ff.).

In Richard's dramatizing of his images he employs, in varying degrees, a number of rhetorical devices for emphasis. They fall into certain classes which re-enforce one another: balanced construction or parison (often antithetical), antimetabole, repetition (particularly anaphora and *traductio,* the unpatterned repetition of a word throughout a passage), plays on words (paranomasia, antanaclasis, polyptoton), and *similiter desinens* or rime. The method may be illustrated in the two passages just quoted. In the Phaëton passage, note how the double sense of "base," the repetitions in several forms, and the antithetical play throughout the language intensify the sense of outrageous impropriety in the action. In the buckets-in-the-well passage antitheses in the language ("emptier"—"full," "down"—"high," "dancing in the air"—"drinking my griefs," etc.) re-enforce the image in all its implications.

Richard needs an audience. The deposition scene (IV. i. 162 ff.), in which he must formally and in public renounce the crown he has already yielded in private, offers him his great occasion—in a pitifully ironic way, his triumph. In his complete powerlessness over events, Richard exercises his greatest power over words to maintain his delusive and momentary control over himself and his audience. He holds his unwilling audience perforce in maximum discomfort while he underscores their breach of faith to him, the martyred victim:

> Yet I well remember
> The favors of these men. Were they not mine?
> Did they not sometimes cry 'All hail!' to me?
> So Judas did to Christ; but He, in twelve,
> Found truth in all but one; I, in twelve thousand, none.
>   (ll. 167-71)

In a series of three dramatic variations on the theme of his abdication he amplifies his fall from power: Bolingbroke's seizure of the crown in the parable of the buckets in the well (ll. 181-89); his own abdication in his symbolic re-enactment of the coronation ceremony in reverse (ll. 204-21); and the ruin of himself and his glory in the smashing of the glass which mirrors his face (ll. 276-91). All of these "episodes" are tightly controlled by the rhetorical devices of balance, repetition, word-play, and rime, in all their refinements.

The buckets-in-the-well episode gives Richard some compensatory pleasure in thinking of the transitoriness of Bolingbroke's "high" position. The uncrowning of himself is important to his self-respect. His insistence on his voluntary action—

> I give this heavy weight from off my head,
> And this unwieldy sceptre from my hand,
> The pride of kingly sway from out my heart;
> With mine own tears I wash away my balm,
> With mine own hands I give away my crown
> (ll. 204-8)

—masks the reality of his helplessness and is edged with cutting irony:

> God pardon all oaths that are broke to me!
> God keep all vows unbroke are made to thee! . . .
> God save King Henry, unking'd Richard says,
> And send him many years of sunshine days!
> (ll. 214-21)

The repetitive phrasing to accompany each gesture emphasizes the ritual significance of the speech.

When he moralizes on the face that shows no deeper wrinkles in the flattering glass, he not only seems to recognize his own follies ("Is this the face which fac'd so many follies,/ That was at last outfac'd by Bolingbroke?"), but also puts himself allusively in a larger framework of transitory human power and its glory. For in the echo of Marlowe in one of his questions,

> Was this face the face
> That every day under his household roof
> Did keep ten thousand men?
> (ll. 281-83)

is heard an oblique allusion to the fall of Troy, the type of earthly kingdoms:

A brittle glory shineth in this face,
As brittle as the glory is the face,
      [*Dashes the glass against the ground.*]
For there it is, crack'd in an hundred shivers.
            (ll. 287-89)

Again, in image and action, the illusion of voluntary control over his fate. What he has controlled is the game he has played with a word, "face," taking it through several meanings and implications and bringing it home again. But if Richard has a power over words, they also, concomitantly, have a power over him. For when he moralizes on the smashed glass—"Mark, silent king, the moral of this sport,/ How soon my sorrow hath destroy'd my face"—and Bolingbroke replies from the world of actuality—"The shadow of your sorrow hath destroy'd/ The shadow of your face"—Richard sets off on an entirely new train of thought, caught by the word "shadow": "Say that again./ The shadow of my sorrow! Ha, let's see. . . ."

Never far below the surface of the play-acting lie rage, bitterness, and grief, ready to break out in sarcastic irony (as often in the remarks to Henry) or in unstaged tears. The bitter wit is chiefly directed at Bolingbroke; the grief is revealed most movingly at the moment when Northumberland insists on his reading aloud the prepared list of his "grievous crimes" and Richard protests: "Must I do so? and must I ravel out/ My weav'd-up follies?" In Richard's home thrust at Northumberland for his broken oath and his charge that all are accomplices,

Nay, all of you that stand and look upon me
Whilst that my wretchedness doth bait myself,
Though some of you, with Pilate, wash your hands,
Showing an outward pity, yet you Pilates
Have here deliver'd me to my sour cross,
And water cannot wash away your sin,
            (ll. 237-42)

the mask is off. "Mine eyes are full of tears, I cannot see." The whole speech is in relatively unfigured blank verse. Again, at the end of the long ordeal, Richard's control breaks, this time

in a rage—but anger does not dull his wit. He has asked leave
to go, and Henry has asked him, "Whither?"

> K. Rich.   Whither you will, so I were from your sights.
> Boling.   Go some of you, convey him to the Tower.
> K. Rich.   O, good! convey! Conveyors are you all,
> That rise thus nimbly by a true king's fall.
>   (ll. 315-18)

Thus, within a rather narrow rhetorical and metrical frame
Shakespeare creates a character and an action with much tonal
range. The style reflects not only Richard's character but also
his conception of his kingly rôle as almost solely a ceremonial
one, perhaps because it is the one way in which he can be
kingly. The substance of kingship, of which the ceremony is the
great symbol, eludes him. His brave, poetic stagings of his symbolic rôle move us with their sad irony.

The welfare of England, a larger issue than Richard's personal failure, is kept before us in the constant reminders of
the country, the scene of the action. The sense of England,
whether as a beloved place or as a commonwealth of men suffering from misrule and civil disorder, is pervasively and movingly conveyed in the poetry. England is Gaunt's "earth of
majesty," his "other Eden, demi-paradise," his "land of such
dear souls, this dear dear land," which Richard exploits as a
landlord, leasing it out "like to a tenement or pelting farm" (II.
i. 40 ff.). England is the Gardener's and his man's "sea-walled
garden," which "is full of weeds, her fairest flowers chok'd up,/
. . . her wholesome herbs/ Swarming with caterpillars" (III. iv.
43-47). It is Richard's "dear earth," sentimentally loved, however misgoverned, whose complexion of "maid-pale peace"
shall be changed to "scarlet indignation" and her pastures'
grass bedewed with faithful English blood (III. iii. 95-100).
To Bolingbroke it is "the fresh green lap of fair King Richard's
land," which, if the King does not meet his demands, the "crim-
son tempest" of the blood of slaughtered Englishmen will be-
drench (III. iii. 42-48). These evocations of the havoc of civil
war, in rich and complex imagery, eloquently suggest the
larger consequences of Richard's tragical history.

These three plays—a tragedy, a comedy, and a tragical history—might be thought of as the climax of Shakespeare's journeyman years, the plays in which he passed his examination as master craftsman.[11] After them nearly everything he writes is done with great freedom and assured ease. The control is no less there, but is less in evidence. The sources of the effects in the rhetoric and in the verse are more complex, less easy to identify. He only returns to these patterned styles for special effects. But I shall not go on with further analyses. These were meant to show how he achieved mastery in the union of story and style, in short, in dramatic language.

Now to return to the larger question I raised at the beginning, the question of the distinctiveness of each of Shakespeare's plays and its relation to differences of style.

I observed that when we know the plays intimately through reading, seeing, and hearing them, we are apt to be struck by the remarkable way in which no play sounds quite like another. It is true that particular situations, especially in the early comedies, may recur with variations: for example, "clowns," whether servants, rustics, or fools, burlesquing in their own actions and language the love affairs of the principal characters, as do one of the Dromios, Launce, Costard, and, with large differences, Bottom and Touchstone. It is also true that certain character types—or rather character rôles—reappear, again most often in the comedies. Such are the comic servants (the Dromios, Launce and Speed, Launcelot Gobbo), the ignorant misusers of language (Bottom, Dogberry and Verges, the Nurse in *Romeo and Juliet,* and Mistress Quickly in the Henry IV plays), the young men about town, in love and playing wit-games (Romeo and his friends, Bassanio and his, even Hamlet with Rosencrantz and Guildenstern), young women in pairs as friends or as mistress and servant-companion, improvising duets in varying harmonies and dissonances, for they are sometimes of contrasting temperaments (Adriana and Luciana, Hermia and Helena), sometimes complementary to one another (Julia and Lucetta, Portia and Nerissa, Rosalind and Celia). Such repetitions as these are owing partly to traditions in comedy (Roman, Italian, Lylyan), and partly to the organization of acting companies and the repertory system in the Elizabethan theater. Even in these recurrent situations and character rôles, however, we are usually less conscious of repetition than of freshness in the handling. And between plays as wholes the differences are always more remarkable than the similarities.

The explanation that naturally occurs to us is that the different stories, each with its proper situations and issues, and especially with its own characters, make the distinctiveness. No one will deny the primary importance of the stuff of the play, that is, of plot and character. But we know, too, that the design and the texture are not separable, except in analysis, from the material, that the "how" is not separable from the "what." The most patent way in which how a thing is said is as important as what is said is in differentiating one character from another. In this individualizing function, the "how" is not with Shakespeare just a matter of speech tags (like Nym's "That's the humor of it," or Pistol's misquotations, his "hollow pamper'd jades of Asia,/ Which cannot go but thirty mile a day"), but of the whole organization and flow of speech, as with Hotspur's helter-skelter volubility; or with Falstaff's easy, lucid prose and his almost casual, yet most telling wit; or with Hamlet's shifts from sustained meditative discourse to rapier wit or impassioned exclamation. Another, less obvious, way in which manner is as important as matter is in the handling of the story itself. Situations and actions are more than just events. In large part our response to a story is controlled by the style in which it is treated; the point has been illustrated in the plays already discussed earlier in the chapter. For later examples compare the largely plain style of *Julius Caesar* with the rich, expansive style of *Antony and Cleopatra*,[12] the one in the language of political urgency, the other in the language of love, war, and empire; or the lyric cadences of the latter with the harsh music of *Coriolanus*. The distinctiveness in style among plays is perhaps most clearly marked in the great tragedies, but it is also certainly felt in other plays, as between the tight formality of *Richard II* and the lively freedom of the Henry IV plays, or between these and *Henry V*, with its fervid battle rhetoric and epic narratives.

Style is made up of a great many components, lexical, grammatical, rhetorical, and prosodic. In a play we are watching and hearing on the stage, when our attention is largely absorbed in what is going on and in discovery of the characters, we cannot be equally well aware of all features of the style. Awareness of style, of course, varies with the listener's interests, knowledge, sensitivity, and familiarity with the play; but, speaking generally, I should judge some features to be more obtrusive than others and more apt to be noticed. Those which, in my judgment, we are most likely to be consciously aware of are these: the large organization of the speeches, whether in monologue or dialogue, whether formally ordered in rhetorical patterns (as in orations or lamentations) or informally loose, suggesting the natural movement of thought (as in a Hamlet soliloquy), whether in verse or in prose, and if in verse whether rimed or unrimed; levels of diction, whether formal or informal, literary or colloquial, educated or ignorant; word-play and wit. Other, subtler features of style which must affect us but which we may not be fully conscious of, unless we know the play very well through reading as well as hearing, are range of vocabulary, niceties of diction (e.g., using a noun as a verb—"knee his throne"), imagery, unless elaborated in long similes or descriptions, syntax (mood, tense, types of sentences), metrical and rhythmic variations in blank verse, or even, sometimes, variations between verse and prose.

Whatever is spoken in a play—in short, all the features of the style—must, we suppose, contribute somehow to the total effect on us, that is, to our felt response, but in different ways and in greatly varying degrees. For instance, noticeably different levels of diction, sometimes re-enforced by contrasts of verse and prose, may serve chiefly for local humor, as with Launce and his dog in *The Two Gentlemen of Verona*, but they may also emphasize a distinction between characters and even set a social tone for the play, as with servants and masters in the *Two Gentlemen*, artisans and aristocrats in *A Midsummer Night's Dream*. A scene of wit may have merely a local effect, as in *Romeo and Juliet* the conversation between Mercutio and the Nurse gives a chance for the random display of Mercutio's wit and the Nurse's stupidity. But in another in-

stance a witty episode may mark a theme or situation of dramatic importance and heighten dramatic irony, as does Mercutio's jesting with Romeo about his old love just when, unknown to the jester, Romeo is on urgent business about his
wedding to Juliet; or as does Hamlet's mockery of Polonius in
the fishmonger and Jephthah dialogues and elsewhere, or of
Claudius, with special mordancy, when the King asks him what
he has done with the body of Polonius.

Shakespeare certainly learned to exploit devices of style for
more than conventional and local uses, as for example with his
extremely varied use of prose, by no means confined to social
distinctions or even to the distinction between high comedy
and low. Here are some examples of a variety of uses. In *As
You Like It*, prose marks a distinction in tone between two
sorts of high comedy; the Duke's idealized life in the woods is
in verse, Rosalind's merry wooing of Orlando, in prose. In
Hamlet prose is the medium for a variety of moods—feigned
and comic madness at the expense of Polonius and others, reflection (as in "What a piece of work"), jangled emotions (as
in the "nunnery" scene), change of pace or pitch in many places.
In *Lear*, prose is used for quick treatment of ongoing action in
the minor plot, for reduction of emotion and pitch at intervals
in the storm scenes or between them, for mental disorder. In
these two tragedies, this subtly varied use of prose in conjunction with the dominant verse amounts to orchestration. It has
much to do obliquely, if not directly, with dramatic effects. We
might go on with illustrations of Shakespeare's inventive uses
of other features of style to extend their dramatic effectiveness,
but such uses are the concern of the essays to follow.

To come back for a moment to the question of what makes
each play sound different from every other. Sensitive readers
have always responded to the distinctive qualities of the language of particular plays. Read Hazlitt on *Macbeth* or *Hamlet*,[13] for example. But impressions of distinctiveness are resist-
ant to analysis, since so many things may be working at once,
co-operatively and inseparably. Quantitative questions of what
features of style contribute more or less to these impressions
are unanswerable, partly because different listeners and read-

ers must vary greatly in their alertness to them, but chiefly
because in experience they are not separable quantities. In any
work of art the whole is more than the sum of its parts. Still,
how a master dramatist uses the many resources of language
to serve the ends of his dramatic art remains a challenging
question. Analysis is the business of criticism, and there remains much to be learned, I think, about the dramatic functioning of Shakespeare's language in its many aspects.

In recent years immense critical attention has been given to
one feature of style which is readily separable in analysis and
which seems promising as a feature of distinction among plays:
that is imagery. Caroline Spurgeon's work on "iterative imagery"[14] in Shakespeare began a long line of criticism focussed on
image patterns in single plays or in groups of plays, and many
generations of students in English, undergraduate and graduate, eagerly searched out new patterns, hitherto unobserved
and unsuspected. Iterative imagery means the repetition in a
given play of certain subjects in the images, such as disease in
Hamlet, animals in *Lear* and *Othello,* food in *Troilus and Cres-
sida,* and so on. Undeniably these running images, where they
are truly such—that is, where they appear in recurrent themes
(such as the rotten state of Denmark perceived by Hamlet) or
in a context which draws attention to them—may be of great
importance in contributing to a distinctive tone in the play in
which they occur. But there is a distinction between hearing
them on the stage and reading them. Unless they are dwelt on
we have less time to become conscious of them in listening
than in reading, not to mention re-reading. What the effects of
iterative images are in the theater is difficult to know. They
perhaps act subliminally to re-enforce impressions we get from
direct statement. Context, whether in listening or in reading, is
always important. In studies of image-patterns, the critical
dangers of image-counting, regardless of the immediate context of the image, and of spinning a web of images which may
come to seem more important than the fable itself have not
always been avoided. The work of a number of scholars has
been corrective and important in keeping the focus on the
function of the images in their dramatic context.[15]

Less attention has been paid to another aspect of images, and that is to their structure—as, for example, in the distinction between a metaphor and a simile, or between a clear and consistent metaphor (of a word, sentence, or longer passage, as in a conceit) and a shifting series of metaphors, often knotted and inconsistent with each other. The stylistic effect is greatly different. I once made a study of such structural differences in the imagery of *Richard II* and *1 Henry IV*, and proposed these as a sign of a watershed in Shakespeare's development.[16] For though in *Richard II* there is some anticipation of the complex image structures characteristic of *1 Henry IV*, in the latter play and afterwards there is very rarely, and only for a special local effect, a return to the formally laid out, sustained metaphors or allegories of *Richard II;* I also suggested the dramatic appropriateness of that different handling of imagery in the two plays. Richard's conceits, worked out elaborately and at length, do catch and hold the attention of an audience, not just for the matter but for the manner. These I have sufficiently illustrated.

Other structural features, such as syntax, have also had little attention with respect to possible common patterns within a given play. Syntax is important stylistically because in a play it is the very fabric of the dialogue. Not only does it carry the thought of the speaker as it is formed (that is, as the author imagines it forming), but in the structure of the sentences (simple, complex, compound; declarative, interrogative, exclamatory) or lack of structure (such as broken phrases) and in shifts of mood (from indicative to subjunctive or imperative), it may also convey habitual attitudes, momentary impulses, hesitations, doubts, special nuances. We know all this, of course, but generally think of syntax as merely expressive of the character or mood of the speaker, or of speakers interacting. In two plays, *Othello* and *King Lear*, I have found Shakespeare using it in a larger way. Dominant syntactical patterns which are used by the central characters extend beyond them to suggest moods and attitudes which are part of the whole dramatic movement.[17] I cannot say whether Shakespeare anywhere else uses syntax in a way so integral to the structure.

In recent years my own explorations of style have been centered in the great tragedies, where the distinctiveness I have
been discussing is most evidently manifested. The essays in this
volume are discrete, each one self-contained. Four of them
were written for special and separate occasions and were not
planned as a sequence. Those on *Hamlet, Antony and Cleopatra,* and *King Lear* were written as lectures, the one on
Othello for a Festschrift.

The essay on *Hamlet* was first designed rather simply as an
observation of the conscious importance Shakespeare gives to
language in this play and as a partial description of how he
uses it freely and inventively for his several dramatic ends. For
this collection the essay has been rewritten and expanded, with
a sharper focus on the stylistic art and with increased attention to the versatility of the language, especially in Hamlet's
speeches—a versatility which in itself gives the play a distinctive quality. Each of the other five essays is on some particular
feature of the play in question, a feature which is both intimately connected with the dramatic movement and contributory to a felt distinctiveness in the style.

In close reading and re-reading, I was consciously looking
for something other than iterative imagery, but did not set out
with any preconceptions of what I should find, except in *Lear.*
After many years of teaching that play and reading it aloud, I
knew that its insistent imperatives were unlike anything else in
Shakespeare, but I had not thought out, beyond character and
obvious theme, how intimately these and other complementary
syntactical patterns were linked to the movement of the action,
and how expressive all these were of the "world" of the play.

I had no preconceived idea of what I should find in *Othello,*
and the discovery of a syntactical pattern of conditional sentences, so sensitively repeated and varied and so perfectly
geared with the interplay of antagonist and protagonist in the
movement to tragedy, was immensely exciting. The distinctive
and controlling feature of *Antony and Cleopatra*—one connected closely with the imagery, but containing it and going
beyond it—seemed to me to be hyperbole, both as a trope and
as a mode of thought informing the entire tragedy. Shake-

speare, like most Elizabethans, is fond of hyperbole, but in no other play of his, I think, can it be said to be essential in just this total way.

Since the four essays had taken me so far into the tragedies, I decided to add pieces on others. For this collection, then, I have written an essay on *Julius Caesar* and one on *Coriolanus*. The one on *Julius Caesar* is on a special feature of the diction, the extraordinarily frequent and varied use of proper names, particularly of "Caesar" and "Brutus," so as to give them a dramatic function. The one on *Coriolanus* is on antithesis, paradox, and dilemma, both as figures and as modes of thought; they are as informing of the play, I believe, as hyperbole is of *Antony and Cleopatra*.

A concluding essay would be out of place, since the questions I have raised in this introductory essay probably have no certain answers. If they do, I do not know them.

No art at all

Language in *Hamlet*

WHAT A MARVEL is *Hamlet!* I mean in the legerdemain by which Shakespeare fools us into thinking Hamlet is a living person, that all those stupid or complaisant or crafty characters at the Danish court are, too—puzzled by him, worried about him, scheming to get at him. With what freedom and ease the language moves, with what shifts and turns and stops! in how many different keys, responsive to all the shades of passion and mood, to the movement of thought, to the inwardness of self-examination, to the ambience of public occasion!— as well to the awful return of a spirit from Purgatory as to the excited springing of a trap to catch royal prey; as well to the sarcastic baiting of a counsellor of state as to the lucid and despairing examination of a bad conscience. So natural, so alive, it all seems that we forget the art. Shakespeare intends us to do just that.

Originally given as a lecture at Los Angeles State College (now California State University, Los Angeles), November 1963, and published, under the title, "The Language of *Hamlet*," in *The Huntington Library Quarterly* 27 (May 1964), 259-78 (© 1964 by the Henry E. Huntington Library and Art Gallery). The essay has been extensively revised.

In a passage exhibiting Polonius humorously, Shakespeare
with tongue in cheek exercises his own formal training in rhetoric. Polonius offers to diagnose for the King and Queen Hamlet's apparent madness:

> My liege, and madam, to expostulate
> What majesty should be, what duty is,
> Why day is day, night night, and time is time,
> Were nothing but to waste night, day, and time;
> Therefore, since brevity is the soul of wit,
> And tediousness the limbs and outward flourishes,
> I will be brief. Your noble son is mad:
> Mad call I it, for to define true madness,
> What is't but to be nothing else but mad?
> But let that go.
>
> (II. ii. 86-95)

Polonius has begun with a deprecatory introduction in the
form of a *praeteritio*, a proposition, a rhetorical definition—all,
he supposes, wittily turned. When the Queen interposes, "More
matter with less art," he takes her remark for a compliment:
"Madam, I swear I use no art at all"—a modest disclaimer
which gives away his pride in it. The joke is, of course, that
concealing his art—the aim of the best orators—is precisely
what he is not doing; he cannot bear that his listeners should
miss any point of his masterly skill.

> That he's mad, 'tis true, 'tis true 'tis pity,
> And pity 'tis 'tis true—a foolish figure,
> But farewell it, for I will use no art.

The reluctant farewell means nothing, for he manages a good
many more foolish figures before he finally concludes his diagnosis with the "declension" of Hamlet into madness.

More seriously and subtly, Shakespeare makes use of another curious device of indirection, this time to conceal his own
art. There are two places in which he affects to quote something, to bring something in from outside the play itself. He
does not, of course, really bring anything in; he composes the
"quotations," but he sets them off in styles quite different from
any style in the body of the play.

One of these pieces is the play within the play, "The Murder of Gonzago" or "The Mouse-trap." This is how it goes:

> Full thirty times hath Phoebus' cart gone round
> Neptune's salt wash and Tellus' orbed ground,
> And thirty dozen moons with borrowed sheen
> About the world have times twelve thirties been,
> Since love our hearts and Hymen did our hands
> Unite comutual in most sacred bands.
> (III. ii. 155-60)

The conceits are formal and rather labored; the riming couplets are in a monotonous rhythm. The argument is largely built on sententious commonplaces: "What to ourselves in passion we propose,/ The passion ending, doth the purpose lose"; or "This world is not for aye, nor 'tis not strange/ That even our loves should with our fortunes change"; or "The great man down, you mark his favorite flies,/ The poor advanc'd makes friends of enemies." The points to be made, those meant to wring the withers of the King and those meant to bring a blush to Gertrude's face, are heavily, even tediously, amplified—not only so that the King and Queen will not miss them, but so that we hardly can, either, for our primary attention must be on Hamlet, and, with Hamlet's, on Claudius and Gertrude. We are not to be absorbed in "The Murder of Gonzago" for its own sake, but to get its message while we are caught up in the excitement of watching these three during the mounting tension marked by Hamlet's pointed comments—"Wormwood, wormwood!"[1] "Let the gall'd jade winch, our withers are unwrung," "Come, the croaking raven doth bellow for revenge!"—until the climax of the King's abrupt rising and the play's abrupt ending. But Shakespeare is also serving another, less evident, purpose, in the sharp differentiation between the styles of the play within the play and the play itself. The conspicuous artfulness of the one enhances the seeming naturalness of the other.

The other most important "quoted" passage is the one on the slaughter of Priam (II. ii. 450 ff.). Hamlet invites the chief player to recite a passage from a play Hamlet likes, evidently a play about Dido and Aeneas, and the speech he recalls is from

Aeneas' tale to Dido on the last events in Troy before it fell.
The style of this tragedy is quite different from that of "The
Murder of Gonzago"; this compels attention to its positive features. Listen to the verse and the diction as Hamlet begins the
recitation:

> 'The rugged Pyrrhus, he whose sable arms,
> Black as his purpose, did the night resemble
> When he lay couched in th' ominous horse,
> Hath now this dread and black complexion smear'd
> With heraldry[2] more dismal: head to foot
> Now is he total gules, horridly trick'd
> With blood of fathers, mothers, daughters, sons,
> Bak'd and impasted with the parching streets,
> That lend a tyrannous and a damned light
> To their lord's murther. Roasted in wrath and fire,
> And thus o'er-sized with coagulate gore,
> With eyes like carbuncles, the hellish Pyrrhus
> Old grandsire Priam seeks.'

The old-fashioned Senecan style had been popular twelve to
fifteen years earlier than Shakespeare's *Hamlet*. The vocabulary is heavy, turgid, highly rhetorical. It is the necrophilous and
Stygian vocabulary of *Thyestes*: "blood," "gules," "coagulate
gore," "sable," "black," "baked," "impasted," "roasted," "dread,"
"dismal," "ominous," "hellish," "damned." Critics have argued a
good deal about whether Shakespeare could possibly have admired this style, and whether he was not intentionally making
fun of it. But Shakespeare's taste in the matter is beside the
point: what matters is that he makes Hamlet admire the speech
—it is "caviary to the general."

As the actor takes over from Hamlet and carries on in fine
histrionic style through the description of the distraught Hecuba,[3] who bursts into clamor at the sight of Pyrrhus making
"malicious sport/ In mincing with his sword her husband's
limbs," Shakespeare lays the groundwork for the dramatic
function of the speech. Hamlet is so struck by the actor's emotion over a fiction, a dream of passion, that he is moved, after
the others leave, to soliloquize on his own imagined lack of
passion in a true cause:

> What's Hecuba to him, or he to Hecuba,
> That he should weep for her? What would he do
> Had he the motive and the cue for passion
> That I have? He would drown the stage with tears,
> And cleave the general ear with horrid speech,
> Make mad the guilty, and appal the free, . . .
> Yet I,
> A dull and muddy-mettled rascal, peak
> Like John-a-dreams, unpregnant of my cause,
> And can say nothing.

The recital piece must be patently "artificial," conspicuously different from the larger piece of art, the play of *Hamlet*, in which it is set. For Hamlet's point to be made, there must be for us, the audience, only one fiction, the account of Pyrrhus' slaughter of Priam and of Hecuba's grief. The old-fashioned diction and rhetoric of the passage must, by contrast, make us think of the language of Hamlet as the very language of men, of Hamlet himself as a living person—as one of us. Absorbed in his response to the actor's recitation, we perhaps do not even notice—at least if we are watching, not reading—that the soliloquy is phrased in the cadences of blank verse, not in the prose of everyday speech. Although the verse should, and probably does, give us a special pleasure, it does not call attention to itself as art, however much it actually is. It does not interfere with our being one with Hamlet in his experience.

Still another short passage is used for the same effect as these two "quotations" from plays Hamlet liked—that is, to divert our attention from the art of *Hamlet*. This passage is a quotation from Hamlet himself, the letter to Ophelia which Polonius reads to the King and Queen. The verses in it startle us with their triteness:

> 'Doubt thou the stars are fire,
> Doubt that the sun doth move,
> Doubt truth to be a liar,
> But never doubt I love.'

(II. ii. 116-19)

Hamlet forstalls our criticism, however, with his own: "O dear Ophelia, I am ill at these numbers. I have not art to reckon my

groans." For Shakespeare to exhibit Hamlet as emphatically no
poet in a play in which he is the chief speaker of lines of ac-
complished poetry is an even more oblique device to make us
move with Hamlet's feelings as if he were a living person, not
a fictional creature. Shakespeare had made use of a similar indirection in the expressive Hotspur's detestation of poetry:

> I had rather hear a brazen canstick turn'd,
> Or a dry wheel grate on the axle-tree,
> And that would set my teeth nothing on edge,
> Nothing so much as mincing poetry.
>
> > (*1 Henry IV*, III. i. 129-32)[4]

Thus far, except for Polonius' aborted oration and the letter
to Ophelia, I have been speaking of language outside the action. We may now turn, in contrast, to the language within the
dramatic action of the play and notice its range.[5] The play
opens with simple, natural talk (albeit in blank verse) as the
sentries change their watch:

> *Fran.*   You come most carefully upon your hour.
> *Bar.*   'Tis now struck twelve. Get thee to bed, Francisco.
> *Fran.*   For this relief much thanks. 'Tis bitter cold,
> And I am sick at heart.
> *Bar.*   Have you had quiet guard?
> *Fran.*   Not a mouse stirring.
> *Bar.*   Well, good night.

But the fearsome awe with which the Ghost—"this dreaded
sight"—must impress us is marked by language which always
imparts dignity to its motion: "With martial stalk hath he gone
by our watch"; "See, it stalks away"; "with solemn march/ Goes
slow and stately by them."

Another style in this first scene is the easy, vivid movement
of Horatio's exposition on the state of things in the kingdom.
First, Marcellus asks what is going on in Denmark, why there
are so many preparations for war, evident in the work round
the clock and round the week at the ordnance factories and
shipyards: "Who is't that can inform me?" Horatio replies:
"That can I,/ At least the whisper goes so." He fills us in on
some past history of a war between Denmark and Norway, and
on the peace treaty made, then continues:

>   Now, sir, young Fortinbras,
> Of unimproved mettle hot and full,
> Hath in the skirts of Norway here and there
> Shark'd up a list of lawless resolutes
> For food and diet to some enterprise
> That hath a stomach in't, which is no other,
> As it doth well appear unto our state,
> But to recover of us, by strong hand
> And terms compulsatory, those foresaid lands
> So by his father lost; and this, I take it,
> Is the main motive of our preparations,
> The source of this our watch, and the chief head
> Of this post-haste and romage in the land.

The syntax is varied, complex, generally loose, though with explanatory interruptions which make for momentary suspensions in the forward movement. Much is said in short space; there is much compression, much metaphorical suggestion, yet the lines move with speed. The homely "post-haste" and "romage" (rummage) give them naturalness and strength. This style might be called the underlying staple of the play, when it is simply moving forward, where no heightening of passion or play of wit is wanted. No special effects are intended, nor is differentiation of character necessarily in question. The same kind of language is spoken by Horatio, Claudius, Laertes, even Hamlet at times. This style is not primarily a matter of character, but of occasion or dramatic function—simply, as I said, of the play's moving forward. Compare Claudius' comment to Gertrude, late in the play, when he has just witnessed mad Ophelia's pitiful performance:

> O Gertrude, Gertrude,
> When sorrows come, they come not single spies,
> But in battalions: first, her father slain;
> Next, your son gone, and he most violent author
> Of his own just remove; the people muddied,
> Thick and unwholesome in their thoughts and whispers
> For good Polonius' death; and we have done but greenly
> In hugger-mugger to inter him.
>
>   (IV. v. 77-84)

Or compare Hamlet, telling Horatio how he discovered the
King's plot against his life:

> Up from my cabin,
> My sea-gown scarf'd about me, in the dark
> Grop'd I to find out them, had my desire,
> Finger'd their packet, . . .
>
> (V. ii. 12-15)

Or even the ghost of King Hamlet, describing the manner of
his death when, as he was sleeping within his orchard, Hamlet's uncle stole upon him,

> With juice of cursed hebona in a vial,
> And in the porches of my ears did pour
> The leprous distillment, whose effect
> Holds such an enmity with blood of man
> That swift as quicksilver it courses through
> The natural gates and alleys of the body,
> And with a sudden vigor it doth posset
> And curd, like eager droppings into milk,
> The thin and wholesome blood. So did it mine, . . .
>
> (I. v. 62-70)

Contrast these speeches with the studied balance and antithesis in Claudius' formal opening speech from the throne:

> Though yet of Hamlet our dear brother's death
> The memory be green, and that it us befitted
> To bear our hearts in grief, and our whole kingdom
> To be contracted in one brow of woe,
> Yet so far hath discretion fought with nature
> That we with wisest sorrow think on him
> Together with remembrance of ourselves.
> Therefore our sometime sister, now our queen,
> Th' imperial jointress to this warlike state,
> Have we, as 'twere with a defeated joy,
> With an auspicious, and a dropping eye,
> With mirth in funeral, and with dirge in marriage,
> In equal scale weighing delight and dole,
> Taken to wife.
>
> (I. ii. 1-14)

This is a politician's speech. Claudius is seeking by his phrasing to make acceptable, and apparently "wise," an action about which there might be some serious questions; above all, trying to make appear harmonious what is by nature antithetical and in some way shocking—"mirth in funeral," "dirge in marriage," "a defeated joy." This figure is what the Elizabethan rhetoricians called *synoeciosis*, or composition of contraries;⁶ here the contraries ought not to be composed. The strain is evident in the grotesque image of "with an auspicious, and a dropping eye."

The falsity of this nice balance between "delight" and "dole" is exposed by Hamlet's first bitter pun—"A little more than kin, and less than kind"—when Claudius tries to draw him into the family circle with his ingratiating "But now, my cousin Hamlet, and my son—." Hamlet refuses the "wisest sorrow," the equality of delight and dole.

> *King.* How is it that the clouds still hang on you?
> *Ham.* Not so, my lord, I am too much in the sun.

The hollowness beneath this composition of contraries is further exposed by Hamlet in his sarcastic reply to his mother, when she urges him to put aside this mourning for his father:

> *Queen.* Do not for ever with thy vailed lids
> Seek for thy noble father in the dust.
> Thou know'st 'tis common; all that lives must die,
> Passing through nature to eternity.
> *Ham.* Ay, madam, it is common.

(The emptiness of this truism in Gertrude's mouth is indicated by her "for ever." We are soon to learn that her husband has been dead less than two months.)

> *Ham.* Ay, madam, it is common.
> *Queen.*   If it be,
> Why seems it so particular with thee?
> *Ham.* Seems, madam? nay, it is, I know not 'seems'.
> 'Tis not alone my inky cloak, good mother,
> Nor customary suits of solemn black,
> Nor windy suspiration of forc'd breath,

> No, nor the fruitful river in the eye,
> Nor the dejected havior of the visage,
> Together with all forms, moods, shapes of grief,
> That can denote me truly. These indeed seem,
> For they are actions that a man might play,
> But I have that within which passes show,
> These but the trappings and the suits of woe.
>   (I. ii. 74-86)

Note the language of this speech, how everything is exaggerated and hyperbolic; in Hamlet's phrasing, the mourning
clothes and the mourning attitudes all appear slightly ridiculous. If we are puzzled by this tone of Hamlet's we are presently, in his first soliloquy, to learn the reason for it. So his
mother dressed, apparently; so she sighed and wept as she followed her husband's coffin:

>   That it should come to this!
> But two months dead, nay, not so much, not two. . . .
> Let me not think on't! Frailty, thy name is woman!—
> A little month, or ere those shoes were old
> With which she followed my poor father's body,
> Like Niobe, all tears—why she, even she—
> O God, a beast that wants discourse of reason
> Would have mourn'd longer—married with my uncle, . . .
>   Within a month,
> Ere yet the salt of most unrighteous tears
> Had left the flushing in her galled eyes,
> She married.
>   (ll. 137-56)

She cannot have meant any of her grief-stricken display, or so
it seems to Hamlet. Hence his pointed, "I know not 'seems'."
His grief is real: "I have that within which passes show."

This speech gives us the key to Hamlet's central question:
What is and what is not? What is the world truly like under its
fine outward show? We hear echoes of the question in many
places, as in Hamlet's bitter charge to Ophelia in the nunnery
scene, reflecting on women generally:

> God hath given you one face, and you make yourselves
> another. You jig and amble, and you lisp, you nickname
> God's creatures and make your wantonness your ignorance.
> (III. i. 143-46)

Shakespeare makes Hamlet always alert to pretense, to false
sentiment, to exaggeration, and often makes him respond in
kind. By parody or exaggeration he exposes the shallowness or
falsity betrayed in the speaker's manner or language. The exposure is done in a purely comic way with Osric, whose modish
lingo Hamlet outdoes: "Sir, his definement suffers no perdition
in you, though I know to divide him inventorially would dozy
th' arithmetic of memory, and yet but yaw neither in respect of
his quick sail, but in the verity of extolment . . ." and much
more of the same (V. ii. 112-15).

Exposure is made in another mood, an intense and passionate mood, with Laertes in the graveyard (V. i. 246 ff.).
The funeral of Ophelia, with its abbreviated rites, is going
forward. Her coffin has been lowered into the grave, and the
Queen has scattered flowers on the body. Laertes cries out:

> O, treble woe
> Fall ten times treble on that cursed head
> Whose wicked deed thy most ingenious sense
> Depriv'd thee of! Hold off the earth a while,
> Till I have caught her once more in mine arms.
> [*Leaps in the grave.*]
> Now pile your dust upon the quick and dead,
> Till of this flat a mountain you have made
> T' o'ertop old Pelion, or the skyish head
> Of blue Olympus.

The speech and the gesture draw Hamlet out of the shadows:

> What is he whose grief
> Bears such an emphasis, whose phrase of sorrow
> Conjures the wand'ring stars and makes them stand
> Like wonder-wounded hearers? This is I,
> Hamlet the Dane!
> [*Hamlet leaps in after Laertes.*]

After they have grappled, been pulled apart, and come out of the grave, Hamlet angrily outdoes Laertes in hyperbolic offers:

> 'Swounds, show me what thou't do.
> Woo't weep, woo't fight, woo't fast, woo't tear thyself?
> Woo't drink up eisel? eat a crocodile?
> I'll do't. Dost thou come here to whine?
> To outface me with leaping in her grave?
> Be buried quick with her, and so will I.
> And if thou prate of mountains, let them throw
> Millions of acres on us, till our ground,
> Singeing his pate against the burning zone,
> Make Ossa like a wart! Nay, and thou'lt mouth,
> I'll rant as well as thou.

Since Hamlet has had no quarrel with Laertes, we are startled with the violence of his outburst. We must understand, I think, that it goes hard with him to be blamed by Laertes for Ophelia's death. Moreover, it seems clear from these lines that he detects a false note in Laertes' ostentatious display of grief. We cannot suppose that Laertes would have let himself be buried as a result of his sudden impulse. Note Hamlet's pejorative verbs: "whine," "prate," "mouth," "rant." Note the precise rhetorical word, "emphasis," for the heightened language. He tells Horatio later that "the bravery" (showiness) of Laertes' grief put him into a towering passion. We are led to ask what Laertes' love for his sister amounted to. He has shown himself to be fond of her, certainly, but with no certain perception of her feelings. Like Polonius he belongs to that world of policy in which love is suspect. Such a simple possibility as Hamlet's love for Ophelia, a love without self-interest, given honestly and unconditionally, her father and her brother never seriously entertained; and hers for him did not count, for she was a green girl. Their prudential counsel to her was good enough as worldly wisdom, no doubt—Lord Hamlet was a prince, out of her star, he could not marry whom he chose, his blaze gave more light than heat, his love was

> a fashion and a toy in blood,
> A violet in the youth of primy nature,

> Forward, not permanent, sweet, not lasting,
> The perfume and suppliance of a minute—
>
> (I. iii. 6-9)

and so on. The only trouble with the advice was that it did
not speak to the truth. Polonius did indeed admit his mistake,
only to fall into another error, namely, that Hamlet had gone
mad for love. He and his son are shown to move on a wholly
different plane of ethical perception from Hamlet's. Between
them they had infected Ophelia with mistrust of Hamlet, and,
however innocently, even Laertes had had a part in wrecking
her life. It is no wonder that Hamlet could say, after Laertes'
hyperboles at the grave, "I lov'd Ophelia. Forty thousand
brothers/ Could not with all their quantity of love/ Make up
my sum."

It is through these quick verbal responses of Hamlet's to the
betraying nuances of language and manner that we are alerted
to the varieties of false-seeming which surround the Prince: the
faddish language of the empty-headed fop, the overblown protestations of the heedless youth, the trite moral commonplaces
of the politic men and the shallow woman, the devious rhetoric
of the astute politician with something to hide. Hamlet is by
no means objective in his witty or passionate responses to the
seemers. But though we may not always assent wholly to his
judgments, we always trust his perceptions. His sensitivity to
the affected or false or strained note is our touchstone of
honesty.

This function of Hamlet's sensitiveness as a touchstone is
important, I believe, in how we are meant to take the Ghost.
Nothing in Hamlet's response, on its first appearance to him,
suggests falsity or duplicity in the Ghost. The skeptical Horatio's conviction assures us, the audience, that the apparition is
to be taken as real, not as a figment of the imagination. Hamlet's reception of the Ghost's message assures us that the
apparition is also to be taken precisely as the ghost of King
Hamlet and that its narration is true. Had Shakespeare intended us to take the apparition otherwise—as "goblin damn'd"
or spirit from hell—we should have expected signs of some sort
to alert us. But the signs point all the other way. And Hamlet,

always sensitive to truth, detects no false note. It is only later, with the horror and the awfulness of the burden upon him, that he is shown to be in doubt of the Ghost's honesty; at its re-appearance in his mother's chamber, his immediate response is again unquestioning belief.

Through his responses to the false notes in the language of others Hamlet is established as the touchstone of truth. This function is dramatically important. For we see the world al-ways through his eyes, and we must trust without question his own honesty of intent. He uses words himself in a great variety of ways, and we must feel, beneath all the exaggerations, the self-reproaches, the rages, the witty jibes, and the bitter taunts, the passionate earnestness in his search for the truth.

Hamlet has many voices, yet they are all Hamlet's. He has also what the rhetoricians called *energeia*—vigor or animation of style. Aristotle equates ἐνέργεια, or activity, with κίνησις, or movement; Quintilian speaks of that "ἐνέργεια, or vigour . . . which derives its name from action and finds its peculiar func-tion in securing that nothing that we say is tame."[7] In Hamlet's style the range and the intensity together are the key to the extraordinary vitality we feel in him. No character in literature has more. We may distinguish in Hamlet principally the lan-guage of passion, the language of mockery, the language of re-flection. There is another voice, too, which ought not to be for-gotten in any analysis of Hamlet's ways of talking, though it appears less frequently. It is the normal, engaging manner of Hamlet in everyday conversation, as when he greets Horatio and Marcellus with spontaneous courtesy: "Horatio—or I do forget myself . . ." and then "Sir, my good friend—I'll change that name with you" (I. ii. 161, 163). Or as when with gra-cious jesting he welcomes the traveling players to Elsinore: "You are welcome, masters, welcome all. I am glad to see thee well. . . . O, old friend! why, thy face is valanc'd since I saw thee last; com'st thou to beard me in Denmark? . . ." (II. ii. 421 ff.). Or as when before the duel he begs Laertes' pardon for the accidental killing of Polonius:

> Give me your pardon, sir. I have done you wrong,
> But pardon't as you are a gentleman. . . .

Sir, in this audience,
Let my disclaiming from a purpos'd evil
Free me so far in your most generous thoughts,
That I have shot my arrow o'er the house
And hurt my brother.

(V. ii. 226-44)

(Nothing better shows up Hamlet's candor against Laertes'
duplicity, for while Laertes answers,

I am satisfied in nature,
Whose motive in this case should stir me most
To my revenge, . . .
I do receive your offer'd love like love,
And will not wrong it,

we know that he intends to fight Hamlet with an unbated foil,
anointed with a deadly poison.) This frank, normal manner of
Hamlet's is, however, rare in a tragedy concerned with his
mental turmoil. The major voices, or modes of speaking, are,
then, the voices of passion, mockery, and reflection. They are,
of course, not always separate. Mockery may enter, and often
does, into the passion (as in the speeches to Rosencrantz and
Guildenstern in the recorder episode, III. ii. 296 ff., and to
Laertes in the graveyard scene, V. i. 254 ff.). And the intensity
of the passion may be expressed in close and logical argument,
as in some of the persuasive speeches to his mother in the
closet scene. But there are speeches we can separate.

We may consider first the mode of passion. Our concern is
with the dramatic purpose of the speech, with Hamlet's response to the situation in which he finds himself. One response
is grief at his father's death, shock at his mother's falsity or
shallowness. This is shown especially well in the first soliloquy
(I. ii. 129 ff.), already commented on and quoted from. Note
how, as Dover Wilson once pointed out,[8] the sentences circle
round and round the vision that he keeps trying to put out of
his mind, but that keeps returning: "That it should come to
this!/ But two months dead, nay, not so much, not two./ . . .
Must I remember? . . . and yet, within a month— . . . A little
month, . . . why, she, even she— . . ." His first response to the

Ghost's disclosure is passionate assent to the charge given him, and physical shock:

> O all you host of heaven! O earth! What else?
> And shall I couple hell? O fie, hold, hold, my heart,
> And you, my sinews, grow not instant old,
> But bear me stiffly up. Remember thee!
> (I. v. 92-95)

Another response is savage hatred of Claudius, often expressed in coarse, ugly, brutal language, as in the Hecuba soliloquy:

> Hah, 'swounds, I should take it; for it cannot be
> But I am pigeon-liver'd, and lack gall
> To make oppression bitter, or ere this
> I should 'a' fatted all the region kites
> With this slave's offal. Bloody, bawdy villain!
> Remorseless, treacherous, lecherous, kindless villain!
> (II. ii. 576-81)

Notice the cadences in the epithets, the falling rhythm, the chiming endings. Or notice the grossly vivid images in the speech when Hamlet comes upon the King at prayer:

> Up, sword, and know thou a more horrid hent:
> When he is drunk asleep, or in his rage,
> Or in th' incestious pleasure of his bed,
> At game a-swearing, or about some act
> That has no relish of salvation in't—
> Then trip him, that his heels may kick at heaven,
> And that his soul may be as damn'd and black
> As hell, whereto it goes.
> (III. iii. 88-95)

His speeches of persuasion to his mother in the closet scene (III. iv) are also speeches of passion, intense and earnest; he paints the enormity of her action in strong colors. She has done

> Such an act
> That blurs the grace and blush of modesty,
> Calls virtue hypocrite, takes off the rose
> From the fair forehead of an innocent love

And sets a blister there, makes marriage vows
As false as dicers' oaths, O, such a deed
As from the body of contraction plucks
The very soul, and sweet religion makes
A rhapsody of words. Heaven's face does glow
O'er this solidity and compound mass
With heated visage, as against the doom;
Is thought-sick at the act.[9]

Hamlet sees the breaking of the marriage vow as a blow
struck at sacred bonds generally, hence at religion itself; he
imagines the response of Heaven to such an act to be a prefiguring of Doomsday. His charges against her of sexual
grossness, or even unnaturalness, at a time when the hey-
day in the blood should be tame and wait upon the judgment, are likewise put in extreme terms. She cannot call it
love; her sense must be apoplexed to allow her to step from
her wholesome husband to this "mildewed ear," his brother:

            O shame, where is thy blush?
Rebellious hell,
If thou canst mutine in a matron's bones,
To flaming youth let virtue be as wax
And melt in her own fire. Proclaim no shame
When the compulsive ardure gives the charge,
Since frost itself as actively doth burn,
And reason panders will.

Under such pressure she does indeed repent. It is just this
intense conviction of Hamlet's and his power of making vivid
to her the immorality of what she has done that move her to
repentance; for he is able to turn her eyes into her very soul
to see "such black and grained spots/ As will not leave their
tinct."

To make sure that her mood of repentance holds, Hamlet
puts positively, for emphasis, what he is enjoining her not to
do:

Not this, by no means, that I bid you do:
Let the bloat king tempt you again to bed,
Pinch wanton on your cheek, call you his mouse,

And let him, for a pair of reechy kisses,
Or paddling in your neck with his damn'd fingers,
Make you to ravel all this matter out,
That I essentially am not in madness,
But mad in craft.

This speech has the quality of *enargeia*,[10] of setting something before the eyes with lively clarity—here, a disgusting clarity. Lest we take the easy way out offered us by the Freudians of reading Hamlet's reproaches as morbid love for his mother, we should remember that, in keeping with the Ghost's admonition not to contrive anything against her, he had charged himself to speak daggers to her, but to use none. The amplification in his speeches—by such methods as hyperbolic diction, exaggerated comparison, and heaping up of detail—is persuasive rhetoric of the emotional kind at its strongest. If we shift the onus of aberrant behavior from Gertrude to Hamlet, we are doing what she does in blaming Hamlet's wild behavior (at the Ghost's sudden reappearance) on his madness. "Lay not that flattering unction to your soul," Hamlet enjoins her, "That not your trespass but my madness speaks."

Hamlet can be as passionate in self-reproach as in reproach to his mother. The Hecuba or "O, what a rogue" soliloquy affords the best example:

                                        Yet I,
A dull and muddy-mettled rascal, peak
Like John-a-dreams, unpregnant of my cause,
And can say nothing; no, not for a king,
Upon whose property and most dear life
A damn'd defeat was made. Am I a coward?
Who calls me villain, breaks my pate across,
Plucks off my beard and blows it in my face,
Tweaks me by the nose, gives me the lie i' th' throat
As deep as to the lungs? Who does me this?
Ha, 'swounds, I should take it; for it cannot be
But I am pigeon-liver'd, and lack gall
To make oppression bitter.
                                   (II. ii. 566-78)

Again, the speech is both vigorous and vivid, because of the
strong colloquial diction, the rhetorical questions, the swiftly
sketched actions. These exaggerated charges against himself
for lack of feeling and for cowardice are demonstrably not
true. This very speech gives the lie to his own charge of dull-
ness. Recognizing the futility of such outbursts, he makes,
himself, the best comment on the quality of the speech:

> Why, what an ass am I! This is most brave,[11]
> That I, the son of a dear father murther'd,
> Prompted to my revenge by heaven and hell,
> Must like a whore unpack my heart with words
> And fall a-cursing like a very drab,
> A scullion![12]
>
> (ll. 582-87)

But the outburst, in his state of "sore distraction," has been a
natural enough response. These final, corrective lines are
Shakespeare's artful way of helping us to interpret the speech
aright.

Another place in which we are made strongly aware of
Hamlet's "sore distraction" is in the "nunnery" scene (III. i),
that scene in which Ophelia and Hamlet are at cross-purposes,
and in which the tension mounts to an almost unbearable pitch.
Here, Hamlet's distraught state is marked by prose, looser
and more wayward than verse can be. Ophelia's image of
Hamlet's reason as like "sweet bells jangled out of time,[13] and
harsh" catches for us the discordant quality of the scene itself.
In *Hamlet* Shakespeare moves easily back and forth between
verse and prose according to occasion, purpose, and mood—not
with an eye to limited rules of decorum, but responsive to
dramatic need. So appropriate, so varied, so "natural" are both
his verse and his prose in this play that in hearing the dialogue
we respond to the change of tone and of nuance without
always noticing the medium.

The voice of "sore distraction" sometimes takes another form,
of "wild and whirling words" that suggest a release from tension, a rebound from some terrible concentration of passion.
The first instance of this is in the somewhat disjointed response

(I. v. 115 ff.) Hamlet makes to Horatio and Marcellus after his interview with the Ghost. We hear the strange note first when he answers Marcellus' call, "Illo, ho, ho, my lord!" with "Hillo, ho, ho, boy! Come, bird, come." We hear it again in his avoidance of direct response to their natural curiosity: "What news, my lord?"

> *Ham.*   There's never a villain dwelling in all Denmark
> But he's an arrant knave.
> *Hor.*   There needs no ghost, my lord, come from the grave
> To tell us this.
> *Ham.*   Why, right, you are in the right,
> And so, without more circumstance at all,
> I hold it fit that we shake hands and part,
> You, as your business and desire shall point you,
> For every man hath business and desire,
> Such as it is, and for my own poor part,
> Look you, I'll go pray.
> *Hor.*   These are but wild and whirling words, my lord.
> *Ham.*   I am sorry they offend you, heartily,
> Yes, faith, heartily.
>
> (I. v. 123-35)

Another example of this release from tension, though in a very different mood, is Hamlet's excitement after the play scene:

> 'Why, let the strooken deer go weep,
>   The hart ungalled play,
> For some must watch while some must sleep,
>   Thus runs the world away.'
>
> (III. ii. 271-74)

The excitement is sustained through much of the conversation with Rosencrantz and Guildenstern that follows. But its disjointedness to them is only Hamlet's impudence; he is quite able to reword the matter, as his recorder lesson shows.

This episode brings us naturally to the mode of mockery, another mode quite as frequent as the mode of passion. It is Hamlet's protection against the spies with which he is beset; he plays up to Polonius' theory that he is mad for love and to

the King's that he may be brooding on ambition. He loves to
feed Polonius the bait that he takes so readily:

> *Ham.*   O Jephthah, judge of Israel, what a treasure hadst
> thou!
> *Pol.*   What a treasure had he, my lord?
> *Ham.*   Why—
>   'One fair daughter, and no more,
>   The which he loved passing well.'
> *Pol.* [*Aside.*]   Still on my daughter.
> *Ham.*   Am I not i' th' right, old Jephthah?
>   (II. ii. 403-10)

And he easily shows up those "sponges" of the King, Rosencrantz and Guildenstern, whose leading questions on ambition
he has turned aside:

> *Ham.*   . . . Will you play upon this pipe?
> *Guild.*   My lord, I cannot.
> *Ham.*   I pray you.
> *Guild.*   Believe me, I cannot.
> *Ham.*   I do beseech you.
> *Guild.*   I know no touch of it, my lord.
> *Ham.*   It is as easy as lying. Govern these ventages . . .
>   (III. ii. 350-57)

Hamlet's wit at the expense of the politicians makes him
the chorus of the play as well as the protagonist, its fool as
well as its hero. These particular "seemers"—Polonius, the King,
and the King's two cat's-paws—he mocks not by outdoing their
language, as he does with Laertes and Osric, but by otherwise
tailoring his method to the character and intelligence of the
victims. Certain features of the mockery, what one might call
the generic features of his assumed madness—a disconcerting
waywardness, shown in his abrupt changes of subject or apparent non-sequiturs, and a perverse habit of misinterpreting
his questioner's word or intent—may appear in any of his encounters. But these tricks are varied to fit the occasion and the
adversary.
  Towards his old schoolfellows he bears no initial ill-will, is

even willing to describe to them his depressed state of mind:
"I have of late . . . lost all my mirth, forgone all custom of exercises," and so on, from "this brave o'erhanging firmament" to
"this quintessence of dust" (II. ii. 291-309). But when, after the
play scene, he perceives that they are still serving as willing
spies of the King, he minces no words in letting them know
that he knows their mission. He first puts them down in jest by
refusing to make them "a wholesome answer" to their message
from his mother and by giving them a crumb for the King
("Sir, I lack advancement"). But then he forces them to play
the uncomfortable game with the recorders. He ends it with his
angry scorn at their incompetence, and at their effrontery in
trying to pluck out the heart of his mystery: ". . . there is much
music, excellent voice, in this little organ, yet cannot you make
it speak. 'Sblood, do you think I am easier to be play'd on than
a pipe? . . ." (III. ii. 296 ff.). Later, when they affect not to
understand his metaphors of the nuts (or apple)[14] kept in the
corner of the jaw to be first mouthed, then swallowed, and of
the squeezed sponge that will be dry again, he dismisses them
as of no consequence: "I am glad of it; a knavish speech sleeps
in a foolish ear" (IV. ii. 12-24).

Hamlet describes Polonius to his face in terms as insulting
as he uses to those two, and with more evident pleasure. No
need to quote his repulsive portrait of old men, with the iden-
tifying sting in the tail of it: "all which, sir, though I most
powerfully and potently believe, yet I hold it not honesty to
have it thus set down, for yourself, sir, shall grow as old as I
am, if like a crab you could go backward" (II. ii. 196-204).
But Polonius, in his fatuous conceit of his own powers of detec-
tion, is more fun to take in than the two dullards, and Hamlet
plays the game of "diseased" wit with him zestfully and often.
He plays it by satisfying the self-appointed clinician's notions
of how a madman should speak and act and thus draws him
into ridiculous responses and situations, as when he willingly
goes along with the transformation of Hamlet's imaginary cloud
from camel to weasel and from weasel to whale (III. ii. 376-
82). The same game is even more fun when Hamlet plays it
(as in the "fishmonger" and "Jephthah" sequences, II. ii. 170-

91, 403-20) so as to confirm the old man's own cherished diagnosis of the cause of Hamlet's lunacy. Hamlet's trick is to draw
Polonius to the lure by a riddling pronouncement, the meaning
of which he makes sure Polonius cannot miss. For example,
after an opening gambit of recognizing Polonius as a fishmonger and moralizing on the word, Hamlet remarks, in two apparent non-sequiturs: "For if the sun breed maggots in a dead
dog, being a good kissing carrion—Have you a daughter?" The
dialogue continues:

> *Pol.*   I have, my lord.
> *Ham.*   Let her not walk i' th' sun. Conception is a blessing,
> but as your daughter may conceive, friend,[15] look to't.
> *Pol.*   [*Aside.*]   How say you by that? still harping on my
> daughter. Yet he knew me not at first, . . .

Polonius, having in his youth suffered much extremity for love,
recognizes the symptoms. He has swallowed the bait, as he
will do again. The fun for Hamlet and for us is in watching the
man who thinks he is hunting the trail of policy so sure get
caught himself, yet never know it.

The game Hamlet plays with Claudius is also a game of impudence, insults, and veiled threats, but it is a far more dangerous, challenging, and interesting game, with a worthier opposite. Although Hamlet talks parabolically and twists meanings in the same perverse ways as with his other victims, he
knows he can leave interpretation to the King, a circumstance
in which he takes perceptible satisfaction. As with Polonius, he
teases Claudius with hints which support the listener's own
suspicions of the cause of his madness. This is the brief conversation the two have just before the play at court opens.

> *King.*   How fares our cousin Hamlet?
> *Ham.*   Excellent, i' faith, of the chameleon's dish: I eat the
> air, promise-cramm'd—you cannot feed capons so.
> (III. ii. 92-95)

But, unlike Polonius, the King does not bite: "I have nothing
with this answer, Hamlet; these words are not mine." Hamlet
turns away with an impertinent reply: "No, nor mine now."

After the King has been caught by "The Mouse-trap," Hamlet is bolder in mockery. In the interchange between them when Claudius demands of Hamlet where he has concealed the body of Polonius (IV. iii. 16 ff.), Hamlet again uses the parabolic form, but this time to preach a gruesome sermon on *vanitas vanitatum* and the grave-worm.

> *King.* Now, Hamlet, where's Polonius?
> *Ham.* At supper.
> *King.* At supper? where?
> *Ham.* Not where he eats, but where 'a is eaten; a certain convocation of politic worms are e'en at him. Your worm is your only emperor for diet: we fat all creatures else to fat us, and we fat ourselves for maggots; your fat king and your lean beggar is but variable service, two dishes, but to one table—that's the end.
> *King.* Alas, alas!
> *Ham.* A man may fish with the worm that hath eat of a king, and eat of the fish that hath fed of that worm.
> *King.* What dost thou mean by this?
> *Ham.* Nothing but to show you how a king may go a progress through the guts of a beggar.

Ignoring both the threat and the impudence, Claudius tries again: "Where is Polonius?" and Hamlet's reply is even naughtier:

> In heaven. Send thither to see; if your messenger find him not there, seek him i' th' other place yourself. But if indeed you find him not within this month, you shall nose him as you go up the stairs into the lobby.

Again, the same disconcerting misinterpretation of the speaker's meaning as we have heard before, but with a sharper edge. The sharpest edge of all is on a piece of sophistical reasoning to which Hamlet treats the King when, later in the scene, he is being packed off to England:

> *Ham.* . . . Farewell, dear mother.
> *King.* Thy loving father, Hamlet.
> *Ham.* My mother: father and mother is man and wife, man and wife is one flesh—so, my mother. Come, for England!

For Hamlet this impudence is a form of relief from the intensity of his passion. It is a relief for us, too. For example, this
scene with the King, with its mordant and macabre humor, follows soon after the intensely emotional scene with his mother.
The exchange between Hamlet and the King in prose lowers
the pitch. And normally the scenes of mockery and wit are in
prose.

We come, finally, to the mode of quiet reflection. Beneath
the passion, the mockery, the wit, there is something profound
—the fundamental questions which the burden imposed on
Hamlet have given rise to; and these questions he can sometimes face and consider in a dispassionate, objective way. He
does so notably in the "What a piece of work is a man" speech,
in the "To be or not to be" soliloquy, in the speech before the
play scene in praise of Horatio, and in the graveyard scene before the entry of the court for the funeral of Ophelia; also to a
lesser degree in the "How all occasions" soliloquy after the
passage of Fortinbras' army. The questions stated or implied in
his reflections are those commonplace, even trite, questions
which we all must ask, yet to which there are no certain answers: What is the world? What is a man? How ought one to
meet the problems of life? What is death?

The first two questions Hamlet answered pessimistically in
the bitter mood of the first soliloquy ("O that this too too
sallied flesh," I. ii. 129 ff.), when the world seemed to him like
an unweeded garden grown to seed, possessed wholly by things
rank and gross in nature. But in acknowledging to his old
schoolfellows his low spirits, he returns to these questions in a
low-keyed, reflective mood, with alternative possibilities expressed in prose (II. ii. 295 ff.). This "goodly frame, the earth,"
with its "majestical roof fretted with golden fire," seems to him
"a sterile promontory," overhung with "a foul and pestilent
congregation of vapors." And man, so noble in reason, so infinite in faculties, so like a god—man, the beauty of the world,
the paragon of animals, is to him the quintessence of dust.
Between these directly antithetical views, no attempt at reconciliation is made. The passage is an oblique way of suggesting
to us, I think, Hamlet's normal idealistic view of the world

before he experienced the shock of disillusion. For he puts the idealistic view objectively, as an accepted truth, the pessimistic one subjectively, as a state of his own mind.

The third question, what is the noblest way for a man to bear the burdens of life, to meet the painful obligations it thrusts upon him, is posed in the "To be or not to be" soliloquy (III. i. 55 ff.). He puts the question in the form of alternatives between patient endurance and bold action confronting danger:

> Whether 'tis nobler in the mind to suffer
> The slings and arrows of outrageous fortune,
> Or to take arms against a sea of troubles,
> And by opposing, end them.

The soliloquy is pitched low, general in its observations, not narrowly focussed on Hamlet's particular problem; and suicide, suggested by the opening proposition, "To be or not to be," comes to the surface only once, with the possibility of ending this "weary life" "with a bare bodkin." The argument moves with the naturalness of thought. Two ideas thread through the soliloquy, the burdens of life and the uncertainty of what lies beyond the bourn of death. The question of whether it is nobler to take arms against a sea of troubles, to meet them head on and hence to risk death, leads naturally to the question of what death is. For if death is like sleep, it is "a consummation devoutly to be wish'd." But if it is like sleep, who knows "what dreams may come/ When we have shuffled off this mortal coil"? Who can know what lies beyond the grave? Who would ever endure the ills of life, and bear its burdens, were it not that the dread of something after death "puzzles the will,/ And makes us rather bear those ills we have,/ Than fly to others that we know not of"?

These are Job's questions. Job, like Hamlet, both longed for death and feared it.

> For so shulde I now have lyen and bene quiet, I shulde have slept then, and bene at rest,/ . . . The wicked have there ceased from their tyrannie, and there they that laboured valiantly, are at rest./ . . . Wherefore is the light given to him that is in miserie? and life unto them that have heavy hearts?/

Which long for death, & if it come not, they wolde even
search it more then treasures.

(3: 13-21)

Are not my dayes fewe? let him cease, and leave of from me,
that I may take a litle comfort,/ Before I go and shal not
returne, even to the land of darkenes and shadowe of death:/
Into a land, I say, darke as darkenes it self, & into the shadow
of death, where is none order, but the light is there as
darkenes.[16]

(10: 20-22)

Hamlet returns twice to the question of how one should conduct one's life. It is implied in his words to Horatio before the
play scene (III. ii. 54 ff.), those words of praise in which Hamlet is at his frank and warmly generous best. This time he takes
up the first of the alternate choices posed in the question he
had asked in the preceding soliloquy: whether it is nobler to
suffer the ills of Fortune or to take arms against them. Hamlet
admires his friend for his stoical superiority to the buffets and
rewards of Fortune, a man—no passion's slave—who has been
"as one in suff'ring all that suffers nothing." But this tranquil
indifference is a choice out of reach of Hamlet, in his own state
of passionate turmoil; not open to him in any case, because of
the solemn charge laid upon him by the Ghost. Hence the
poignancy we feel in Hamlet's admiration for this ideal of
noble equanimity.

The same question is again provoked in Hamlet when he
comes upon the army of Fortinbras on the way to fight the
Poles (IV. iv. 32 ff.). He sees "the imminent death of twenty
thousand men,/ That for a fantasy and trick of fame,/ Go to
their graves like beds." The mood this time is not as objective
as in the earlier reflections on how to meet the ills of Fortune.
Because Hamlet feels shamed for his inaction by the example
of Fortinbras, he puts the alternatives of passivity and of action quite differently, no longer as of equal value; on the one
hand, "to sleep and feed" in bestial oblivion, allowing man's
godlike reason "to fust in us unus'd"; or, on the other, to make
"mouths at the invisible event" and to expose "what is mortal

and unsure/ To all that fortune, death, and danger dare,/ Even
for an egg-shell." Between such alternatives there can be only
one possible choice:

> Rightly to be great
> Is not to stir without great argument,
> But greatly to find quarrel in a straw
> When honor's at the stake.

And Hamlet has far greater argument to stir for than has Fortinbras. The astonishing thing to Hamlet in this encounter is
the realization that by Fortinbras and his men death goes un-
regarded. He once again blames himself for "thinking too precisely on th' event," and the event he is thinking on is surely
death. This soliloquy has an important dramatic function. It
clears the air for Hamlet by moving death as an obstacle to
action out of the center of his vision.

Not that death is banished from Hamlet's consideration, or
from ours. As the play draws to an end it is death, never far
from the surface, which becomes the dominant motive. But
Hamlet, returning from what seems to him the providential
adventure with the pirates, can now look at death from an
altered perspective and in a universal way. It is in a graveyard
(V. i) that we first see him on his return to Denmark. He
makes the skulls tossed up in the digging of a new grave the
occasion for a speculative and moralizing sermon on the Dance
of Death. For one thing is certain: whatever death may be, it
is what we must all come to in the end, king and beggar alike.
The variations on the theme are done in a vein of detached
irony. The grave, the grave-worm, the stinking chapless skull
that a sexton can knock about with a spade, dust—these are the
common end, the end for the politician, who would circumvent
God and whose pate the gravedigger overreaches; for the
courtier, who could say "Good morrow, sweet lord"; for the
lawyer, with his quiddities and his quilleties; for the buyer of
land, with his fines, his double vouchers, his recoveries, whose
fine pate is full of fine dirt; for the lady in her chamber, who
painted an inch thick; for Yorick the jester himself, who
mocked at the pretensions of beauty and power, and who,

chap-fallen, has not one gibe now to mock his own grinning; for Caesar and Alexander, the very types of worldly power, whose "clay/ Might stop a hole to keep the wind away."[17]

It is in a simple and thoughtful way that the truth comes to Hamlet at last—the answer to what to do about the terrible burden of revenge laid on him by the ghost of his father. The answer is spoken quietly, when Horatio urges him to heed his premonition and not to take part in the fencing-match with Laertes:

> *Hor.* If your mind dislike any thing, obey it. . . .
> *Ham.* Not a whit, we defy augury. There is special providence in the fall of a sparrow. If it be now, 'tis not to come; if it be not to come, it will be now; if it be not now, yet it will come—the readiness is all. Since no man, of aught he leaves, knows what is't to leave betimes, let be.[18]
>   **(V. ii. 219-24)**

The unspoken noun is, of course, "death." The language in the passage is biblical and stoical, and the speech is in prose—this time not for mockery, but for quietness. The answer is simply readiness for whatever may come. When Hamlet is ready, the problem disappears. The answer has been forming since his return, as his report to Horatio on his escape has shown, earlier in the scene. Confidence has come with his surrender to a larger purpose: "There's a divinity that shapes our ends,/ Rough-hew them how we will" (ll. 10-11). And to Horatio's warning that the fate of Rosencrantz and Guildenstern will be shortly known from England, Hamlet has replied: "It will be short; the interim is mine,/ And a man's life's no more than to say 'one'" (ll. 73-74).

The final readiness, then, is to take death when it comes. For this is what Hamlet's coming to terms with himself and his world means, has meant from the beginning, when the Ghost returned to lay the fearful charge upon him. It means acceptance of death.[19]

Hamlet has a final great fling of passion when he is mortally wounded and discovers the treachery of the King and Laertes. He cries out, "O villainy! Ho, let the door be lock'd!/ Treach-

ery! Seek it out." And he has a final bitter pun, as he forces
Claudius to swallow the poisoned drink intended for him,
with the pearl, or "union," dissolved in it: "Is thy union here?"

But in spite of so many words spoken during the play, so
many wild and whirling words, so much unpacking of his
heart, so much bitter and witty comment on the uses of this
world, so much probing and questioning of things, Hamlet's
final feeling is the deeply poignant one of failure: This was not
the way it was to have been at all, with so much done that
should not have been done, so much unsaid that ought to be
said. The final sad irony for Hamlet, so scrupulous in seeking
the truth and in searching for the right thing to do, is that he
should be thought a common assassin.

> Had I but time—as this fell sergeant, Death,
> Is strict in his arrest—O, I could tell you—
> But let it be. Horatio, I am dead,
> Thou livest. Report me and my cause aright
> To the unsatisfied.

Hamlet, who must himself join the Dance of Death, puts an
end to words with the final poignant word for the ultimate
mystery: "The rest is silence."

If, in our intense absorption, we have ceased to think of
Hamlet as a character in a play, the flourish of trumpets for
Fortinbras and the dead march as the body of Hamlet is carried off the stage end the illusion. They return us from Shakespeare's world of art to ours of common day.

Iago's *If*—

Conditional and Subjunctive in *Othello*

V ERY SOON after the opening of what is often called the temptation scene (III. iii) in *Othello*, Cassio, who has been talking with Desdemona, walks away as Othello and Iago enter, and this interchange takes place:

Iago. Ha? I like not that.
Oth. What dost thou say?
Iago. Nothing, my lord; or if—I know not what.
Oth. Was not that Cassio parted from my wife?
Iago. Cassio, my lord? No, sure I cannot think it, . . .

Iago's "if" is the great central *if* in the play. It is vague and incomplete, with neither condition nor conclusion stated. It is the small hole in the dike which, persistently widened by Iago, will let in the destroying flood. If Cassio's stealing away from Desdemona means something sinister, if Desdemona is not a

First written under the title, "Iago's 'If—': An Essay on the Syntax of *Othello*," for *The Drama of the Renaissance: Essays for Leicester Bradner*, ed. Elmer W. Blistein (Providence: Brown University Press, 1970; © 1970 by Brown University), pp. 69-99. The original essay has been slightly revised.

faithful wife, if Cassio is not a true friend, if certainties are not certainties, chaos is come again. For Othello cannot entertain *if*'s. He cannot live as Hamlet does, weighing possibilities, holding hypotheses, thinking of consequences. To be once in doubt is once to be resolved. This casual but calculated "if" has been prepared for by others in the play, and will be followed by others. Indeed, if we look closely, as I propose we do, we see that conditional sentences (by no means all Iago's) mark the stages of the action. When they express doubt they are disruptive of the assurance expressed in Othello's unqualified declarative sentences. Under Iago's *if*'s Othello's verse turns to prose and even syntax goes momentarily to pieces. The conditionals of possibility are verticals coming up from below, first touching, then penetrating, the horizontal movement, distorting and disrupting it. They are like molten rock which, thrusting itself up from below into old sedimentary beds, heaves up, twists, cracks, and dislimns their level planes.

I propose to look at the syntax of *Othello*, for it is in the interplay of assertion and negation that the bare bones of a fable are given dramatic life and sensibility. Syntax is the most intimate way to show movement of mind; it is the dramatist's most refined tool in shaping monologue or dialogue. Revelation of character may or may not be in question; always important is the dramatic structure which the syntax helps to shape. In *Othello*, as in every one of his plays, Shakespeare uses syntax to create special effects appropriate to particular situations—as, for instance, in the dominant syntax of exclamation, command, and question in the three scenes of public disturbance begun by Iago (I, i and ii; II. iii; V. i). But in this play (as in *Lear* and perhaps others), Shakespeare does something more: he uses syntax, I believe, to inform in a subtle way his larger dramatic structure. It is with this second use that I shall be principally concerned.

There are two large syntactical patterns, I would say, which operate in the drama as a whole. These are chiefly sentences expressive of possibility in varying degrees (that is, conditional sentences of varying structure and mood) and operative within a framework of sentences expressive of certainty (mainly declarative sentences, not greatly complicated, in the indicative

mood). The conditional sentences function in the way they do
because they are intimately allied with the way in which action
in the play is motivated and understood. The non-conditional
declarative pattern must be looked at first, because it is the
ground which the conditional pattern partly supports, partly
disturbs.

The dominant voices in the play are Othello's and Iago's.
Othello's first. If one takes Othello's love of Desdemona as the
primary theme of the play, in a major key, one may perhaps
call Othello's directness and simplicity the tonic chord. His
normal sentences are declarative, in the indicative mood, often
simple in construction; if compound or complex, they are not
greatly extended or involved. This is the way he is introduced
to us (I. ii) when Iago rushes to him to warn him that Brabantio and his kin are coming to arrest him: "'Tis better as it is";
"Not I; I must be found"; "I fetch my life and being/ From
men of royal siege." The assertions which help establish
Othello's *ethos*[1] are not hedged with concessions and doubts.
They are candid but brief, not emphatic because they need not
be; they imply a natural confidence in himself, a confidence
born of an innate self-respect and based on experience in the
tented field; "The world is thus and so; I am thus and thus; I
shall do what I need to do." He moves with quiet authority
into the military man's imperatives when necessary: "Keep up
your bright swords, for the dew will rust them"; "Hold your
hands,/ Both you of my inclining, and the rest." Or, more
sharply when disorder is threatened, as in the tumult on Cyprus: "Hold, for your lives!" "Silence that dreadful bell."
"What's the matter . . . ? Give me answer to 't."

At the beginning, Othello has the same confidence in his
love for Desdemona and in hers for him as in his profession;
and his affirmations are as simple and frank:

> That I have ta'en away this old man's daughter,
> It is most true; true I have married her.
>
> (I. iii. 78-79)

> She lov'd me for the dangers I had pass'd,
> And I lov'd her that she did pity them.
>
> (ll. 167-68)

It is a confidence truly placed. Desdemona's declarations of love are as direct and as unqualified as his.

> I am hitherto your daughter. But here's my husband.
> (l. 185)

> My heart's subdu'd
> Even to the very quality of my lord.
> I saw Othello's visage in his mind,
> And to his honors and his valiant parts
> Did I my soul and fortunes consecrate.
> (ll. 250-54)

There are, of course, normal variations of sentence pattern in Othello's speech, which is always sensitively responsive to any immediate situation. But we may take the uncomplicated sentences in the indicative mode, sometimes re-enforced by the imperative of wish or command, as the warp of his speech. To change the figure, it is in these that we hear the characteristic and distinctive notes of his speech.

His style is not always what one would call plain. But even when it is marked, as it often is, by courtly diction, richness of imagery, and beauty of rhythm, it rests on a base of directness of apprehension and simplicity of structure. The images are uncomplicated, given in similes or metaphors not greatly extended, certainly always lucid, rarely in mixed or knotted tropes.

The counterstatement to Othello's love, Iago's malicious hatred of Othello, also opens in a major key and is also simply declarative in form. The hatred is stated at the outset (I. i) in plain terms, first in Iago's racy circumstantial narrative to Roderigo about Othello's promotion of Cassio to the lieutenancy:

> *Rod.*   Thou toldst me thou didst hold him in thy hate.
> *Iago.*   Despise me if I do not . . . ,

and then in his promise to get even: "I follow him to serve my turn upon him." The assertion of hate (made both to Roderigo and in soliloquy) is insisted upon: "I have told thee often, and I retell thee again and again, I hate the Moor" (I. iii. 364-66, 386). Iago's mind, seen straight into, when he is talking to him-

self (hence to us) or to Roderigo, is always vulgar and obscene. His plainness, therefore, quite as direct in assertion as
Othello's, is in a wholly different key. Plain also is the mask of
blunt soldier he wears to meet the world. The interesting thing ·
is that the mask is remarkably like his own face. There are only
shadings of difference in the language (to Othello it is cleaned
up a little), or none at all (as in his obscenities to Brabantio
about the Barbary horse and the old black ram). The essential
difference is in the intent. His opening statement to Roderigo,
true as we find it to be, is yet less candid than it seems, since
he uses it to manipulate this stupid cat's-paw. His natural cynicism (the ethos Shakespeare invents for him) need hardly
change its tone; or if it does, only enough to seem, in the context of its directed use, a healthy realism. Iago often assumes
the style of the homely moralist. He states general moral truths
(or seeming truths) in aphorisms or sentences ("Poor and content is rich"), gives examples and analogies, draws plausible
but subtly false conclusions, or misapplies the lesson, as in his
homily to Roderigo on the hoary text that our bodies are our
gardens, to cultivate as we will (I. iii. 320 ff.).[2] The differences
in style, whether in prose or verse, are governed by the decorum of the person or of the scene as a whole; the verse to
Othello is as plain, if not as vulgar, as the prose to Roderigo.
The rhetoric of simplicity is a subtle mask, and he wears it with
pleasure.

Iago's pattern of declarative sentences, therefore, differs from
Othello's in two fundamental ways—in quality and in relation
to the truth. Iago's prosy, if lively, vulgarity is counterpointed
against Othello's poetic grace. Othello's assertions match the
truth of himself and the truth he sees; up to the point of his
deception they mirror reality. Iago's do not. His "honest" statements, sometimes true, sometimes false, sometimes partly one,
partly the other, always devious in intent, do not reflect the
world as it is. In fact, the truth of love which Desdemona and
Othello know Iago does not even recognize. To him love would
appear to be, as he defines it to Roderigo, "merely a lust of the
blood and a permission of the will" (I. iii. 334-35).

Iago's method of operation is to introduce doubt into Othel-

lo's confidence. The conditional sentence expressing a condition
assumed to be possible is the subtlest of his grammatical and
logical tools.

We might consider the conditional sentence itself for a moment. It expresses relations in the world of contingent possibilities. Take the form in which the relation between condition and conclusion is assumed to be necessary: If *this* is true,
then *that* is; if *this* should happen, then *that* would. The question in such a sentence is not about the conclusion, but about
the condition on which the conclusion or consequence is, or
seems to be, contingent. (In the alternative "seems" there is a
trap, for even if *this* is true, *that* only may be. It is a trap Iago
knows very well how to set.) The probability of the condition's
existing or occurring has to be assessed on a scale of degrees.
Probability amounting to certainty is at one end—what may be
and is; improbability, also amounting to certainty, is at the
other—what might conceivably be, but is not. Uncertainty lies
in an indeterminate middle zone between. When the condition
is assumed to be only possible, it has obviously less predictive
force than when it is assumed to be fact. There is room, however, in nice distinctions of mood and tense, to suggest variations of relation (or rather, feeling about the relation) between
condition and conclusion. Shakespeare uses such distinctions
with more subtlety than we are accustomed to in modern English, in which the indicative mood so often usurps the preroga-
tive of the subjunctive in conditional sentences of possibility.
The condition contrary to fact has many uses. Suppose we say,
"If *this* were true (believing it not to be), *that* would happen";
this statement carries us by implication to an assertion in the
indicative: "But *this* is not true; therefore *that* will not happen."
By using the conditional form, however, we can do something
we cannot in a simple assertion. We may intend a relieved
"Thank goodness it is not true!" or a wistful "If only it were!"
Condition contrary to fact offers subtle possibilities of variation
(which we shall find illustrated in *Othello*). It is a form capa-
ble of the most delicate nuances in expressing our responses to
the contingencies among which we live. For excluded possibilities may affect us as much as open ones. They remind us of

limits beyond which we cannot go, but sometimes, too, of our incredible escapes. And only to imagine the exclusion of the possibilities we live by may give us either our worst fears or our strongest certainties. Possibilities still unrealized hold the door open to the future, hopefully or fearfully. But we do not put contemplation of them aside because they are over—when they have lived in act, died forever, or never come into being. These make our thankful deliverances, our regrets, or our frustrations. What if it had not happened! If only it had not! If only it had!

One way in which Shakespeare establishes Othello's ethos is to make him rarely speak in *if*'s. He quickly creates for us in these early scenes (I. ii, iii) an illusion of a full and adventurous past for Othello, a past in which the possibilities appear to have been always successfully dealt with or successfully escaped from. Here he is now, assured and serene, taking what comes, asking few questions, not worrying about contingencies, not thinking too precisely on the event. He uses few conditional sentences in the first two acts—that is to say, before Iago disturbs him. Most of those he does use are in forms nearest improbability; they imply his confidence that the world will not be upset. One sort is the condition contrary to fact in the subjunctive: "Were it my cue to fight, I should have known it/ Without a prompter" (I. ii. 83-84). The other form has the condition in the indicative or subjunctive and the consequence in the imperative or optative subjunctive:

> when light-wing'd toys
> Of feather'd Cupid seel with wanton dullness
> My speculative and offic'd instruments,
> That my disports corrupt and taint my business,
> Let housewives make a skillet of my helm,
> And all indign and base adversities
> Make head against my estimation!
> (I. iii. 268-74)

This is a strong form of asseveration, having almost the force of an oath. It calls for an unwished consequence to follow upon an incredible condition: If I am not what I am, then let this

shame fall on my head. Conditions contrary to fact, subtly
varied in form, often asseverative, recur in Othello's speech to
the end of the play. How they are placed at strategic points in
the action, usually as forewarnings, we shall see as we go along.

Iago, on the other hand, is continually holding the door open
to hitherto unthought of possibilities. To Roderigo it is the door
to the enjoyment of Desdemona; to Othello it is the door to the
unbounded darkness of nightmare. He keeps it open by a dex-
terous game of rhetoric, one which also includes a game of
false logic. He manipulates events so that his conclusions seem
to follow on the conditions he has pointed to. The "seem" is
important, because there is never a necessary relation between
Iago's arranged and predicted condition and the conclusion
supplied. He works by false enthymemes, arguing from a sign
that seems a true one but is not.[3] He traps Othello by the fal-
lacy of multiple cause, and can do so because, having suggested the cause he wants believed, he can then bring off the
effect he has foreseen. Interestingly enough, Iago does not
think too precisely on the event either. The conditional possibilities he phrases for himself are simply the confident opportunist's, with only an immediate consequence perceived: If I
can do this, so much will be done; then we'll see what next. He
moves easily up the stairs, one at a time, in a *gradatio* of
achieved possibilities: "If this poor trash of Venice . . . stand
the putting on . . ."; "If I can fasten but one cup upon him . . .";
"If consequence do but approve my dream . . ." It always does
—or almost.

The two fundamental conditions of the story, the given ones
with which we start, are Iago's revengeful hatred of Othello
and Othello's and Desdemona's love of each other. The drama
is to be built out of the drive of the hatred to destroy the love,
beginning with the antagonist's cry of "Poison his delight," and
ending with the agonist's destruction of his wife and of himself.[4] Two other conditions are also given in the story, and it
is with the leverage they give the villain that he operates
against the hero. The first of these complicating conditions is
the disparity between Othello and Desdemona—in race, nation,
age, social background, and experience: between Othello the

black Moor, in middle years, a soldier of fortune with an adventurous, far-traveled past, an "extravagant and wheeling
stranger," and Desdemona the fair Venetian, "a maiden never
bold," young, homekeeping, and innocent. The second complicating condition is the position and character of Cassio, the
handsome and gracious young Florentine whom Othello trusts,
whom he has promoted over Iago to the vacant lieutenancy,
and who, we later learn, was an intermediary between him and
Desdemona in his wooing. Iago's game begins by opening up
the possibilities of doubt which would seem to lie in the disparity between Othello and Desdemona—doubt, that is, of the
quality and permanence of their love. His first move against
Othello, by slander and through Desdemona's father, does not
work. But then, by bringing in the second condition, the attrac-
tiveness and familiar manners of the youthful Cassio, and by
linking it with the doubts already raised about the strangeness
of the marriage, he wakens a destructive jealousy in Othello
and successfully makes him the agent of his own ruin.

Conditional sentences in asseverative form, set as they are
in the frame of unqualified declarative sentences, mark with
strong emphasis at the beginning of the play the given conditions of love and hate. Then, in varying forms, conditional
sentences mark the entry and manipulation throughout the
play of the complicating conditions. We shall examine the most
crucial ones to observe how they operate with the movement
of the action—with Iago's undermining thrusts at Othello's
peace and with the movement of Othello's mind from assured
certainty to doubt of Desdemona's love; next to certainty of
her disloyalty—the false certainty which leads to murder; then
back quickly through doubt of his cause to the final certainty of
her love and of his irretrievable mistake. Every move to the
catastrophe is marked by a conditional clause—an *if*, a *when*,
a *but that*.

The play falls into three major movements, to which we may
give the old grammarians' terms of *protasis, epitasis,* and *catastrophe.*[5] The protasis, or presentation, comprising the first act,
lays down the initial circumstances of the story, introduces the
principal characters, emphasizes the opposition of Iago to

Othello out of which the drama will grow, and prepares the
ground for Iago's future operations. The epitasis, or intensifying of the action, comprising Acts II through IV, ties the knot
of complication, with Iago breaking Cassio and moving Othello
to the point of murder. The catastrophe, or overturn, comprising the last act, brings the tragic consequence in the murder of
Desdemona, the recognition by Othello of what he has done,
and his suicide.

You will recall how boldly the play opens, not with the hero,
but with the villain—the hatred before the love, the Serpent
before Adam and Eve. Shakespeare starts the run towards tragedy swiftly and at once. Iago makes the necessary exposition
of circumstances (the promotion of Cassio, the marriage of
Othello); states his feeling (hatred), his motive (disappointed
ambition), his intent (revenge); adumbrates his future methods of operation (his use of Roderigo as a tool, his initiation of
a public disturbance to cause fear and confusion, his rhetoric
of innuendo, slander, and affected honesty); and makes his first
move against Othello's peace, all in the first scene. The two
conditional sentences of Iago's which we must not miss are the
two in his speech of self-declaration, defining him for us un-
equivocally:

> It is as sure as you are Roderigo,
> Were I the Moor, I would not be Iago.
> In following him, I follow but myself;
> Heaven is my judge, not I for love and duty,
> But seeming so, for my peculiar end;
> For when my outward action doth demonstrate
> The native act and figure of my heart
> In complement extern, 'tis not long after
> But I will wear my heart upon my sleeve
> For daws to peck at: I am not what I am.
>   (I. i. 56-65)

Taken together, the obvious condition contrary to fact ("Were
I the Moor") and the imagined condition ("when my outward
action . . .") with its preposterous conclusion serve to announce
his rôle as antagonist, emphasize his absolute difference from
the agonist, and declare in essence what his mode of operation

against him will be. The conditionals are two forms of exclud-
ing possibilities; hence they work to establish certainties. They
are emphatic ways of telling us, the audience, to keep our eyes
open to Iago's covert operations.

In the second scene, when Othello first appears, he also is
given a speech of self-declaration, which may be set against
Iago's. Before we see Othello, Iago has blackened his name in
gross obscenities to Brabantio and has roused a hue and cry
after him for his elopement with Desdemona. Before we have
witnessed for ourselves the quality of the love, Iago has ob-
scured it in a murky cloud of ugliness and doubt. When in the
second scene the outcry moves to Othello's door, it is quieted
by his calm and assured authority: "Keep up your bright
swords, for the dew will rust them"; "Hold your hands,/ Both
you of my inclining, and the rest." In the magic of a few brief
sentences Shakespeare creates a figure which, in its simplicity
and dignity, expunges the memory of the leering preface. The
sun shines all the brighter for the clouds which have stained it.
In the same way as his character, the love appears for the first
time in its true and proper light. Iago's speech of self-declaration, for the audience's sake, is now matched by Othello's:

> 'Tis yet to know—
> Which, when I know that boasting is an honor,
> I shall promulgate[6]—I fetch my life and being
> From men of royal siege, and my demerits
> May speak, unbonneted, to as proud a fortune
> As this that I have reach'd; for know, Iago,
> But that I love the gentle Desdemona,
> I would not my unhoused free condition
> Put into circumscription and confine
> For the sea's worth.
>
> (I. ii. 19-28)

Othello's parenthesis, ironic in its condition contrary to fact,
sets the decent reticence of the man conscious of his own worth
against the practical concealment of the double-tongued. Iago,
in his busy duplicity, says, "I am not what I am." Othello says
directly what he is.

In the second conditional sentence, the love is affirmed *simpliciter,* without need of description, but in a form which leaves no doubt of its worth. Here is the love and the cost, the choice and the consequence. The expected form of such a condition contrary to fact would be: "If I did not love Desdemona, I would not . . ." But putting the conditional verb in the positive rather than in the negative quite alters the emphasis, places it on the true condition, not the untrue one, marks its acceptance with no undertone of regret, makes the statement imply, "This is the only condition for which I would have paid such a price." The value of both the love and the free life is enhanced. Yet Othello's first words spoken of his love sound, unknown to him, with the dark undertone of prophecy. The cost will be more than anything Othello can imagine.

In this speech, Shakespeare has put for us in other terms than Iago's the unusualness of the marriage. Iago's way of looking at it—as lust on Othello's part, unnaturalness on Desdemona's—is the only one, however, which Desdemona's father can credit. Since his gentle daughter's voluntary part in such a union is unimaginable to him, Brabantio has found a way out in the only condition he can understand: the use of charms or drugs. He enters soon after Othello's speech to confront him and order his arrest:

> O thou foul thief, where hast thou stow'd my daughter?
> Damn'd as thou art, thou hast enchanted her,
> For I'll refer me to all things of sense,
> If she in chains of magic were not bound,
> Whether a maid so tender, fair, and happy,
> So opposite to marriage . . .
> Would ever have, t' incur a general mock,
> Run from her guardage to the sooty bosom
> Of such a thing as thou—to fear, not to delight!
> Judge me the world, if 'tis not gross in sense
> That thou hast practic'd on her with foul charms,
> Abus'd her delicate youth with drugs or minerals
> That weakens motion.
>   (I. ii. 62-75)

Brabantio makes his charge formally in an *ad hoc* trial of
Othello before the Duke and Senate of Venice (I. iii). The
episode has, in brief form, most of the features of a trial:
charge, questioning of the defendant, defendant's reply, including a narrative of his past, questioning of a witness, dismissal of charges. The syntax is partly interrogative, but mainly
assertive on both sides.

At one point, Othello, requesting that Desdemona be called to
speak for him, solemnly sets his condition against Brabantio's:

> If you do find me foul in her report,
> The trust, the office I do hold of you,
> Not only take away, but let your sentence
> Even fall upon my life.
>> (I. iii. 117-20)

Desdemona's testimony, as candid and unqualified as Othello's
in his account of his wooing, settles the matter, and Brabantio
must perforce dismiss his charge.

> Come hither, Moor:
> I here do give thee that with all my heart
> Which but thou hast already, with all my heart
> I would keep from thee.
>> (ll. 192-95)

Do we hear an echo of Othello's acceptance of the same condition? "But that I love the gentle Desdemona, I would not . . ."
The same phrasing, but in another key. The same unalterable
condition, but with all the difference of meaning, to father and
husband, between separation and union. Brabantio's last word
also carries a condition:

> Look to her, Moor, if thou hast eyes to see;
> She has deceiv'd her father, and may thee.
>> (ll. 292-93)

Othello sees the truth now with unaided vision; but Iago will
help him readily enough to false glasses. Again, there lies in
the condition, unperceived of the speaker, a prodigious irony

which time will bring to birth. Othello rightly replies, "My life upon her faith!"

This forensic episode is of great importance. Othello has been tried for a supposed crime and the case has been dismissed for want of evidence. Before the self-evident truth of the love, the charge of unnaturalness has melted like snow in June. The very strangeness between the conditions of Othello and Desdemona which has called the love in question is, given the transparent honesty of the two, the best guarantee of its truth, as, later on, Othello's first, unprompted response to Iago's doubts is to tell him, "She had eyes, and chose me."

It does not matter to Iago that he has failed in his first attempt to bring Othello into disrepute. He promises Roderigo to find a way to succeed another time: "If sanctimony and a frail vow betwixt an erring barbarian and a super-subtle Venetian be not too hard for my wits and all the tribe of hell, thou shalt enjoy her" (I. iii. 355-58). These are the terms of the marriage he has seen, or chosen to see, from the beginning. In the soliloquy which ends the act he hits on a hopeful way to break the union apart, by making something of Cassio's charming person and "smooth dispose." The act ends as it began, in an affirmation of Iago's hate, but now with a promise as well: "Hell and night/ Must bring this monstrous birth to the world's light."

Bringing the monstrous birth to light is the business of the epitasis, or second movement of the play, in which Iago moves Othello to a jealous and murderous rage. This long movement is broken into smaller movements, each marking a stage of Iago's maneuverings, or of Othello's passion, or of both together. But first there is a prelude to the whole. The "high-wrought" tempest which we hear of as the second act opens serves double duty, for it is both a fortunate dismissal of the Turkish threat and an omen of a more dreadful tempest to come in the mind and life of Othello. It is disorder of a huge kind, like the storm in *Lear*. Yet, the elements, "as having sense of beauty, do omit/ Their mortal natures, letting go safely by/ The divine Desdemona." That we should not miss the portent,

Shakespeare makes Othello say, on his finding Desdemona safely landed ahead of him:

> O my soul's joy!
> If after every tempest come such calms,
> May the winds blow till they have waken'd death!
> And let the laboring bark climb hills of seas
> Olympus-high, and duck again as low
> As hell's from heaven!
>
> (II. i. 184-89)

For Othello, who knows that after tempests such calms do not always come, the wish is a way of emphasizing the relief of this escape, the happy reunion, the feeling that any hardship or fear would be worth this conclusion. The condition might almost be true. For us, who see Iago standing by, weaving his spider's web for Cassio out of the young man's courtesies to Desdemona, the contrariness to fact is absolute, the wish for another tempest like a defiance of the omens. Another prophetic conditional comes immediately:

> If it were now to die,
> 'Twere now to be most happy; for I fear
> My soul hath her content so absolute
> That not another comfort like to this
> Succeeds in unknown fate.

This clearly improbable condition with its conclusion in the superlative is a way of acknowledging the joy, the perfection of such a moment—and its rarity, too, for "happy" also means "fortunate." The joy and the fear are complementary. We must take the speech as something like the classical tragic hero's fear of too much good fortune and meant primarily as a warning to us. It is not, as the interchange between him and Desdemona makes clear (ll. 193-99), a pessimistic expectation on his part. It is only Iago and we who must perceive the full truth of the conclusion. As Othello kisses his wife, with the prayer, "And this, and this, the greatest discords be/ That e'er our hearts shall make!" Iago promises,

> O, you are well tun'd now!
> But I'll set down the pegs that make this music,
> As honest as I am.

The first discord Iago creates is another tumult—the drunken fight in the Court of Guard on the night of their arrival in Cyprus (II. iii). This oblique move, against Cassio, is of course preparatory to the direct move against Othello yet to be made. As Iago considers how to use to his advantage the evening of celebration Othello has allowed the garrison, he states the condition on which he will operate, Cassio's weak head for liquor:

> If I can fasten but one cup upon him,
> With that which he hath drunk to-night already,
> He'll be as full of quarrel and offense
> As my young mistress' dog.
>
> (ll. 48-51)

He can, and does, and the consequences follow: Cassio enmeshed in a brawl, Montano the Cypriot governor seriously wounded, Othello scandalized and angry, Cassio dismissed in disgrace from his lieutenancy. In this maneuver Iago has also satisfied a second and larger condition he had mused upon:

> If consequence do but approve my dream,
> My boat sails freely, both with wind and stream.
>
> (ll. 62-63)

Consequences have approved his dream, and Iago's boat is well launched, on course for the larger prize.

Before the scene ends, Iago has arranged, out of the young officer's desperate need to be reinstated, a new condition, that Cassio will ask Desdemona to intercede with Othello for him. Iago's game is to work the condition two ways. To Cassio the argument that if Desdemona speaks for him he will have a better chance with Othello, must be made to seem compelling, and under Iago's persuasion it does. In point of fact, intercession would not have been necessary, for Othello has said, according to Emilia (III. i. 46-49), that he "needs no other suitor but his likings" to reinstate Cassio when he can expediently do so. Still, Desdemona's word would have done no harm—far from it.

"Let him come when he will," Othello replies to her first impor-
tunings; "I will deny thee nothing" (III. iii. 75-76). But of
course Iago intends it to do great harm. To Othello the condition, "If Desdemona speaks for Cassio," must be made to seem
to require the conclusion, "she is false to me." The spurious
enthymeme must seem to be a true one. Iago's method will be
to predict as a possibility what he knows will happen, and at
the same time prepare Othello's response to it by supplying
ahead of time a false interpretation. Unlike the brawl, the outcome of which had to depend on a certain amount of luck, the
new condition he has arranged he can take wholly into his own
hands.

The temptation scene (III. iii) opens with Desdemona's
promise to help Cassio, a promise assured by the conditions of
her integrity: "If I do vow a friendship, I'll perform it/ To the
last article." Iago, entering with Othello in time to see Cassio
leave, can now bring out his most cunning tools to work an upheaval in Othello's mind. Recall once again the exchange between the two:

> *Iago.* Ha? I like not that.
> *Oth.*   What dost thou say?
> *Iago.* Nothing, my lord; or if—I know not what.
> *Oth.* Was not that Cassio parted from my wife?
> *Iago.* Cassio, my lord? No, sure I cannot think it,
> That he would steal away so guilty-like,
> Seeing your coming.
>
>   (ll. 35-40)

The exclamation of surprise, the strong assertion of disapproval,
the tentative "if" begins a long and intense dialogue between
himself and Othello, a dialogue which occupies more than one
scene and which does not end for another 860 lines (until IV.
i. 214). The dialogue is broken by short episodes in which Desdemona's insistent suit for Cassio is renewed and in which
the business of the handkerchief is introduced and continued.
Each of these episodes supplies Iago with new "evidence" to
work with, so that after each interruption the dialogue is resumed with a bolder line and with increased suffering and dis-

order in the mind of Othello. The whole has three parts: the
movement to doubt, the movement to conviction, the movement to proof.

How this whole long movement toward "proof" will end is
foretold in Othello's lines of unconscious prophecy, spoken,
soon after Iago's "if," as Desdemona leaves with her husband's
consent to see Cassio:

> Excellent wretch! Perdition catch my soul
> But I do love thee! and when I love thee not,
> Chaos is come again.
>
> (ll. 90-92)

His love of Desdemona, the condition of his life, is twice affirmed in the imagined consequences of its unimaginable negation. Trembling with the burden of our superior awareness, we
watch Iago make his nothing into a seeming something, shape
his formless *if* into a credible phantasm, flesh it out with seeming substance. The first stage is to awaken an uncertainty
Othello cannot stand, to hint at something monstrous without
saying what it is, yet to prepare for the revelation by little
cautionary lectures on reputation and jealousy. Othello's rising
impatience, expressed in a series of conditionals truer than he
knows—

> By heaven, thou echo'st me,
> As if there were some monster in thy thought
> Too hideous to be shown. . . .
> . . . thou criedst, 'Indeed!'
> And didst contract and purse thy brow together,
> As if thou then hadst shut up in thy brain
> Some horrible conceit
>
> (ll. 106-15)

—comes to a climax as he tries to break out of the maddening
phantasmagoria:

> Why? why is this?
> Think'st thou I'ld make a life of jealousy?
> To follow still the changes of the moon
> With fresh suspicions? No! to be once in doubt
> Is once to be resolv'd. . . .

> No, Iago,
> I'll see before I doubt; when I doubt, prove;
> And on the proof, there is no more but this—
> Away at once with love or jealousy!
>   (ll. 176-92)

But Iago's reminders of the differences between him and his wife and of Brabantio's warning dash his spirits. This is Iago's moment to bring out his prediction with its false conclusion:

> Yet if you please to hold him [Cassio] off awhile,
> You shall by that perceive him and his means.
> Note if your lady strain his entertainment
> With any strong or vehement importunity;
> Much will be seen in that.
>   (ll. 248-52)

The condition of Desdemona's love, the very thing that confirmed it, is being made to seem the negation of it; her innocence and her earlier reluctance to marry are being turned into Venetian subtlety. Othello, feeling himself a stranger in such a world, is at the mercy of Iago's evidently superior knowledge. He promises his own condition of future action:

> If I do prove her haggard,
> Though that her jesses were my dear heart-strings,
> I'ld whistle her off, and let her down the wind
> To prey at fortune.
>   (ll. 260-63)

With the "if" at the beginning of the dialogue, Iago's muddy stream entered Othello's clear one. The two currents at first ran side by side, not mingling. But now the discoloring has begun and will not end until the mainstream is thoroughly fouled. Desdemona is later (III. iv. 140-43) to say, with true observation of the condition if not the cause of her husband's troubled mind: "Something sure of state . . . / Hath puddled his clear spirit." Iago has a different explanation: "The Moor already changes with my poison."

The first half of the temptation scene has brought Othello to doubt. The next brings him to certainty and decision. At the

first interruption of the dialogue the sight of Desdemona as she
enters clears his mind, and his right impulse makes him say:
"If she be false, O, then heaven mocks itself!/ I'll not believe't"
(III. iii. 278-79). For a breathing space things are stood up-
right again. But it is the last time they will be. For now Desdemona drops her handkerchief; and Emilia, who finds it, gives
it to Iago, with an upside-down condition of fearful import to
us:

> *Emil.*   What will you do with't, that you have been so earnest
> To have me filch it?
> *Iago.*   [*Snatching it.*] Why, what is that to you?
> *Emil.*   If it be not for some purpose of import,
> Give't me again.
>   (ll. 314-17)

Now Iago, with the handkerchief in his pocket, begins to
shape his obscene phantasm with free and bold invention.

This second half of the scene, the movement to certainty, is
different in tone from the first. It is prefaced by Iago's great
cue lines for Othello's re-entrance:

> Look where he comes! Not poppy, nor mandragora,
> Nor all the drowsy syrups of the world
> Shall ever medicine thee to that sweet sleep
> Which thou ow'dst yesterday.
>   (ll. 330-33)

Othello has crossed a bridge into another country. He has begun to inhabit the realm of perdition he spoke of so innocently
at the beginning of the scene, and he now looks back to the
place he knows to be forever beyond recovery.

>   O now, for ever
> Farewell the tranquil mind! farewell content!
> Farewell the plumed troops and the big wars
> That makes ambition virtue! . . .
> Farewell! Othello's occupation's gone.
>   (ll. 347-57)

The price of his marriage, once so gladly accepted, is being
exacted. While Iago's busy brain continues to invent more in-

genious traps and more refined tortures, Othello's mind moves
out into great imaginative reaches of perception and feeling.
At one point of intense dramatic irony, he turns on Iago with a
possibility that is a true description of Iago's *modus operandi:*

> If thou dost slander her and torture me,
> Never pray more; abandon all remorse;
> On horror's head horrors accumulate;
> Do deeds to make heaven weep, all earth amaz'd;
> For nothing canst thou to damnation add
> Greater than that.
>
> (ll. 368-73)

But it is a truth he must not be allowed to recognize. With
Iago's offended protest that "to be direct and honest is not
safe," the moment of insight has passed, and Othello, tortured
by a divided mind, calls for proof:

> I think my wife be honest, and think she is not;
> I think that thou art just, and think thou are not.
> I'll have some proof. . . .
>   If there be cords, or knives,
> Poison, or fire, or suffocating streams,
> I'll not endure it. Would I were satisfied!
>
> (ll. 384-90)

The time has come for another of Iago's false enthymemes. He
prepares the way for its psychological reception:

> If imputation and strong circumstances
> Which lead directly to the door of truth
> Will give you satisfaction, you might have't.
>
> (ll. 406-8)

The imputation and strong circumstances he supplies at once
in the form of two lies, one the vivid and lewd narrative of
Cassio's dream, the other a statement that he has today seen
Cassio wipe his beard with the handkerchief Othello had given
his wife. "If it be that—," Othello begins. Iago widens the condition and supplies the plausible but false conclusion: "If it be
that, or any that was hers,/ It speaks against her with the other
proofs." Convinced by emotion and false logic, Othello cannot

even wait on the possibility: "O blood, blood, blood!" Othello's
current must run, if not to love, then to vengeance:

> Like to the Pontic Sea,
> Whose icy current and compulsive course
> Nev'r feels retiring ebb, but keeps due on
> To the Propontic and the Hellespont,
> Even so my bloody thoughts, with violent pace,
> Shall nev'r look back, nev'r ebb to humble love,
> Till that a capable and wide revenge
> Swallow them up.
>
> (ll. 453-60)

He kneels to make a solemn vow of revenge. This is the moment of decision, from which there is no turning back.

The third stage in this long dialogue is the movement to
visible "proof"—that is, to the exhibition of the handkerchief in
Cassio's hand. In Othello's mind this stage is the final movement to chaos. It is preceded by another interlude (III. iv), this
time a discordant antiphony between Desdemona's insistence
to Othello that he keep his promise to hear Cassio's appeal and
Othello's to her that she fetch the handkerchief. Othello's demand is accompanied by his story of the handkerchief and the
grave conditions which possession of it imposes on the owner.
The Egyptian who gave it to his mother had told her:

> while she kept it,
> 'Twould make her amiable, and subdue my father
> Entirely to her love; but if she lost it,
> Or made a gift of it, my father's eye
> Should hold her loathed, . . .
> To lose't or give't away were such perdition
> As nothing else could match.
>
> (ll. 58-68)

What wonder that the frightened Desdemona lies, "It is not
lost; but what and if it were?" What indeed! The rest of the
interlude keeps us aware of Iago's mischief with the handkerchief, for we see Cassio, who has found it in his room, giving it
to Bianca to have the pattern copied.

The dialogue between tormentor and tormented is resumed in a new scene (IV. i), which is chaos enacted. Under the pressure of Iago's indecent suggestions and perverse "if's"—"If they do nothing, 'tis a venial slip;/ But if I give my wife a handkerchief—"; "What/ If I had said I had seen him do you wrong?"—Othello's sentences break down and he falls in a fit: "Lie with her? lie on her? . . . It is not words that shakes me thus. Pish! Noses, ears, and lips. Is't possible? Confess? Handkerchief? O devil!" A successful period is put to Iago's manipulation when his condition "If it be that . . ." is fulfilled and he can point out the handkerchief passing between Bianca and Cassio. Othello is torn almost to incoherence with the conflict between what his own experience of Desdemona tells him and what Iago has led him to see.

> Ay, let her rot, and perish, and be damn'd tonight, for she shall not live. . . . O, the world hath not a sweeter creature! she might lie by an emperor's side and command him tasks.
> *Iago.* Nay, that's not your way.
> *Oth.* Hang her, I do but say what she is. . . . But yet the pity of it, Iago! O Iago, the pity of it, Iago!
>   (ll. 181-96)

Iago proposes strangling in the bed she has contaminated, he offers to be "undertaker" for Cassio, and the long dialogue is over. A trumpet announces the emissary from Venice, come to call Othello home.

This epilogue to the scene provides Iago with his moment of triumph. After the shocked Lodovico has seen Othello strike Desdemona, Iago hints at Othello's ruin in the fine duplicity of a pious wish:

> He's that he is. I may not breathe my censure.
> What he might be—if what he might he is not—
> I would to heaven he were![7]
>   (ll. 270-72)

This is surely the masterpiece of all conditional sentences.

Although the stage leading to proof has ended, one more

scene rounds it out. It is the "gate of hell" scene (IV. ii), in
which Othello, having viewed with his own eyes the evidence
of guilt, interrogates the supposed criminal. It is forensic, like
the scene which ended the protasis, although more loosely so.
This time the legal procedure of question and answer, statement and denial, is distorted in purpose and operation, for the
prosecuting attorney is also the plaintiff and he has no ears to
hear the truth. The defendant rests her oath of denial on the
condition of a true definition:

> No, as I am a Christian.
> If to preserve this vessel for my lord
> From any other foul unlawful touch
> Be not to be a strumpet, I am none.
> (ll. 82-85)

In the midst of this cruel process, Othello expresses another
of his great poetic insights into experience, yet one dreadfully
ironic in the untruth on which it is founded:

> Had it pleas'd heaven
> To try me with affliction, had they rain'd
> All kinds of sores and shames on my bare head, . . .
> I should have found in some place of my soul
> A drop of patience; . . .
> But there, where I have garner'd up my heart,
> Where either I must live or bear no life;
> The fountain from the which my current runs
> Or else dries up: to be discarded thence!
> (ll. 47-60)

He weighs excluded possibilities against the one which seems
to have come into being: If only it had been that, not this!

Emilia has "the office opposite to Saint Peter" and keeps the
gate of hell. Part of the dramatic irony with which the scene is
saturated comes from her clear-eyed perception and downright
statement of the true relations between conditions and conclusions. This logical sequence, spoken in answer to Othello's
questioning before the interview with Desdemona, has everything which Iago's *if*'s do not:

> I durst, my lord, to wager she is honest;
> Lay down my soul at stake. If you think other,
> Remove your thought; it doth abuse your bosom.
> If any wretch have put this in your head,
> Let heaven requite it with the serpent's curse!
> For if she be not honest, chaste, and true,
> There's no man happy; the purest of their wives
> Is foul as slander.
>
> (ll. 12-19)

And when Othello has left and Iago himself is present, Emilia in a strong asseverative conditional hits the truth precisely:

> I will be hang'd if some eternal villain,
> Some busy and insinuating rogue,
> Some cogging, cozening slave, to get some office,
> Have not devis'd this slander. I will be hang'd else.
>   *Iago.*   Fie, there is no such man; it is impossible.
>   *Des.*   If any such there be, heaven pardon him!
>
> (ll. 130-35)

Desdemona's optative subjunctive is counterpointed by Emilia's: "A halter pardon him! and hell gnaw his bones!" Desdemona's own solemn asseveration, in a pitiful appeal to the author of her ruin, follows:

> Here I kneel:
> If e'er my will did trespass 'gainst his love,
> Either in discourse of thought or actual deed, . . .
> Or that I do not yet, and ever did,
> And ever will (though he do shake me off
> To beggarly divorcement) love him dearly,
> Comfort forswear me!
>
> (ll. 151-59)

The catastrophe occupies the last long scene of the play (V. ii). It is foreshadowed poetically by the bedchamber scene (IV. iii): "If I do die before thee," Desdemona says to Emilia, "prithee shroud me/ In one of these same sheets." Emilia has laid the wedding sheets on the bed, Desdemona sings her forlorn Willow Song, and they talk of the conditions under which women betray their husbands. Emilia would do it if the world were the price; Desdemona, not for the world.

The ground for the catastrophe is cleared by Iago's last maneuverings to get Cassio and Roderigo killed (IV. ii. 172 ff.), his last promise to Roderigo ("If thou the next night following enjoy not Desdemona, . . ."), his last conditions of operation ("If you will watch his going thence, . . ."); then (V. i. 12-21) his assessment of alternative possibilities—

> Now, whether he kill Cassio,
> Or Cassio him, or each do kill the other,
> Every way makes my gain . . .

—and finally his recognition that his own fate hangs on the success of this last act of violence:

> If Cassio do remain,
> He hath a daily beauty in his life
> That makes me ugly; and besides, the Moor
> May unfold me to him; there stand I in much peril.

"This is the night/ That either makes me, or fordoes me quite." The scene (V. i) is another one of tumult, of swords clashing in the dark, of outcries and arrests, like those beginning the protasis and epitasis; but this time it is a hugger-mugger. Cassio, though seriously wounded, escapes with the daily beauty of his loyalty unimpaired to make Iago ugly.

The long last scene falls into three parts, the deed of violence, the discovery or recognition, and the suicide. The first part opens with Othello's illumined awareness of the finality of his act of execution on Desdemona:

> Put out the light, and then put out the light:
> If I quench thee, thou flaming minister,
> I can again thy former light restore,
> Should I repent me; but once put out thy light,
> Thou cunning'st pattern of excelling nature,
> I know not where is that Promethean heat
> That can thy light relume.
>
> (V. ii. 7-13)

This is awareness only in idea, clothed in the beauty of metaphor. When the deed is done—not as it was meant to be, sternly
and in justice, but angrily and in violence—it is followed by an
anticlimax of bewilderment about the merely practical question of what to do next. At this moment, with Emilia's cry, the
immediate world is at the door; reality strikes in the homeliest
of ways and is inexpressible:

> If she come in, she'll sure speak to my wife.
> My wife, my wife! what wife? I have no wife.

Recognition, or discovery, begins with Emilia's insistence on
Desdemona's fidelity (ll. 130 ff.). The recognition Othello has
to make is that the monster Iago has shown him, the monster
for which he has killed his wife, has never been anything but
a monstrous fantasy, housed in his own mind. The recognition
is so bewildering and so damning that he must resist it:

> O, I were damn'd beneath all depth in hell
> But that I did proceed upon just grounds
> To this extremity.

This is one of his old forms of asseveration, based on a condition he believes to be contrary to fact; only now the affirmation
is not a promise for the future but a justification of the past.
Another follows:

> Nay, had she been true,
> If heaven would make me such another world
> Of one entire and perfect chrysolite,
> I'd not have sold her for it.

The lines are heavy with the nearly unbearable irony that the
condition is most true. Do we hear Desdemona's voice, as she
prepared to lie down on her wedding sheets? "Beshrew me, if
I would do such a wrong/ For the whole world."

But when, with Emilia's testimony about the handkerchief,
Othello's awakening is complete, the recognition of the truth
is so dreadful that he can imagine only damnation:

> Now—how dost thou look now? O ill-starr'd wench,
> Pale as thy smock! when we shall meet at compt,
> This look of thine will hurl my soul from heaven,
> And fiends will snatch at it.

The conjunction is temporal, not "if" but "when." An "if" follows as he makes a wounding, but not fatal, thrust at Iago: "If that thou be'st a devil, I cannot kill thee." The consequence seems to approve the condition.

The *if*'s are over. We are again in a world of fact, monstrous but true. At last a crime has been committed, and it is Othello's. Were he tried he must this time be found guilty. In place of a trial we have his last formal speech (ll. 338-56). It is cast fittingly in the hortatory imperative to express a plea in the strongest possible way: "I pray you, . . . / Speak of me as I am; . . ./ Set you down this;/ . . . say besides, that in Aleppo once, . . ." Notice that the form of his plea, though imperative, implies a condition: If you tell the truth impartially, without a bias either extenuating or malicious, you will be bound to say these things about me. His hearers must then speak

> Of one that lov'd not wisely but too well;
> Of one not easily jealous, but being wrought,
> Perplexed in the extreme; of one whose hand,
> Like the base Indian,[8] threw a pearl away
> Richer than all his tribe; of one whose subdu'd eyes,
> Albeit unused to the melting mood,
> Drops tears as fast as the Arabian trees
> Their medicinable gum.

The obligation is on us to understand the speech precisely. The relation of the condition to its conclusion is necessary. The truth is this and no other. To read the speech otherwise, with reservations about Othello's motives or the psychology of jealousy, is not to have attended to the syntax of the play in its dramatic functioning. From beginning to end there has been a precise discrimination between the true and false relations of a condition to its conclusion. Iago's monster was created from the false relation. The imperative form of this last speech is an adjuration to Othello's hearers (and to us) to speak of him truly and justly.

But notice that Othello is also declaring something. What his hearers are bound to report are his final affirmations—of his love, his jealousy, his folly, and his remorse. They are the only declarations he can make; the old simple truth cannot be had again. The final declaration in the speech—a report of the act of justice he did on a turbaned Turk—is, with the utmost economy, caught up in the final adjuration that his witnesses report the act of justice he does at this instant on himself.

Othello's last sentences are nevertheless simply declarative:

> I kiss'd thee ere I kill'd thee. No way but this,
> Killing myself, to die upon a kiss.

Simple as they are, they go beyond the kiss before the murder and tie the end to the beginning. The tragedy lies all between.

Give me the map there!

Command, Question, and Assertion in *King Lear*

K*ING LEAR* sounds markedly different from any other of the tragedies. It gives the sustained impression of a world less immediate and contemporary than the other tragedies do, regardless of their particular historical or temporal setting. The world of *Lear* is archaic and remote—not only in time, but from the everyday naturalness and variety of discourse one hears in *Hamlet* or *Julius Caesar* or even *Antony and Cleopatra*. The moments of natural simplicity in speech, as in the scene of Lear's reconciliation with Cordelia, may therefore be almost unbearably moving. The general remoteness is proper to the fable, which, in its simplified characters and in its simple moral alternatives of good and evil, takes us into the world of fairy-tale—fairy-tale vastly stretched, indeed,

Delivered first as the Fred S. Tupper Memorial Lecture at the George Washington University, 11 April 1969, and subsequently at McGill University and at the Shakespeare Institute, Ashland; published in *Shakespeare's Art: Seven Essays*, ed. Milton Crane (Chicago: The University of Chicago Press for the George Washington University, 1973; © 1973 by the George Washington University), pp. 55-70. The essay has been somewhat revised.

92

and transformed into tragedy; nevertheless, still fairy-tale at base. Shakespeare has fitted his setting and his style to his fable so intimately that we feel we are seeing a drama of human suffering through enlarging and filtering lenses; or that we are listening to the music of it, composed in unexpected keys with harsh dissonances and rare harmonies.

Something of our impression of remote grandeur must come from the vague and featureless setting of largely unnamed places and of uncertain distances; from a storm so cosmic that Lear can call on the thunder of it to

> Strike flat the thick rotundity o' th' world!
> Crack nature's moulds, all germains spill at once
> That makes ingrateful man.

We are aware also that the style of Lear has something to do with this impression of a more primitive world than is found elsewhere in the tragedies. Does the impression come from the imagery of savage animals matching the savage hearts of men? from the sense of pain and stress in the physical images of being wrenched, broken apart, struck, torn, pierced, racked, flayed, scalded?[1] Does it come from the language—the sometimes archaic vocabulary? the density or deliberateness of the phrasing, its stiffness or harshness? Listen to Gloucester telling his tormentors why he has sent the King to Dover:

> Because I would not see thy cruel nails
> Pluck out his poor old eyes, nor thy fierce sister
> In his anointed flesh rash[2] boarish fangs.
> The sea, with such a storm as his bare head
> In hell-black night endur'd, would have buoy'd up
> And quench'd the stelled fires;
> Yet, poor old heart, he holp the heavens to rain.
> If wolves had at thy gate howl'd that dearn[3] time,
> Thou shouldst have said, 'Good porter, turn the key.'
> All cruels else subscribe.
>
> (III. vii. 55-65)

Does the impression come from the larger features of the speeches—the rhetoric of fiat, pronouncement, objurgation, imprecation, petition, interrogation? Doubtless from all these, and

more, together: from imagery, diction, figure, syntax, meter.[4]
In a performance the effects on our minds are immediate and
interacting. But the causes may, in part, be separately analyzed
(as the imagery has been), to the increase of our understanding of Shakespeare's art and of our pleasure in it. I say "in part"
because the whole will always elude analysis; who can "with
counters sum the . . . proportion" of its infinite?

I have chosen to concentrate on the syntax, for in *King Lear*
I believe it to be an important and distinctive component of
the style, one which does much to give it its peculiar stamp. A
close look at the syntax discovers, as in *Othello,* a recurrent
pattern, but a very different one. The analysis is rhetorical and
grammatical at once; I have looked persistently beneath the
rhetorical structure to identify the repeated syntactical building blocks of so much of it.

When King Lear walks on the stage within a few lines of the
opening of the play, he addresses the court with a declaration
of his intentions, much of it cast in the imperative mood:

> Mean time we shall express our darker purpose.
> Give me the map there. Know[5] we have divided
> In three our kingdom; and 'tis our fast intent
> To shake all cares and business from our age,
> Conferring them on younger strengths, while we
> Unburthen'd crawl toward death.

He has struck at once his own most characteristic syntactical
mood, and with it one of the distinguishing moods of the
tragedy, for it is Lear's voice which will dominate the play. In
no other Shakespearian tragedy do we hear so imperious a
voice—so continually demanding, ordering, exclaiming, im-
precating, pronouncing.

Lear's oftenest heard note is the note of command, whether
the syntax be formally in the imperative mood ("Know this!"
"Do that!") or whether it be in some other. A variant of the
imperative is the "Let it be done" or "May it be done" construction, which takes the place of the Latin hortative or imperative
subjunctive. Lear uses this construction frequently as a form
of command ("Let me not stay a jot for dinner," I. iv. 8) or of

urgent wish, as in his prayers to the gods: "O, let me not be
mad, not mad, sweet heaven!/ Keep me in temper, I would not
be mad!" (I. v. 46-47). Even the indicative mood is for him
often a declaration of unalterable intention, expressive of the
same dominance of will as in the commands:

> The barbarous Scythian . . .
> shall to my bosom
> Be as well neighbor'd, pitied, and reliev'd,
> As thou my sometime daughter.
>> (I. i. 116-20)

If we listen sensitively, we shall also become aware in Lear's
part of two other common types of sentence, both in the indicative mood. One is the interrogative sentence, variously
used, the other the declarative sentence used for simple, unqualified assertions.

The pattern of syntax is set in the first scene. Lear follows
his announcement of retiring from government and of dividing
his kingdom among his three daughters in a planned ceremony.
He asks each of the daughters in turn how much she loves him.
These questions are not truly queries, but demands; they are
asked to dramatize the gift-giving, not to learn the answers,
which he thinks he knows already.

> Tell me, my daughters . . . ,
> Which of you shall we say doth love us most,
> That we our largest bounty may extend
> Where nature doth with merit challenge? Goneril,
> Our eldest-born, speak first.

Goneril makes a fulsome reply, that she loves him better than
eyesight, space, and liberty, no less than life, grace, health,
beauty, honor; and Lear marks off her portion on the map. He
next puts the question to Regan,

> What says our second daughter,
> Our dearest Regan, wife of Cornwall? Speak,

receives a similar fulsome reply (that she takes no joy in anything but her father's love), and in turn designates her portion.
Then he questions Cordelia:

> Now, our joy,
> Although the last, not least,[6] . . .
>   what can you say to draw
> A third more opulent than your sisters? Speak.

Clearly he had intended the best portion for her. Note the dialogue which follows the question to her.

> Nothing, my lord.
> Nothing?
> Nothing.
> Nothing can[7] come of nothing. Speak again!

Lear's question, "Nothing?" is one of shocked incredulity. The declaration, "Nothing can come of nothing," is a flat assertion of an apparent truism: "Nihil ex nihilo." The use of the interrogative in Lear's part is to vary from such demanding or exclamatory questions early in the play to questions of genuine inquiry later on. The declarative sentence will continue to be used for plain unqualified assertions, often aphoristic or sententious, but later these will be reflections of new experience, not just automatic responses to a situation.

To return to the dialogue between Lear and Cordelia. To his angry order, "Speak again!" she replies in a statement which seems clear and is yet a riddle—a profound one, the answer to which is not to be learned until nearly the end of the play:

> Unhappy that I am, I cannot heave
> My heart into my mouth. I love your Majesty
> According to my bond, no more nor less.

His question put in terms of quantity has begot a reply in kind, and Goneril's and Regan's insincere protestations of love have provoked a sarcastic nicety of distinction in Cordelia's terms:

> Why have my sisters husbands, if they say
> They love you all? . . .
> Sure I shall never marry like my sisters,
> To love my father all.

Her statement is followed by another balanced interchange of question and answer:

> *Lear.*   But goes thy heart with this?
> *Cor.*   Ay, my good lord.
> *Lear.*   So young, and so untender?
> *Cor.*   So young, my lord, and true.

The awful fiat of disinheritance, attested by a frightening oath, follows at once:

> Let it be so: thy truth then be thy dow'r!
> For by the sacred radiance of the sun,
> The mysteries of Hecate and the night;
> By all the operation of the orbs,
> From whom we do exist and cease to be;
> Here I disclaim all my paternal care,
> Propinquity and property of blood,
> And as a stranger to my heart and me
> Hold thee from this for ever.

The syntactical patterns of command, question, and assertion have been established. The three "themes" or "subjects"—if we may use a strictly musical metaphor—have been stated. As the play progresses, they will be varied and developed in complex harmonies and dissonances until they are brought to a resolution at the end.

We might say that these matters of syntax are only a matter of character. But we have heard Cordelia's plain assertions balancing Lear's plain questions ("Nothing?" "Nothing"; "So young, and so untender?" "So young, my lord, and true"). Moreover, Lear's voice is not the only one in which we are to hear commands, hortatory prayers, emphatic assertions of intent, astonished questions, and sententious declarations. Listen to Kent, for instance, expostulating with Lear on his fatal decision to divide his kingdom and banish Cordelia:

> Be Kent unmannerly
> When Lear is mad. What wouldest thou do, old man?
> Think'st thou that duty shall have dread to speak
> When power to flattery bows? To plainness honor's bound
> When majesty falls to folly. Reserve thy state,
> And in thy best consideration check
> This hideous rashness.

> (I. i. 145-51)

And again,

> Revoke thy gift,
> Or whilst I can vent clamor from my throat,
> I'll tell thee thou dost evil.

> (ll. 164-66)

It is extraordinary to what a degree the syntax of other speakers in the play reflects Lear's. Goneril and Regan are busy with commands; so are Gloucester and, later, Edmund. Cordelia's prayers—if different in tone from her father's, having more in them of supplication than command—are yet like his in syntax:

> All blest secrets,
> All you unpublish'd virtues of the earth,
> Spring with my tears; be aidant and remediate
> In the good man's distress!

> (IV. iv. 15-18)

So likewise are Gloucester's prayers: "Kind gods, forgive me that and prosper him!" (III. vii. 92).[8] And Gloucester's questions are as amazed as Lear's.[9] Edgar's and Cordelia's are as full of shock at the discovery of unwelcome truths.[10] Goneril, Regan, and Cornwall ask questions, too—not in wonder, however, but in hatred; they turn questions into torturing interrogations.[11] The Fool is always asking questions for the sake of the gnomic or parabolic answers he supplies to them.[12] Unqualified assertions on everybody's part are the commonest type of declarative sentence in the play. Kent, Edgar, and Albany can be at times as aphoristic as Lear.[13]

The fact that these types of sentences are repeated to some degree in the speech of other characters than Lear indicates that they are not limited in function to the distinguishing of character. Lear's syntax does indeed reflect his. It is the primary means by which we are made aware of his temperament and habits of mind; or, put more critically, it is the primary means by which a dramatic character called "Lear" is created. But in what it suggests the syntax goes beyond anything Shakespeare wants to have us understand about Lear himself. It is

an important means by which we enter (on a deeper level than
formulated ideas) the peculiar universe of this play—of this
play as distinct from any other; for the universe of the play is
artistic as well as moral. Possibly this is a way of saying that
the universe of the play is the same as Lear's universe. But in
any case what is suggested is something beyond "character" in
the ordinary, limited sense of the term. The "world" of a tragedy is created not only by what is said but by how it is said.
Scrutiny will show that the grammatical structure has as much
to do as the other resources of the language—diction, imagery,
figure, prosody—in creating the universe of this tragedy. And I
think the reason is that the syntax is so intimately appropriate
to the fable, as Shakespeare conceived it.

The Lear story is a folk-tale at base. The essence of the tale
is that in a test of love put to his three daughters, a father fails
to understand the riddling answer of the youngest: "I love you
as much as salt"; he must learn the value of salt by being deprived of it before he realizes that this youngest daughter is the
only one who loves him truly. Although the old story was
moved into a political context by Geoffrey of Monmouth's graft
of it in the twelfth century on British legendary history, and
although it was further sophisticated in its subsequent retell-
ings in chronicle and in drama, the folk-tale motifs of the love-
test, the youngest-best, and a riddle answerable only after
experience, remained a part of it.[14] And so did they in Shakespeare. He did nothing to obliterate the motifs and conven-
tions of folk- or fairy-tale; in fact, they determined his artistic
point of view in the handling of action, character, and even
language. The story from Sidney's *Arcadia* which he used to
parallel and complicate the Lear plot, the story of the old king
of Paphlagonia and his two sons,[15] whom Shakespeare turned
into Gloucester, Edgar, and Edmund, helped him to expand
the universal meaning of the Lear story and convert it to tragedy. In the *Arcadia* the episode of the Paphlagonian king was
a moral exemplum on the theme of kindness and unkindness,
that is, of naturalness and unnaturalness in filial relations.
Shakespeare enlarged the theme to encompass the breaking of
bonds on all levels of relationship: between father and child,

brother and brother, sister and sister, king and subject, man and the gods. He changed Cordelia's riddle, the old loving-like-salt riddle, which in Geoffrey had become, "As much as thou hast, so much art thou worth, and so much I love thee,"[16] to "I love you according to my bond." And he deepened the theme to sound the very nature of love.

It will be seen that the generally not very complicated syntax of the play—with its plain and emphatic declaratives, its commanding or hortatory imperatives—fits the fairy-tale world of absolutes: good and evil, truth and falsehood, love and hate. In a fairy-tale, also, questions are posed for the sake of answers, which are either gnomic or riddling; the riddles must contain some element of ambiguity or irony and must not be understood until the hero has discovered their meaning by a test or by experience. In the Henry plays, and in tragedies conceived in more realistic terms, such as *Julius Caesar* and *Coriolanus*, there is a good deal of persuasive argument, logical or emotional, before decisions are made or altered. Deliberative rhetoric requires a complex and varied syntax for the consideration of possibilities, the weighing of alternatives, the nice adjustment of principle to expediency. But in *King Lear*, the King has made his first decision, to divide his kingdom and give up the responsibility of governing it, before the play opens; he makes his second one, to banish Cordelia and divide her portion between the other two daughters and sons-in-law, without deliberation. The action in the main plot, after he has made the second, and fatal, decision, is a series of shocking and explosive confrontations, not of events arising from earlier decisions and leading to new ones. Lear has, indeed, surrendered the possibility of further free decision. His part, until late in the play, is therefore passive in the strict sense of the word; he can do nothing but suffer in the process of learning and accepting his mistake.

The intrigues of the sisters and of Edmund which carry the action forward are quickly motivated, simply conceived, and easily managed. The intrigue of Edmund against his brother is even crude, without much attention to plausibility in detail. Much of the preparation for the dénouement, such as the part played by Kent and Gloucester in the return of Cordelia to aid her father, is merely hinted at, never worked out. For this kind of plot, where motivation is often taken for granted, credulity is stressed, emotion is unshaded, action is unsubtle, and persuasion is by force, no very complex or subtle syntax is wanted. This is not to say that the play is smooth in the hearing or reading. Far from it. Boldness in diction, grammar, trope, and meter make the going slow and sometimes rough. Much of the style is craggy. But it is not often complex sentences that make it so.[17]

It is interesting to note that conditional sentences, which in *Othello* accompany every significant move in the action, are relatively sparse in *King Lear*. The very core of Othello's tragedy is his betrayal by false conditions, which he is made to believe are true; the conditional sentences in his part and in Iago's occur in nearly every possible grammatical variation in the indicative and subjunctive moods. In *King Lear* conditional sentences occur largely in the parts of the Fool and of the plotting characters, i.e., Edmund, Goneril, and Regan. Their special purpose in the Fool's part I shall return to a little later. In the "practisers'" parts they remind us merely of the possibilities recognized and exploited by the opportunist: "If he distaste it, let him to my sister" (I. iii. 14), or "If I find him comforting the King, it will stuff his suspicion more fully" (III. v. 20-21). These are very like the similar ones Iago speaks in soliloquy as he improvises his successive moves against Othello. It is significant, surely, that there are few conditional sentences in the speeches of Lear, and that those few are memorable.[18] The world the King inhabits at the beginning of the play is a world of certainties and absolutes, not a world of uncertainties or contingencies. Within the reach of his power his commands bring obedience. To him it is a clearly defined world of privileges and obligations, without conditions or doubts. He never says: "If this were so, I should do such and such," but always, "Let this be so."

Lear's discovery through experience is in part a discovery of the world of contingency, in which conditions govern all relations. Perhaps he did not so much fail to recognize contingency as to suppose that he alone could set all the conditions. The most crucial condition he discovers is that his authority and the respect he assumes to be due him under the title of king—"the name, and all th' addition to a king"—are not absolute, but are contingent on his power. That given away, his commands are worthless. When "the sway, revenue, execution of the rest" are gone, his "addition" disappears. He is later to extend his discovery to other experiences than his own—for instance, to the general realm of justice:

> Plate sin with gold,
> And the strong lance of justice hurtless breaks;
> Arm it in rags, a pygmy's straw does pierce it.
> (IV. vi. 165-67)

But Lear does at the start believe in at least one contingency, that is, that love is given in proportion to benefits received. This means that he has things precisely upside down. What Cordelia's love will teach him is that love is the one true absolute, given without measure and without condition.

The conflict in Lear's mind, therefore, is not a debate leading to decision, but a resistance to discovery of unwelcome truths. The syntactical form which counterpoints his imperatives is the question in the indicative mood. The counterpointing begins with his shocked question to Cordelia, when the first crack appears in the certainties of his world. "Nothing, my lord." "Nothing?" As other cracks appear and deepen, the incredulous exclamatory questions ("Are you our daughter?") shade into questions about his own identity as father and as king ("Who is it that can tell me who I am?"). These give place, as his experience teaches him more, to general questions on human society and the nature of man. To some of his questions he supplies the answers with the aphoristic assertions I have mentioned. They are not necessarily the right answers. These must be found, if at all, in the implications of the tragedy as a whole.

To follow the varied use of these sentence patterns throughout the play one needs to have the text in hand and ample time to study it in. In this essay I shall try to throw into relief, in the principal scenes of the Lear plot, the interplay and function of the three "themes" (to revert to the musical metaphor) and so to indicate the direction the development takes.

Lear makes the first discovery of his mistake in his stipulated monthly sojourn at his eldest daughter's castle (I. iii, iv). Fulfilling her agreement with Regan to "do something, and i' th' heat," Goneril orders her servants to "come slack of" their services to him, picks a quarrel with him over his hundred attendant knights, threatens that if he does not reduce their number she will do it herself, makes it appear that they are quarreling and brawling, but actually sees to it that her servants stir up trouble so that she may "breed from hence occasions" to complain. This behavior is so incredible to Lear, considering that he has given her half his kingdom, that he demands of her who she is ("Are you our daughter?" and "Your name, fair gentlewoman?" I. iv. 218, 236) and who he is:

> Does any here know me? This is not Lear.
> Does Lear walk thus? speak thus? Where are his eyes?
> Either his notion weakens, his discernings
> Are lethargied—Ha! waking? 'Tis not so.
> Who is it that can tell me who I am?
> > (I. iv. 226-30)

The same note of unsettling astonishment is struck as in his "Nothing?" to Cordelia's "Nothing." The Fool knows the answer, and interposes *sotto voce*, "Lear's shadow." Lear's questions are put sarcastically, in exasperated frustration, but beneath them is the deeper note of uncertain identity. If he is not recognized as father and as king, then who is he? Who is Lear if he is not these things? He calls for his horses to be saddled that he may ride off to Regan's, and, in the most terrible curse in the play, calls down on Goneril the retributive judgment of Nature, that she be sterile; or, if not, that her child

> be a thwart disnatur'd torment to her.
> Let it stamp wrinkles in her brow of youth,
> With cadent tears fret channels in her cheeks,
> Turn all her mother's pains and benefits
> To laughter and contempt, that she may feel
> How sharper than a serpent's tooth it is
> To have a thankless child!

His discovery that Goneril had already dismissed half his train of knights before she even requested him to do it brings down on her another curse. Trying to control his tears, Lear storms

out with the confident assertion that he has a daughter left who
will flay Goneril's "wolvish visage."

But something else has been going on in this scene. The Fool
has been asking Lear questions, in the form of posers or riddles
so that he may supply the witty answers. Since they are all
variations on the theme of Lear's folly in giving up his crown
or of banishing the wrong daughter, they emphasize the same
truths that Lear's own questions of vexed astonishment show
him so reluctant to accept.

> *Fool.* . . . Can you make no use of nothing, nuncle?
> *Lear.* Why, no, boy, nothing can be made out of nothing.
> (I. iv. 130-31)

We have heard this before. The Fool gives the axiom a new
twist:

> Prithee tell him, so much the rent of his land comes to. He
> will not believe a fool.

Lear's comment, "A bitter fool," prompts a new question:

> *Fool.* Dost thou know the difference, my boy, between a
> bitter fool and a sweet fool?
> *Lear.* No, lad, teach me.

And so the Fool does, by an acted-out demonstration that Lear,
whom nobody but himself counselled to give away his land, is
the bitter fool, he the sweet one.

> *Lear.* Dost thou call me fool, boy?
> *Fool.* All thy other titles thou hast given away; that thou
> wast born with.

Sometimes the situation is reversed and Lear asks the question,
as at the end of the preceding passage, but the interchange is
only a variant on the same riddling game.

> *Fool.* . . . How now, nuncle? Would I had two coxcombs
> and two daughters!
> *Lear.* Why, my boy?
> *Fool.* If I gave them all my living, I'ld keep my coxcombs
> myself. There's mine, beg another of thy daughters.
> (ll. 104-9)

The Fool's answers, like the last one, are full of *if*'s, for it is precisely the world of contingency that he is teaching Lear about. "Nay," he says to Kent, "and thou canst not smile as the wind sits, thou'lt catch cold shortly. . . . if thou follow him [Lear], thou must needs wear my coxcomb" (ll. 100-104). The Fool's parabolic riddles[19] and plain assertions of obvious truths are choric in effect; but they also perhaps suggest what is running in Lear's own mind, for at one point he recognizes his dreadful mistake:

> O most small fault,
> How ugly didst thou in Cordelia show!
> Which, like an engine, wrench'd my frame of nature
> From the fix'd place; drew from my heart all love,
> And added to the gall. O Lear, Lear, Lear!
> Beat at this gate that let thy folly in
> And thy dear judgment out!
>
> (ll. 266-72)

The mood is still imperative, but the commands are to himself.

Warned by Goneril of Lear's departure, Regan and her husband leave home to afford an excuse for not taking her father in; and it is at Gloucester's castle that father, daughter, and son-in-law meet. In this scene (II. iv) we hear again the incredulous questions,

> Deny to speak with me? They are sick? they are weary?
> They have travell'd all the night? Mere fetches, . . .
>
> (ll. 88-89)

and the angry imprecations,

> You nimble lightnings, dart your blinding flames
> Into her scornful eyes! Infect her beauty,
> You fen-suck'd fogs, drawn by the pow'rful sun,
> To fall and blister!
>
> (ll. 165-68)

But there is now a marked difference from the earlier scenes, for Lear slips from the offensive to the defensive. He now tries, with evidently increasing inner stress, to maintain a front against a truth too dreadful for him to acknowledge—that his

second daughter, as the Fool had predicted, tastes as like the
first "as a crab does to a crab." He keeps insisting, against all
the signs—the sight of Kent his messenger in the stocks, Cornwall's and Regan's refusal at first to see him, Regan's coldness
when she does—that his daughter's eyes "do comfort, and not
burn," that it is not in her to cut off his train or "oppose the
bolt" against his coming in, that she better knows "the offices
of nature, bond of childhood,/ Effects of courtesy, dues of
gratitude." Throughout the scene he struggles to keep his temper lest he be overwhelmed by rising hysteria. Therefore he
looks for any excuse to convince himself that what he sees with
his own eyes, hears with his own ears, is not true. But the sight
of Kent in the stocks, reminding him of an intentional insult to
himself, keeps reviving his anger; and he returns over and over
to the same question: "Death on my state! wherefore/ Should
he sit here?" "Who put my man i' th' stocks?" "Who stock'd
my servant?"

After the entry of Goneril (l. 188), whom he greets with a
now familiar admonitory question ("Art not asham'd to look
upon this beard?"), and after the shocking sight of Regan's
welcome to her ("O Regan, wilt thou[20] take her by the hand?"),
the sisters in a turn-about take over the questioning, and by its
means conduct a disingenuous argument that would reduce
him to complete dependency on them. Harping on his dotage
and telling him that Goneril knows what she does in cutting
his train in half, Regan begins:

> What, fifty followers?
> It is not well? What should you need of more?
> Yea, or so many? sith that both charge and danger
> Speak 'gainst so great a number? How in one house
> Should many people under two commands
> Hold amity? 'Tis hard, almost impossible.
>   (ll. 237-42)

In these questions we hear the same surprise, the same suggestion of unreasonableness, as in Lear's questions, but with
the difference that these are smoothly turned into a plausible
but specious argument. Goneril warms to it and to the method:

> Why might not you, my lord, receive attendance
> From those that she calls servants or from mine?

And Regan chimes in with her amen: "Why not, my lord?"
When she tells him that she will allow him no more than
twenty-five, he decides he must make the hard choice of returning with Goneril, whose allowance of fifty means to him
that she has twice Regan's love. But Goneril resumes the questions with greater eloquence and greater speciousness:

> Hear me my lord:
> What need you five and twenty? ten? or five?
> To follow in a house where twice so many
> Have a command to tend you?

Regan moves the argument to its inevitable end: "What need
one?" This brings Lear's protesting cry, "O, reason not the
need!" and with it his penetrating insight into distinctively
human needs; a man lives on a purely animal level if he seeks
no more than the base satisfaction of physical needs. His reply
is more truly reasoned than theirs.

> . . . our basest beggars
> Are in the poorest thing superfluous.
> Allow not nature more than nature needs,
> Man's life is cheap as beast's. Thou art a lady;
> If only to go warm were gorgeous,
> Why, nature needs not what thou gorgeous wear'st,
> Which scarely keeps thee warm.

Decorum, ceremony, courtesy, elegance—things which give
dignity and beauty to life—come only when man is able to live
beyond his animal needs. Civilized man does not live by bread
only. This is the first wise speech of Lear, the first in which he
moves out beyond himself in the utterance of a general truth.
　　But what he most needs at this moment is patience:

> But for true need—
> You heavens, give me that patience, patience I need!

and he pitifully asks the gods to touch him with noble anger,
not to let "women's weapons, water-drops," stain his man's

cheeks. The form of the petition is the same as in his curses, but the tone is different. As he goes out into the rising storm, he makes a threat of vengeance. We hear the familiar syntax, but this time his imagination falters. The future of strong determination is now empty of content:

> No, you unnatural hags,
> I will have such revenges on you both
> That all the world shall—I will do such things—
> What they are yet I know not, but they shall be
> The terrors of the earth!

Defiance replaces command; he is threatening only to himself:

> You think I'll weep:
> No, I'll not weep.
> I have full cause of weeping, but this heart
> Shall break into a hundred thousand flaws
> Or ere I'll weep. O Fool, I shall go mad!

The scene ends with Regan's command to Gloucester, "Shut up your doors," and with Cornwall's echo of it in remorseless finality:

> Shut up your doors, my lord, 'tis a wild night,
> My Regan counsels well. Come out o' th' storm.

Gloucester has no authority in his own house. Power has fully passed to the cruel and the wicked.

Out in the storm (III. i, ii, iv) Lear "strives in his little world of man to outscorn/ The to-and-fro-conflicting wind and rain" (III. i. 10-11). The imperatives of petition and of command are indistinguishable in form, almost as if he could himself command the elements:

> Blow, winds, and crack your cheeks! rage, blow!
> You cataracts and hurricanoes, spout
> Till you have drench'd our steeples, drown'd the cocks!
> You sulph'rous and thought-executing fires,
> Vaunt-couriers of oak-cleaving thunderbolts,
> Singe my white head!
>
> (III. ii. 1-6)

Still, he knows that in his helplessness he is at their mercy—
"Here I stand your slave"—and protests the injustice of their
attack on him:

> But yet I call you servile ministers,
> That will with two pernicious daughters join
> Your high-engender'd battles 'gainst a head
> So old and white as this.

And again, but with a shift to the third person and the petitory
subjunctive:

> Let the great gods,
> That keep this dreadful pudder o'er our heads,
> Find out their enemies now.

Their true enemies are those whose covert crimes are undi-
vulged and unwhipped of justice, the perjured, the concealers
of evil hearts like his daughters, the simulars of virtue. They
are the ones to "cry/ These dreadful summoners grace." He,
Lear, is "a man/ More sinn'd against than sinning." This is a
truth indeed, for his faults were vanity, not hypocrisy; the
anger of hurt pride, not malice.

Lear's widening vision of the nature of evil, a vision so bitter
that he prays the "all-shaking thunder" to flatten the globe,
crack nature's moulds, and destroy all the seeds of mankind
(III. ii. 6-9), includes also a new awareness of suffering:

> Poor naked wretches, wheresoe'er you are,
> That bide the pelting of this pitiless storm,
> How shall your houseless heads and unfed sides,
> Your loop'd and window'd raggedness, defend you
> From seasons such as these? O, I have ta'en
> Too little care of this! Take physic, pomp,
> Expose thyself to feel what wretches feel,
> That thou mayst shake the superflux to them,
> And show the heavens more just.
>   (III. iv. 28-36)

Question, assertion, and command are all there, but altogether
different in emphasis and direction from anything we have
heard before. The disturbing question, even though it can be

asked only because of Lear's own immediate experience in the
storm, is not centered in himself; it is not a demand for an
answer, not an angry exclamation, not even an expression of
bewilderment as to who he is, but a question of genuine hu-
manitarian concern: How are the unfed, the unclothed, the
homeless, to endure seasons such as these? The assertion, "I
have ta'en too little care of this," is a simple admission of his
own negligence and irresponsibility. The hortatory command,
"Take physic, pomp," is addressed to rulers in general, not
merely to himself.

But this high pitch, whether in prayer to the elements or in
solemn adjuration to himself, is not sustained throughout these
scenes. His three principal sentence patterns, his three "themes,"
are sometimes modulated into another key, with a new note of
tenderness. When Kent would lead him to shelter in a hovel
he has found, Lear thinks first of his Fool:

> Come on, my boy. How dost, my boy? Art cold?
> I am cold myself. Where is this straw, my fellow?
> The art of our necessities is strange
> And can make vile things precious. Come, your hovel.
> Poor Fool and knave, I have one part in my heart
> That's sorry yet for thee.
>   (III. ii. 68-73)

Lear is discovering who he is. Between his speeches we have
been hearing the Fool's wry and pitiful "sentences": "O nuncle,
court holy-water in a dry house is better than this rain-water
out o' door" (ll. 10-11); "He that has a house to put 's head in
has a good head-piece" (ll. 25-26). To his melancholy song on
the way of the world,

> 'He that has and a little tine[21] wit—
>   With a hey ho, the wind and the rain—
> Must make content with his fortunes fit,
>   For[22] the rain it raineth every day,'
>   (ll. 74-77)

Lear assents: "True, boy. Come bring us to this hovel."
During the two storm scenes Lear's new perceptions are in-

terrupted by the realization of his helplessness as "a poor, in-
firm, weak, and despis'd old man" and by his struggle for self-
control:

>   —filial ingratitude!
> Is it not as this mouth should tear this hand
> For lifting food to't? But I will punish home.
> No, I will weep no more. In such a night
> To shut me out? Pour on, I will endure.
> In such a night as this! O Regan, Goneril!
> Your old kind father, whose frank heart gave all—
> O, that way madness lies; let me shun that!
> No more of that.
>   (III. iv. 14-22)

Note again the incredulous questions, the exclamations, the
declarations of future intent; but now they oscillate between
shock and defiance, or between shock and the impulse to
weep. The sight of Edgar as poor mad Tom, who is routed out
of the hovel (1. 46), is all that is needed to end the King's
slender hold on sanity. His questions take a sudden, irrational
turn which yet marks his fixation:

> Didst thou give all to thy daughters? And art thou come to this?
>
>   ·   ·   ·   ·   ·
>
> Has his daughters brought him to this pass?
> Couldst thou save nothing? Didst[23] thou give 'em all?

These questions lead to the next:

> Is it the fashion that discarded fathers
> Should have thus little mercy on their flesh?
> Judicious punishment! 'twas this flesh begot
> Those pelican daughters.

Poor Tom now becomes to Lear the source of wisdom, a learned
Theban, from whom he can learn the secrets of the universe:
"What is the cause of thunder?" He is fascinated with this Tom
o' Bedlam—in rags, houseless, reduced to drinking "the green
mantle of the standing pool"; to eating "the swimming frog, the
toad, the todpole, the wall-newt," and "cow-dung for sallets";

possessed by the foul fiend, who has "laid knives under his pillow, and halters in his pew."

Contemplation of Edgar's state leads Lear to his central question and to his observation, categorically stated, on the nature of man himself:

> Thou wert better in a grave than to answer with thy un-
> cover'd body this extremity of the skies. Is man no more than
> this? Consider him well. Thou ow'st the worm no silk, the
> beast no hide, the sheep no wool, the cat no perfume. Ha!
> here's three on's are sophisticated. Thou art the thing itself:
> unaccommodated man is no more but such a poor, bare, fork'd
> animal as thou art. Off, off, you lendings! Come, unbutton
> here.

(III. iv. 101-9)

With the onset of madness, Lear's speech does not lose its coherence or customary syntax. The sequence in this speech of wondering question, sententious assertion, and imperious command follows a pattern close to that in the apostrophe, earlier in the scene, to the "poor naked wretches" out in the storm at the mercy of the elements. But that speech was wholly rational; this is not, altogether. This speech is at the nadir of Lear's experience; he thinks he has discovered what man truly is, and that he must therefore reduce himself to this essential state. Clothes are taken as the symbols of corrupt, civilized man; they are mere borrowings, sophistications of nature, and must therefore be discarded. We remember, however, Lear's earlier intuition in the "O reason not the need" speech. There he had said, "Allow not nature more than nature needs,/ Man's life is cheap as beast's." It is indeed! Is, then, this unaccommodated state a desirable state to return to? He did not think so then, when he was sane. And is Tom, eating "the old rat and the ditch-dog," the thing itself? Is man no more than a poor, bare, forked animal? The implications of the assertion are ambiguous. It may be well to remember who this "poor Tom" is in himself. He is Gloucester's son, a victim of his brother's ambition and his father's credulity, yet the one whose selfless love will save his father. "Is man no more than this?" is the great central question of the play. If it is answered, as I believe it is, it is answered not explicitly, but implicitly, in the characters—those who love as well as those who hate—and in the experiences of Lear and of Gloucester, that is to say, in the tragic action itself.

After Lear's descent into madness and his spiriting away by Kent to Dover, it is Gloucester's turn to find the truth by suffering and to be rescued by his outcast son Edgar, the same Poor Tom who prompted Lear's crucial question. Like Lear, Gloucester suffers the shock of confrontation with the ugly truth, but the admission of his mistake is swifter, the disillusion more sudden and savage. In the scene (III. vii) in which Cornwall and Regan question him for his knowledge of the landing of Cordelia with an army and his part in the escape of the King, questions are put to a new use—to brutal interrogation, not to find out the truth, but to force the answers the questioners want. When Gloucester tries to reply that he has a letter from one of neutral heart, they deny his answer and close in on him with antiphonal insistence:

Corn.	Cunning.
Reg.	And false.
Corn.	Where hast thou sent the King?
Glou.	To Dover.
Reg.	Wherefore to Dover? Wast thou not charg'd at peril—
Corn.	Wherefore to Dover? Let him answer that.
Glou.	I am tied to th' stake, and I must stand the course.
Reg.	Wherefore to Dover?

(III. vii. 49-55)

His courageous answer that he would not see Regan's cruel nails pluck out Lear's poor old eyes brings on him his own blinding. He is told that Edmund, on whom he calls for help, was his betrayer, and he is "thrust . . . out at gates" that he may "smell his way to Dover." This is Regan's order. Cornwall adds, "Turn out that eyeless villain." Under the new rule, questions are instruments of terror and commands are the orders of naked power.

We last saw Lear being taken in a litter to Dover, where Cordelia awaited him. But somewhere along the way he es-

caped from his caretakers to wander alone. Shakespeare now
brings him and Gloucester—the madman and the blind man—
together on the heath (IV. vi. 80 ff.). Lear, again feeling himself "every inch a king" and with the old authority in his voice,
preaches to Gloucester on the evil state of the world, a world
Gloucester, in his blindness, sees now only "feelingly." This
state has been partially exemplified in the actions of the evil
characters, but here it is put in general and more inclusive
terms; the episode has, therefore, a choric quality. At moments
Lear imagines himself, the king, to be acting as a chief magis-
trate; he exercises his power on the bench absolutely and cyni-
cally. The questions he asks are cynical questions: "See how
yond justice rails upon yond simple thief. . . . change places,
and handy-dandy, which is the justice, which is the thief?" (ll.
151-54). The questions are answered with cynical commands,
and the commands are defended by cynical assertions of the
ubiquity of lust, cupidity, hypocrisy, and injustice, as in these
sequences:

> When I do stare, see how the subject quakes.
> I pardon that man's life. What was thy cause?
> Adultery?
> Thou shalt not die. Die for adultery? No.
> The wren goes to't, and the small gilded fly
> Does lecher in my sight.
> Let copulation thrive; for Gloucester's bastard son
> Was kinder to his father than my daughters
> Got 'tween the lawful sheets.
>
>   (ll. 108-16)

Or this one, in which the assertions are more sententiously put:

> Thou rascal beadle, hold thy bloody hand!
> Why dost thou lash that whore? Strip thy own back.
> Thou hotly lusts to use her in that kind
> For which thou whip'st her. The usurer hangs the cozener.
> Through tatter'd clothes small vices do appear;
> Robes and furr'd gowns hide all. Plate sin with gold,
> And the strong lance of justice hurtless breaks;
> Arm it in rags, a pygmy's straw does pierce it.
>
>   (ll. 160-67)

This sequence ends with a general pardon:

> None does offend, none, I say none. I'll able 'em.
> Take that of me, my friend, who have the power
> To seal th' accuser's lips.

Since all offend, judged and judge alike, none offends. In place of justice, corruption in the court; in place of responsible authority, power alone. He ends his preaching to Gloucester with a counsel of patience drawn from ancient commonplaces on this vale of tears:

> Thou must be patient; we came crying hither.
> Thou know'st, the first time that we smell the air
> We wawl and cry.

And why do we?

> When we are born, we cry that we are come
> To this great stage of fools.

I said that this devastating vision of a corrupt world—a world in which women are Centaurs, "a dog's obey'd in office," and "robes and furr'd gowns hide all"—was choric, in a way, extending as it does beyond anything Lear is shown to have experienced directly. But it is not the whole truth of the world of the play. Gloucester's bastard son, we know, was not kinder to his father than Lear's elder daughters "got 'tween the lawful sheets." And there beside the two old men stands Edgar, still unrecognized, the slandered and outcast son, who has saved his father from suicide and despair. His own comment on the meeting of the madman and the blind man is a truly choric one: "I would not take this from report; it is,/ And my heart breaks at it" (ll. 141-42). In the next scene (IV. vii), Lear is to come back to sanity, under the ministration of Edgar's counterpart, Cordelia.

This is, above all, a quiet scene, unadorned, and without heightening of any sort. The imperious voice is gone. As the King wakes after his long, restorative sleep (l. 41), the first questions are Cordelia's tender, courteous ones, delicately restoring a right relation to him of both love and reverence:

"How does my royal lord? How fares your Majesty?" The returning pain of consciousness makes him protest:

> You do me wrong to take me out o' th' grave:
> Thou art a soul in bliss, but I am bound
> Upon a wheel of fire, that mine own tears
> Do scald like molten lead.

Lear's questions are of bewilderment at where he is: "You are a spirit, I know; when did you die?"; of pitiful uncertainty at his own pathetic state:

> Where have I been? Where am I? Fair daylight?
> I am mightily abus'd;

and of unbelieving wonder at a sight he fears cannot be true:

> Do not laugh at me,
> For (as I am a man) I think this lady
> To be my child Cordelia.
> *Cor.* And so I am, I am.
> *Lear.* Be your tears wet? Yes, faith, I pray weep not.

"Be your tears wet?" is the old incredulous question—"So young, and so untender?"—reversed, and in a new key, not of anger but of wonder and hope. The answer to the riddle of Cordelia's loving according to her bond is at hand. Lear prepares himself for the worst and makes his confession:

> I pray weep not.
> If you have poison for me, I will drink it.
> I know you do not love me, for your sisters
> Have (as I do remember) done me wrong.
> You have some cause, they have not.

The conditional sentence, "If you have poison for me, I will drink it," may remind us of the love-test, when it was Lear who set the condition: "What can you say to draw/ A third more opulent than your sisters?"—that is, if you say you love me best, I shall give you the richest part of my kingdom. The condition he now imagines is again *quid pro quo,* but with the situation reversed, and the consequence of acceptance not reward but punishment. The terms are strictly just, but quite as impossible to Cordelia as were the first. Her reply to his "You have some cause, they have not," is simply, "No cause, no cause." No conditions, no contingencies, no quantities. Lear's last words in the scene are a simple petition and a simple assertion.

>   You must bear with me.
> Pray you now forget, and forgive; I am old and foolish.

Recognition and acceptance are complete.

The last three scenes of the play (V. i, ii, iii) are given over to the complicated dénouement, in which the British defeat the French invaders; Lear and Cordelia are captured and sent to prison; the evil sisters destroy each other; Edmund is mortally wounded by his brother Edgar in a formal trial by combat; Kent and Edgar, who have stood faithfully by master and father, are recognized and recount their own pilgrimages. It seems as if right and justice, under Albany, will prevail after all. But before the combat Edmund had ordered the deaths of Lear and Cordelia in prison, and his countermanding order, given when he was about to die himself, comes too late. Before the two went off to prison (V. iii. 26), we had heard Lear's idyllic vision of his reunion with Cordelia:

>   Come, let's away to prison.
> We two alone will sing like birds i' th' cage;
> When thou dost ask me blessing, I'll kneel down
> And ask of thee forgiveness;

and we had heard his happy renunciation of sublunary and transitory power:

>   we'll wear out
> In a wall'd prison, packs and sects of great ones,
> That ebb and flow by th' moon.

Now we are to see Lear return with Cordelia dead in his arms:

> Howl, howl, howl, howl![24] O, you are men of stones! . . .
>   She's gone for ever!
> I know when one is dead, and when one lives;
> She's dead as earth.
>   (V. iii. 258-62)

The old Lear is not gone: he shows again the mighty grief, the rage which gave him strength to kill Cordelia's hangman, the impatience when the others close around him: "A plague upon you, murderers, traitors all!/ I might have sav'd her; now she's gone for ever!"

He phrases two conditional sentences—as we have seen, a form not common with him:

> Lend me a looking-glass.
> If that her breath will mist or stain the stone,
> Why then she lives.

He is evidently given a feather to hold to her lips, for he says, in excited delusion,

> This feather stirs; she lives! If it be so,
> It is a chance which does redeem all sorrows
> That ever I have felt.

The second condition follows from the first. The sight moves Kent, Albany, and Edgar to speak chorically, in question and petition:

> *Kent.*   Is this the promis'd end?
> *Edg.*   Or image of that horror?
> *Alb.*   Fall and cease.

A vision of the Judgment, and a prayer for surcease.

Now Albany makes a solemn declaration of intent, a promise which is like a command, to restore justice and order:

> All friends shall taste
> The wages of their virtue, and all foes
> The cup of their deservings.

All friends? Cutting into this promise comes Lear's protesting, heartbroken, unanswerable question, his last one, on the ultimate injustice of Cordelia's death:

> Why should a dog, a horse, a rat, have life,
> And thou no breath at all?

Her breath has not stained the stone, the feather has not stirred, his sorrows will not be redeemed.

> Thou'lt come no more.
> Never, never, never, never, never.
> Pray you undo this button. Thank you, sir.
> Do you see this? Look on her! look! her lips,[25]
> Look there, look there!

He dies in the illusion that she is coming back to life. The three modes of command, question, and assertion which opened the play—the three "themes," if we return to our musical metaphor —have been brought to a close in Lear's own voice.

The final speech of the play, Albany's,[26] is a simple statement of the magnitude of the tragedy. This statement is without a command, without a question, without a sententious assertion, without a declaration, even, of future intent:

> The weight of this sad time we must obey,
> Speak what we feel, not what we ought to say:
> The oldest have[27] borne most; we that are young
> Shall never see so much, nor live so long.

What should be in that 'Caesar'?

Proper Names in *Julius Caesar*

'Brutus' and 'Caesar' what should be in that 'Caesar'?
Why should that name be sounded more than yours?
Write them together, yours is as fair a name.

THE NAME of Caesar does sound throughout the tragedy in a quite extraordinary way. Brutus's, too, though more seldom than Caesar's. It is of course normal in dramatic dialogue for the name of an important character to be frequently on the lips of other characters. Such repetition is almost unconscious as the dramatist falls into the habit of natural dialogue. The iteration of "Caesar" in this play, however, is so extreme that we must take it to be done for a special effect, and the secondary iteration of "Brutus" is sufficiently frequent to bring his name, also, to the level of our awareness as a significant name.[1]

If it does nothing else, keeping Caesar's name so insistently before us tells us that the play is certainly in some sense about Caesar. In an affective way, the repetition accompanies every movement of the plot: Caesar's return to Rome in triumph, the fear of his ambition which motivates a conspiracy to assassinate him, the preparation for the assassination, the killing itself, and the consequences of that crime. In the widest and simplest sense the play (like several sixteenth-century plays before it) is about the fall of Caesar. In treating a man and a theme so famous in history and legend, it is perhaps not surprising that Shakespeare should choose to focus with such intensity on the name itself. For to the sixteenth century the name of Julius Caesar was instantly evocative of many things: the greatness of Rome in its palmy days, Caesar's own greatness as ruler of Rome and the world, the instability of fortune and the falls of princes, the evils of power and of tyrannicide. The most important thing about Caesar's name, one might say, was the fame of it.

In Shakespeare's play Caesar's name is dinned into our ears in waves of iteration until the end of the funeral oration. Then there is a lull, while we listen to the sordid business which occupies the Caesarians and the republicans alike. Yet the name never wholly ceases to be present. It comes up more than once in the quarrel between Brutus and Cassius, and it returns with significant emphasis at the key moments of the dénouement.

We hear less about Brutus than about Caesar, and more from him. Still, at times his name rings in our ears. Whereas we are most often conscious of "Caesar" as a single name, repeated alone and for its own sake, we are most aware of "Brutus" when it is paired with or set in opposition to "Caesar." This most noticeable use of the name underlines Brutus' position as Caesar's primary antagonist. Since Brutus and Cassius are so dependent on one another, one might expect that the frequency of repetition of Cassius' name, alone or paired with Brutus's, would also be high, but it is far less than that of Brutus's.[2] And pairing of the two names, so common in tradition, is not very frequent in the play.[3] There is little sense of twinning, none of interchangeability, much less of that strange common identity the two have in Chaucer's "Monk's Tale" and in Lydgate's *Fall of Princes*, where they are run together as "Brutus Cassius."[4] Instigator of the conspiracy Cassius certainly is, but once Brutus has made his decision to join it, he also becomes its leader. Its mistakes as well as its achievements are his. The strong implication of Brutus' primacy which Shakespeare found in Plutarch he further strengthened. He also intensified in his own way the irony of the assassination inherent in Caesar's known fondness for Brutus. And he made Brutus, the an-

tagonist, as much a tragic hero as the protagonist. Many feel
that Brutus is indeed the "true" hero of the play. Debate on
such a matter, however, is futile. Whatever terms one uses, the
play is "about" the one as much as it is "about" the other,
though it is about them in different ways. Their tragedies are
inseparable, each one depending on the other.[5] The manner in
which their names are consciously paired or set off against
each other re-enforces this structural relation.

Another special way in which Brutus' name appears—that is,
together with the name of his ancestor, Junius Brutus—links
him with Rome and Roman republicanism in a strong bond of
traditional obligation and patriotism, a bond which is the
strongest motive in his decision to join the conspiracy against
Caesar. And "Rome," if we count with it the adjective and adjective noun "Roman," is the third name to strike the ear with
some special significance in its repetition.[6]

In short, in dramatizing this great event in history and the
great issue of Roman freedom which occasioned it, Shakespeare has chosen to give special and unusual emphasis to the
very names of the chief actors,[7] and to the name of Rome itself.
There was nothing new for him in giving imaginative life
within the framework of a play to persons and events of history. He had been doing it with increasing richness and subtlety in the English history plays for seven or eight years before
he came to *Julius Caesar*—imagining, for instance, the Richard
Plantagenet who could give up a crown and the Henry Bolingbroke who could take one. Moreover, as poets are apt to be,
he had already been teased by the relation between name and
person or thing: "that which we call a rose . . ." Remember
Richard II's faith in the reality of the kingly name: "Is not the
king's name twenty thousand names?/ Arm, arm, my name!"[8]
and the part this "realism" played in his tragedy. This time, in
Julius Caesar, Shakespeare raised an explicit question about
name and person with respect to two men of the greatest fame.
Although the question, "What should be in that 'Caesar'?" is
Cassius' question, put for an immediate dramatic purpose, it
still reverberates when we have finished the tragedy.

Let us now turn to the play to see how the names function

dramatically. We may begin by taking a look at the second scene, when the principal characters appear for the first time, and by noticing how the various uses of "Caesar," "Brutus," and "Rome" are begun;[9] also how the very issue of names is forcibly raised.

This is the day of the Lupercalia. Caesar makes two brief appearances, one before the race and one after the episode in which he is offered the crown. On the first appearance (I. ii. 1-24), the use of his name in the third person helps establish a certain ceremoniousness. Although Antony naturally answers his summons directly ("Caesar, my lord?"), and although the Soothsayer calls his name urgently and imperatively ("Caesar!"), he is spoken of by others in the third person, as in Casca's call for order ("Peace ho, Caesar speaks"), in Antony's graceful flattery ("When Caesar says 'Do this,' it is perform'd"), in Cassius' order to the Soothsayer ("Fellow, come from the throng, look upon Caesar"). He also speaks of himself in the third person. This form follows naturally enough in the phrasing of his response to the Soothsayer's call:

> Who is it in the press that calls on me?
> I hear a tongue shriller than all the music
> Cry 'Caesar!' Speak, Caesar is turn'd to hear,

and we perhaps hardly remark it. But it is a habit which will assume much significance as the play continues.

On Caesar's exit (l. 24), Brutus and Cassius engage in earnest conversation about Brutus' disturbed mind, and now it is Brutus' name which is spoken, by both of them and in the third person, thus distancing him as a subject to be talked about. Brutus pleads,

> But let not therefore my good friends be griev'd
> (Among which number, Cassius, be you one)
> Nor construe any further my neglect
> Than that poor Brutus, with himself at war,
> Forgets the shows of love to other men.

And Cassius reports he has heard

> Where many of the best respect in Rome
> (Except immortal Caesar), speaking of Brutus

And groaning underneath this age's yoke,
Have wish'd that noble Brutus had his eyes.

At the sound of trumpets and of shouting (1. 78), the talk turns
on the danger of Caesar's becoming king, and Cassius begins
to sow seeds of distrust in Brutus' mind. The theme, in which
"Caesar" is constantly reiterated with sarcastic overtones, is the
incongruity of Caesar's physical weakness and his pretensions
to greatness. "This man," who could not make good his own
challenge to Cassius to swim the Tiber, and who has the falling
sickness, "is now become a god."

At the second flourish and shout (1. 131), Cassius takes occasion to set the names of Brutus and of Caesar side by side.
The ground has been laid to deflate Caesar's, to reduce it to a
mere name, with the implication that the man behind the name
is far less than he pretends to be, and at the same time subtly
to elevate Brutus's:

> 'Brutus' and 'Caesar': what should be in that 'Caesar'?[10]
> Why should that name be sounded more than yours?
> Write them together, yours is as fair a name;
> Sound them, it doth become the mouth as well;
> Weigh them, it is as heavy; conjure with 'em,
> 'Brutus' will start a spirit as soon as 'Caesar'.
> Now in the names of all the gods at once,
> Upon what meat doth this our Caesar feed
> That he is grown so great? Age, thou art sham'd!
> Rome, thou hast lost the breed of noble bloods!
> When went there by an age since the great flood
> But it was fam'd with more than with one man?
> When could they say, till now, that talk'd of Rome,
> That her wide walks encompass'd but one man?
> Now is it Rome indeed and room enough,
> When there is in it but one only man.
> O! you and I have heard our fathers say
> There was a Brutus once that would have brook'd
> Th' eternal devil to keep his state in Rome
> As easily as a king.

In this way, Brutus and Caesar have been set side by side, with
the issue of freedom and tyranny drawn. The name of Rome

has been evoked to suggest a republican past when men were free, and an ancestral Brutus recalled as an example of bold patriotism. Brutus, with his oblique reply in the third person, shows that he understands, and is not averse to playing the rôle Cassius has hinted he should play:

> chew upon this:
> Brutus had rather be a villager
> Than to repute himself a son of Rome
> Under these hard conditions as this time
> Is like to lay upon us.

At this moment (l. 177) Caesar returns, with an angry spot on his brow, and stays only long enough to draw for Antony's benefit a sharp portrait of Cassius, with his "lean and hungry look." In view of what we have heard Cassius saying about Caesar's inflated name, Caesar's prelude to the portrait is electrifying:

> Would he were fatter! but I fear him not.
> Yet if my name were liable to fear,
> I do not know the man I should avoid
> So soon as that spare Cassius.

A *notatio* of an envious man follows and is concluded by a general observation:

> Such men as he be never at heart's ease
> Whiles they behold a greater than themselves,
> And therefore are they very dangerous.

The portrait is rounded off with a return to his own name:

> I rather tell thee what is to be fear'd
> Than what I fear; for always I am Caesar.

Caesar, on his second appearance, has assumed an ideal rôle, one in which the name of "Caesar" takes on a supra-personal meaning.

With Caesar's exit (l. 214), we hear in Casca's irreverent prose an account of the episode which took place off stage—the offering of the crown three times, Caesar's refusal of it twice,

and the ignominious ending of the matter in his falling down
in an epileptic fit. The scene closes with Cassius' comment to
himself on the situation, his intent to have writings thrown in
at Brutus' window ("all tending to the great opinion/ That
Rome holds of his name; wherein obscurely/ Caesar's ambition
shall be glanced at"), and a premonitory hint to the audience:
"after this let Caesar seat him sure,/ For we will shake him, or
worse days endure."

The several ways in which names are to be used with dramatic significance have been laid down in this scene—the iteration of Caesar's name, the focussing on the name itself both
detached from the man and joined with the man, the pairing
of Brutus' name with Caesar's, and the bringing in of "Rome"
as a third, richly connotative name with reference to which
the other two are somehow to be weighed.

Let us look first at "Caesar," the dominant name of the play.
It will be convenient to order the discussion by the formal
ways in which the name is used: in direct address to Caesar by
others, in the third person by others when he is not present
but also when he is, and in the third person, of himself, when
he is the speaker. I shall comment first on references to Caesar
when he is absent, since these are a running guide to the action
and our responses to it; next on how he is spoken to, and of,
when he is present; and finally on the most distinctive form, his
references to himself by name in the third person.

With certain exceptions to be spoken of presently, he is the
theme of every man's talk from the time the commoners incur
the reproach of the tribunes by rejoicing in his triumph (I. i.
31) until Antony rings changes on his name in the funeral
oration. We hear him belittled by Cassius and Casca in the
scene of the Lupercalia (I. ii). He is the theme, of course, of
Cassius' persuasion of Casca on the night of the ominous
thunderstorm (I. iii), of Brutus' self-examination and decision
(II. i. 1-58), of the conspirators' debate on whom else to kill
(II. i. 154-91), of the Soothsayer's conversation with Portia
on the morning of the assassination (II. iv), of Brutus' self-
justification in his public speech in the Forum after the assas-

sination (III. ii. 13 ff.), and, finally, of Antony's oration in the
same place (III. ii. 72 ff.). Obviously, talk about Caesar is not
objective, since all except the Soothsayer (whose business is
not judgment but prophecy) are interested parties on one side
or the other. Brutus' occasional comments on Caesar are the
only ones free of the distortion of personal feeling about him.

The most eloquent speeches about Caesar are of course
Antony's—guarded in praise when, after the assassination,
Antony is still uncertain of Brutus' reception of him, bold when,
alone with Caesar's corpse, he gives his own feelings full rein,
and bolder still as he manipulates the response of the people
from approval of the conspirators to violent and murderous
hatred. Although he comes "to bury Caesar, not to praise him,"
before he is through Caesar is "noble Caesar," "great Caesar,"
"sweet Caesar," the generous friend of the Roman people,
martyred in their service.

Until Caesar is dead, then, we hear nothing positively good
about him and afterwards nothing bad. Clearly, the talk about
him, so abundant, and so charged with feeling, is not aimed at
giving us a detached judgment of Caesar, but at controlling
our responses to the action—sympathy with the conspirators in
their credible fear of "Caesarism," but pity for Caesar in the
manner of his death.[11] Antony's choric soliloquy (III. i. 254-75),
which predicts the second half of the action, the revenge of
Caesar's spirit on the conspirators, and which suddenly makes
us recollect the enormous fame of Caesar ("the noblest man/
That ever lived in the tide of times"), prepares the way for a
shift to a quite impersonal basis in our response to Caesar.
Judgment on him, and sympathy for him, as a person will both
become irrelevant. We shall assent to the justice of the revenge,
but our sympathies will be freed to return to Brutus and Cassius, now in a more considered way.

It is interesting to note in these first three acts that there are
significant, if only momentary, intervals when Caesar's name is
not mentioned. There are two which are especially interesting.
The first is the scene of the portentous storm (I. iii). For
seventy-one lines of mounting suspense its features are de-

scribed in the conversation between Cicero and Casca, then
between Cassius and Casca, before Cassius brings them all to
bear on the present "monstrous state" of Rome.

> Now could I, Casca, name to thee a man
> Most like this dreadful night
> That thunders, lightens, opens graves, and roars
> As doth the lion in the Capitol—
> A man no mightier than thyself, or me,
> In personal action, yet prodigious grown,
> And fearful, as these strange eruptions are.

Casca voices the implication: " 'Tis Caesar that you mean; is it
not, Cassius?" and Cassius circumspectly replies, "Let it be
who it is." Cassius moralizes only by analogy. The effect on the
audience is to bring the night's terrors to a focus in the name of
Caesar, but in a different sense from Cassius' intent. We know
that the monstrous state they are instruments of fear and
warning to will be not Caesar's tyranny but his death.

The second such significant pause is in the talk of the conspirators at Brutus' house (II. i. 101-53). Caesar's name is not
for a time after the convening spoken at all; the decision is
assumed to have been made and argument to be past. The
moment is big with his unspoken name, the more effective
because there is no talk of operative details. But the name
comes into the open with Decius' question of policy, "Shall no
man else be touch'd but only Caesar?" (l. 154) and with Cassius'
urging that Mark Antony, "so well belov'd of Caesar," should
not outlive Caesar. In Brutus' eloquent dissent, on the theme
"Let's be sacrificers, but not butchers, Caius," he uses Caesar's
name nine times in twenty-seven lines. In his futile wish to
separate the killing of Caesar's spirit from the killing of his
body, he is, like Cassius earlier, though without devious intent,
seeking unsuccessfully to separate the significant name from
the fleshly man.

After the climax and reversal, in the new urgencies faced
by Caesarians and republicans alike, Caesar's name subsides.
Yet the thought of him is an undercurrent in the quarrel between Brutus and Cassius (IV. iii), for it surfaces in ways

which reveal their own tender spots. Once the theme which joined them, Caesar now divides them. In a strange, ironic way, he has become a standard to appeal to, to set their own behavior against.

"Remember March, the ides of March remember," admonishes Brutus in his charge against Cassius of condoning, even participating in, bribe-taking. Brutus, like Othello, is concerned about "the cause"; he still holds to the distinction between sacrifice and murder. And to him Caesar is great, being gone.

> Did not great Julius bleed for justice' sake?
> What villain touch'd his body, that did stab
> And not for justice? What? shall one of us,
> That struck the foremost man of all this world
> But for supporting robbers, shall we now
> Contaminate our fingers with base bribes?
> And sell the mighty space of our large honors
> For so much trash as may be grasped thus?

Cassius, you recall, felt in Caesar's royal airs a personal affront to himself as an independent and self-sufficient person. He was always touchy about maintaining his personal equality with Caesar.[12] So now, at the highest point of the quarrel, in the midst of charge and countercharge, Caesar becomes the bone of contention in a more personal way than in Brutus' lines:

> *Cas.* When Caesar liv'd, he durst not thus have mov'd me.
> *Bru.* Peace, peace, you durst not so have tempted him.
> *Cas.* I durst not?
> *Bru.* No.
> *Cas.* What? durst not tempt him?
> *Bru.*   For your life you durst not.

Finally, hurt at Brutus' charges and lack of charity, Cassius bares his breast and offers Brutus his dagger. Caesar again stands between them, now on a note of jealousy:

> Strike as thou didst at Caesar; for I know,
> When thou didst hate him worst, thou lov'dst him better
> Than ever thou lov'dst Cassius.

The postlude to the scene is the appearance to Brutus of the ghost of Caesar (ll. 275 ff.): "Thy evil spirit, Brutus." No need to speak the name.

As the action draws to a close with the Battle of Philippi, Caesar's name is evoked by Antony and Octavius as a reproach and a threat to Brutus and Cassius and by the latter as their nemesis. In Antony's taunt flung at them before the battle (V. i. 30 ff.), the scene of the killing is vividly and sarcastically recalled. The burden of the taunt is the hypocrisy before the butchery. There is some free invention as well as exaggeration in the sketch:

> In your bad strokes, Brutus, you give good words;
> Witness the hole you made in Caesar's heart,
> Crying, 'Long live! hail, Caesar!'

And again, when he charges them with not threatening before they struck:

> Villains! you did not so, when your vile daggers
> Hack'd one another in the sides of Caesar.
> You show'd your teeth like apes, and fawn'd like hounds,
> And bow'd like bondmen, kissing Caesar's feet;
> Whilst damned Casca, like a cur, behind
> Struck Caesar on the neck. O you flatterers!

The act is cast in the ugliest terms. But the amplifying strikes the conspirators, especially Brutus, with his betrayal of friendship, where they are most vulnerable. Then Octavius promises the avenging of Caesar's three-and-thirty wounds unless he, "another Caesar," is himself killed by the "traitors."

Caesar *is* avenged in the outcome and is acknowledged to be by the victims—once by Cassius, when he kills himself on "this good sword/ That ran through Caesar's bowels" (V. iii. 41-42), and three times by Brutus: first when he is brought to view Cassius' body (V. iii. 94-96)—

> O Julius Caesar, thou art mighty yet!
> Thy spirit walks abroad, and turns our swords
> In our own proper entrails;

secondly, when he reports the two appearances to him of Caesar's ghost and knows his hour is come (V. v. 17-20), and, finally, when he is about to commit suicide (V. v. 50-51): "Caesar, now be still./ I kill'd not thee with half so good a will." Caesar's ghost is laid.

So much for Caesar when, not present, he is yet spoken of. Talk about him, as I have said, is a means of guiding our responses to the action and of marking the unifying features of the plot. When he is present, the interplay of the several forms of the second and third persons, of direct and indirect address, is a wonderfully adroit way of moving back and forth between Caesar the man and Caesar the public figure.

What was at once noticeable in the scene we have looked at in detail (I. ii) was that when Caesar was present he was sometimes spoken of as "Caesar" in the third person rather than directly addressed. And this form continues to be used in the play up to his death. There may be in the habit a remnant of the old polite form, still heard in Elizabethan courtly English. In any case, the use of it depersonalizes Caesar, separates him from the speakers, makes us at the moment more conscious of his position than of his character, as when Decius Brutus tells him, in the midst of direct address, that "the Senate have concluded/ To give this day a crown to mighty Caesar" (II. ii. 93-94). The two forms of address, direct and indirect, combining urgency with deference to his function, appear in Artemidorus' plea that his suit be read: "O Caesar, read mine first; for mine's a suit/ That touches Caesar nearer. Read it, great Caesar" (III. i. 6-7). The consciousness of Caesar's position is often re-enforced by epithets—"great Caesar," "mighty Caesar," "most noble Caesar." Since, however, most of the persons surrounding Caesar are unfriendly to him, misliking his semi-royal state, the employment of the third person makes room for ambiguities and ironies, as when Decius subtly persuades Caesar not to yield to Calphurnia's fears: "If Caesar hide himself, shall they not whisper,/ 'Lo, Caesar is afraid'?" (II. ii. 100-101). Only Antony's, the Soothsayer's, and Artemidorus' third person is honestly dignifying.

Direct address, being expected, is less noticeable. But it likewise can be employed for special effects. It may bear the stress of the Soothsayer's warning on Caesar's first appearance ("Caesar!" "Beware the ides of March"; I. ii. 12, 18); or of Artemidorus' clamorous insistence on the fatal morning ("Hail, Caesar! read this schedule"; "O Caesar, read mine first . . ."; "Delay not, Caesar, read it instantly"; III. i. 3, 6, 9). It has a similar but more sinister urgency, again on that morning (III. i. 33-57), in the way in which the conspirators press Metellus Cimber's petition on Caesar with their familiar "thou's." But this matter I shall postpone briefly until I can treat the episode as a whole in connection with Caesar's use of his own name.

The most moving example of direct address is Antony's to Caesar's dead body, as if Caesar were alive (III. i. 148-50). Much of the effect comes from his using the familiar "thou," something we had not heard him speak to Caesar living.

> O mighty Caesar! dost thou lie so low?
> Are all thy conquests, glories, triumphs, spoils,
> Shrunk to this little measure? Fare thee well!

The simplicity and intimacy in such a question have the immediate effect of heightening the pity and the irony of Caesar's fall from "mighty Caesar" to simple "thou." The restatement of this irony in Antony's second address to the corpse, when he is alone with it (III. i. 254-57)—

> O, pardon me, thou bleeding piece of earth,
> That I am meek and gentle with these butchers!
> Thou art the ruins of the noblest man
> That ever lived in the tide of times

—amplifies the greatness of Caesar. His "personality" ceases to be important.

Most striking of all the forms is Caesar's speaking of himself in the third person by his own name.[13] This form, like the third person others use of him in his presence, emphasizes his assumed impersonal rôle as "Caesar," for so used "Caesar" is at least as much a concept as a personal name and at times almost becomes a title. Caesar appears alive in only three scenes—

twice in I. ii, on the Lupercal, before and after the offering of the crown; in II. ii, at home on the crucial morning of the ides of March, the morning after Calphurnia's prophetic dream; and in III. i, on the same morning, making his way to the Capitol, taking his seat there, and being brought down by the conspirators.

In the first of these scenes (I. ii), you recall, Caesar emphatically establishes himself in his ideal rôle by explicitly equating the first person with the third (ll. 211-12): "I rather tell thee what is to be fear'd/ Than what I fear, for always I am Caesar."

In the second of the scenes (II. ii), on the morning of the crucial decision, to go or not to go to the Senate meeting, the iteration of his name is most marked. In his twenty-three lines up to the entrance of Decius (at l. 56), he speaks it eight times. His reiterated intent, in spite of Calphurnia's ominous dream and the unfavorable reports of the augurs, keeps the conceptual Caesar uppermost:

> Caesar shall forth; the things that threaten'd me
> Ne'er look'd but on my back; when they shall see
> The face of Caesar, they are vanished.

Again:

> What can be avoided
> Whose end is purpos'd by the mighty gods?
> Yet Caesar shall go forth; for these predictions
> Are to the world in general as to Caesar.

Still again:

> The gods do this [i.e., give bad auguries] in shame of
>   cowardice;
> Caesar should be a beast without a heart
> If he should stay at home to-day for fear.
> No, Caesar shall not; Danger knows full well
> That Caesar is more dangerous than he.
> We are two lions litter'd in one day,
> And I the elder and more terrible;
> And Caesar shall go forth.

The rhythmically repetitious "Caesar shall go forth" is almost incantatory.

When, for Calphurnia's sake, Caesar has changed his mind and agreed not to go, the apparent disjunction of the private man from the public man must be glossed over:

> Shall Caesar send a lie?
> Have I in conquest stretch'd mine arm so far
> To be afeard to tell greybeards the truth?
> Decius, go tell them Caesar will not come.

Finally, a more natural personal note is struck as under Decius persuadings he returns to his first intent:

> How foolish do your fears seem now, Calphurnia!
> I am ashamed I did yield to them.
> Give me my robe, for I will go.

The resolution of the conflict without and within is reflected in his speech. He addresses his companions in a relaxed and gracious way:

> Good friends, go in, and taste some wine with me,
> And we, like friends, will straightway go together.

In the last of these three scenes (III. i), Shakespeare manipulates the shifts in person to give us the subtlest shadings of Caesar's response to the increasing pressure and rising tension of the moments before the assassination. Hesitations behind him, on his way to the Senate he is again insulated in his rôle as "Caesar," and the personal note of appeal to him in Artemidorus' demanding cries is totally without force: "What touches us ourself shall be last serv'd." As he takes his seat to begin the day's business, he is all Caesar: "Are we all ready? What is now amiss/ That Caesar and his Senate must redress?" (ll. 31-32). Metellus petitions him in a combination of adulation and familiarity:

> Most high, most mighty, and most puissant Caesar,
> Metellus Cimber throws before thy seat
> An humble heart.

Although Caesar replies in kind, with the familiar "thou," to chide him for his "couchings" and "lowly courtesies," his is the debasing "thou" of a superior to an inferior: "If thou dost bend, and pray, and fawn for him,/ I spurn thee like a cur out of my way." He still holds to the majestic rôle:

> Be not fond
> To think that Caesar bears such rebel blood
> That will be thaw'd from the true quality . . .

and

> Know, Caesar doth not wrong, nor without cause
> Will he be satisfied.

On his refusal, Metellus shifts to the flattering third person and prepares the way for Brutus' approach:

> Is there no voice more worthy than my own,
> To sound more sweetly in great Caesar's ear
> For the repealing of my banish'd brother?

Brutus, though familiar, maintains a stiff honesty:

> I kiss thy hand, but not in flattery, Caesar;
> Desiring thee that Publius Cimber may
> Have an immediate freedom of repeal.

But Cassius, also familiar, enjoys a grim, ironic, premonitory joke:

> Pardon, Caesar! Caesar, pardon!
> As low as to thy foot doth Cassius fall,
> To beg enfranchisement for Publius Cimber.

Caesar, taken off guard by Brutus' appeal, replies to all three in the first person. Beset and on the defensive, he lowers himself almost to their person-to-person level:

> I could be well mov'd, if I were as you;
> If I could pray to move, prayers would move me:
> But I am constant as the northern star,
> Of whose true-fix'd and resting quality
> There is no fellow in the firmament.

Yet in matter the speech is simply an enlargement of the
theme, "for always I am Caesar," still another declaration of
the identity of "I" and "he, Caesar."

> . . . men are flesh and blood, and apprehensive;
> Yet in the number I do know but one
> That unassailable holds on his rank,
> Unshak'd of motion; and that I am he,
> Let me a little show it, even in this—
> That I was constant Cimber should be banish'd,
> And constant do remain to keep him so.

The insistence on his unassailability and on his Olympian remoteness is at this point anticipatory irony of the most intense
kind, for all the conspirators close in around him, and at
Casca's signal strike him down. Within four lines he is dead.

How are we to take this third-person habit of Caesar's? this
deliberate use of his own name? As evidence of character? As
a manifestation of the *hubris* of the tragic hero whom the gods
mean to destroy? As a way to suggest the greatness Caesar had
assumed in tradition, hence to prepare the way for the magnitude of his fall? These several ways of looking at the
speeches in question need not be incompatible, provided one
entertains all the quick impressions one receives in the theater,
or even the more thoughtful impressions from reading, and
does not insist on an exclusive and consistent intellectualized
theory.

Shakespeare does, in his usual deft way, give the illusion of
a living person, one hardly endearing and one with nearly as
many weaknesses as strengths. The incomplete, but striking,
portrait is much at variance with the impression we get from
Plutarch's biography, taken as a whole, of an ambitious, tough-
minded, and unscrupulous man, indeed, but also of an imaginative, large-spirited, often generous man, and certainly a bold
and decisive one. It is naturally tempting to concentrate on the
obsession with self and the rôle-playing of Shakespeare's
Caesar as if the causes of these traits could be laid bare in
some deep-rooted psychological conflict. The danger, when the
critical focus is on Caesar "the man," lies in overdoing analyses

of motives which would be proper to an actual person but which must be largely irrelevant to a limited and illusory *dramatis persona*. Moreover, Shakespeare presents Caesar only at one moment in time, not necessarily conceived of as the habitual Caesar, but only as the Caesar about to go to his doom.

Therefore, what about *hubris?* Self-confidence, trust in his own genius, seems to have been characteristic of the actual Caesar all his life. In his latter days, at the height of his power, some historians[14] represent him as increasingly arrogant, contumelious in his behavior towards the Senate, dangerously insolent in taking on himself excessive honors, and irreligious in disregarding, or even openly defying, unfavorable omens. Sir Thomas Elyot in *The Governour* vividly catches this quality of infatuation in the once "moste noble Cesar," now "radicate in pride,"

> who, beinge nat able to sustaine the burden of fortune, and envienge his owne felicitie, abandoned his naturall disposition, and as it were, beinge dronke with over moche welth, sought newe wayes howe to be advaunced above the astate of mortall princes. Wherfore litle and litle he withdrewe from men his accustomed gentilnesse, becomyng more sturdy in langage, and straunge in countenance, than ever before had ben his usage.[15]

This picture of the infatuated Caesar falls in with the convention of *hubris* in the tragic hero, especially familiar to the Renaissance in Senecan tragedy.[16] Megalomania expressed in boasting was a standard feature of the part in sixteenth-century Caesar plays, and it is possible to relate the obsessive speeches of Shakespeare's Caesar to the same tradition.[17] His difference from his predecessors is that he is more convincing, not a mouthpiece for inflated rhetoric, but endowed with *energeia,* a vitality of imagined speech and behavior which creates a highly credible dramatic illusion. That Shakespeare intended a strong impression of infatuation in Caesar's speeches on that tense morning of the ides of March is shown in the comment he gives Calphurnia at her husband's defiance of the auguries,[18] manifesting *hubris,* insolence, of the most dangerous kind. To his third reiteration of his intent, "And Caesar shall go forth," she remonstrates,

> Alas, my lord,
> Your wisdom is consum'd in confidence.
> Do not go forth to-day.

(II. ii. 48-50)

The third suggested way of looking at Caesar's speeches, one which does not destroy the illusion of a living person and does not conflict with the dramatic device of *hubris,* perhaps even strengthens it, is to bring to bear on the speeches the rôle Caesar played in the medieval tradition of tragedy, that of the Falls of Princes.[19] One of the uncertainties in the play is how to take Caesar—as the tyrant Cassius would have him or as Antony's "noblest man that ever lived in the tide of times." Doubtless, as not quite either. Still, the uncertainty we feel about him in Shakespeare appears to reflect the divided opinion of him in history and in tradition. Among ancient historians and other writers, some were favorable (as was Sallust), some unfavorable (as were Cicero, Lucan, and Dio Cassius), still others (indeed most) in between or both at once (as were Plutarch and Appian), with little attempt, usually, to reconcile his better and his worse qualities. The same may be said of Renaissance treatments of him; contrary views and double views persisted.[20] Most of the early Caesar plays were ambivalent, too. In the anonymous *Caesar's Revenge,* for instance, Caesar is at one moment a tyrant and a threat to Rome, at another a man of generosity and mercy; a ranting egotist who boasts that Rome will rule the world and that he will rule both, yet one who refuses the crown for virtue's sake and denies ambition. It is well to remember that in the early Falls of Princes tradition, such a distinction (as between Caesar the ambitious tyrant and Caesar the noble statesman) was not central, for the irony lay in the subjection of such a man of power to the whim of Fortune and in the magnitude of his fall. In Chaucer's "Monk's Tale," the fall of the vicious Nero was as much a tragedy as the fall of the wise and manly Caesar. Even

when, as in *The Mirror for Magistrates,* the fallen great were
represented as being punished for the crimes their ambition led
them to commit, the earlier irony was not lost sight of. In so
far as the apparently contradictory views of fortune and of
retribution were accommodated at all, the ambitious man who
sought high place was seen not only as specially liable to the
temptation of crime, but also as more strongly exposed to the
envy of others and to the operation of fortune than the un-
ambitious man.[21] To be content with one's humble lot was
safest from every point of view. The focus was not on merely
human, but on cosmic morality. The theme of *vanitas vanitatum* did not disappear, as Richard II's poetic sermon on the
death of kings reminds us.[22] Whatever the judgment of historians about the actual Caesar, in the *de casibus* framework he
was one of the two greatest men in pagan antiquity, Alexander
being the other. The fates of these two were not just examples
among many, but were the very types of *casus illustrium
virorum* (the misfortunes befalling famous men), for each had
established an empire over much of the civilized world and
each was stricken down at the height of his power.[23] In Hamlet's moralizing on the Dance of Death theme, the two are in-
terchangeable symbols of the ultimate irony of ambition: "Why
may not imagination trace the noble dust of Alexander till 'a
find it stopping a bunghole? . . . Imperious Caesar, dead and
turn'd to clay,/ Might stop a hole to keep the wind away."

The language of Caesar's speeches in Shakespeare's play
should perhaps be read as the language of this "mightiest
Julius." In the Renaissance Caesar plays, one often has the
impression that the hero is speaking as "the foremost man of all
this world" would be expected to speak, that he is fulfilling a
rôle as the "idea" of Caesar, or as the expositor of his own
fame. Perhaps Shakespeare, likewise, made his Caesar speak
as if he were himself conscious of what he was to become in
tradition; or, to put the matter more artistically, as if Shakespeare intended the speeches to serve an extra-personal, an-
achronistic purpose, a purpose less representational than conceptual. However Caesar's language is to be interpreted, his
emphatic assumption of the position of greatness which tradi-

tion was to assign him is of great importance dramatically. It fits the Falls of Princes theme. In the climactic first scene of the third act, in which we have heard, just before the stabbing, Caesar's most exalted statements of his Olympian position, Shakespeare gives to Antony, at his first sight of the mangled body, the choric comment on his death already quoted. It is in the *de casibus* vein:

> O mighty Caesar! dost thou lie so low?
> Are all thy conquests, glories, triumphs, spoils,
> Shrunk to this little measure?
> (III. i. 148-50)

The extent of Caesar's fall was irony enough for Renaissance tragedy, yet Shakespeare deepened the irony enormously. He gave the rôle his Caesar attempted to assume a profound moral turn. The theme, in Caesar's iteration of his own name, is always constancy—the constancy of the man unafraid to die:

> What can be avoided
> Whose end is purpos'd by the mighty gods?
> Yet Caesar shall go forth;
> (II. ii. 26-28)

of the man unmoved by others' opinion of him:

> Shall Caesar send a lie?
> Have I in conquest stretch'd mine arm so far
> To be afeard to tell graybeards the truth?
> (II. ii. 65-67)

of the man unswayed by passion or flattery:

> Be not fond
> To think that Caesar bears such rebel blood
> That will be thaw'd from the true quality
> With that which melteth fools—I mean sweet words,
> Low-crooked curtsies, and base spaniel fawning.
> (III. i. 39-43)

Is the rôle the Julius of the play sees himself in the rôle of the potentate, the one on which so much of the psychological criticism centers? Although he enacts it, it is not the one he articulates. That is rather the rôle of the constant man. But he dares, in his last moments of tragic infatuation, to think that his constancy is perfect and unique—almost as if in his steadfastness of purpose he, alone of men and like the Northern Star, could stand above the tide of times, not subject to Fortune's turning wheel:

> men are flesh and blood, and apprehensive;
> Yet in the number I do know but one
> That unassailable holds on his rank,
> Unshak'd of motion; and that I am he,
> Let me a little show it, even in this—
>
> (III. i. 67-71)

Hence the special poignancy and the intense irony of the way in which his fall comes—at that instant and by the most unexpected hand: "*Et tu, Brute?*" The third person most simply yet eloquently marks his last words: "Then fall Caesar!" His last act—to compose his garments and stand quietly to receive the blows—is one of constancy.

The moving query to Brutus brings us to a consideration of Shakespeare's significant employment of Brutus' name. Although it appears a little less than three-fifths as often as Caesar's (partly because Brutus is less talked about than Caesar, more often seen talking or being talked to), it is yet second to Caesar's in frequency and importance. The frequency, however, may seem less than it is, for the name is used in more varied ways, often more spontaneous, hence less obtrusive, ways than Caesar's.

For instance, direct address to Brutus occurs most often in the give-and-take of dialogue between equals, as with Portia and Cassius. In these reciprocal interchanges we are apt to pay little attention to the name itself, unless it shifts from the second person to the third. The third person used of Brutus when he is present is naturally not the ceremonial sort of thing it is with Caesar, and the conceptualizing it accomplishes is altogether different. Yet it is quite as important in dramatic function.

When Portia speaks of her husband in the third person, as she mainly does in the scene with him (II. i. 233 ff.), she sets off the difference of the present Brutus from his habitual self:

> could it [impatience] work so much upon your shape
> As it hath much prevail'd on your condition,
> I should not know you Brutus,

and marks his separation from her:

> Dwell I but in the suburbs
> Of your good pleasure? If it be no more,
> Portia is Brutus' harlot, not his wife.

In its greater intimacy and therefore poignancy, the whole tone of the episode is very different from Calphurnia's with her husband; the handling of the dialogue is characteristic of the greater fullness and inwardness with which Brutus is everywhere presented to us than is Caesar. With Brutus we are given a sense, by small touches here and there, of a personal and reflective life outside the political sphere of the action. To this active sphere, although his comments on death and on constancy suggest a reflective side, Caesar is rather closely confined, and he is always on show. We never witness Caesar in "undress"; Brutus, several times. Hence Caesar is much more formidable, less readily apprehended, than Brutus.

Something of the same thing as in the Portia scene happens in the quarrel scene (IV. iii) between Brutus and Cassius, when each at moments speaks of the other in the third person. It is a way of standing aside to look at their strained friendship; a way to set off what each once knew the other to be from what each now seems to be.

> *Bru.*   Was that done like Cassius?
> Should I have answer'd Caius Cassius so?
> When Marcus Brutus grows so covetous
> To lock such rascal counters from his friends,
> Be ready, gods, with all your thunderbolts,
> Dash him to pieces!
>
> (ll. 77-82)

> *Cas.*   Hath Cassius liv'd
> To be but mirth and laughter to his Brutus
> When grief and blood ill-temper'd vexeth him?
>
> (ll. 113-15)

Shakespeare makes Brutus, like Caesar, sometimes speak of himself in the third person by his own name, but in more varied ways and never insistently. He does it a couple of times in the quarrel scene, once in anger and somewhat self-righteously (in the first of the two passages just quoted), and once, as Cassius does of himself, when he returns to his deeper feeling:

> from henceforth,
> When you are over-earnest with your Brutus,
> He'll think your mother chides, and leave you so.
> (ll. 121-23)

He does it also when, taking leave of Cassius before Philippi, he speaks as a Stoic, determined to retain his liberty:

> Think not, thou noble Roman,
> That ever Brutus will go bound to Rome;
> He bears too great a mind.
> (V. i. 110-12)

For the most part, however, in partial contrast to Caesar, Brutus demonstrates rather than talks about the constancy of the stoical man. Brutus uses the third person of himself in still a third, most significant, way, when he thinks of himself as a Roman republican and patriot, assimilated to the ancestral Brutus as tyrant-slayer; but his rôle-playing gives nothing like the impression of obsession with self that Caesar's does. Brutus adopts his rôle for the sake of Rome;[24] Caesar, his, for his own sake. It is interesting that Caesar never mentions Rome, and Romans only once, when he is telling Decius how in Calphurnia's dream "many lusty Romans," smiling, bathed their hands in the blood flowing from Caesar's statue (II. ii. 78-79). We hear of Romans, of course, in Antony's reading of Caesar's will (III. ii. 240-51), but not in direct quotation: "To every Roman citizen he gives . . ."; "he hath left you . . ." In any case the words are not heard from Caesar's mouth, now stilled, but from Antony's, and with his implication of generous motives.

Let us now turn, then, to the key scenes in this antagonism

of Brutus to Caesar, and notice how the name of Brutus is used by himself and others to sharpen this central dramatic opposition. There are five scenes, or groups of scenes, to consider, each at a significant point in the movement of the plot: the first (I. ii), Cassius' initial attempt to move Brutus against Caesar; the second (II. i), Brutus' self-interrogation and decision; the third (III. i), the assassination and the temporary truce between Antony and the republicans; the fourth (III. ii), the orations of Brutus and of Antony to the Roman people, the turning point against the republicans; the fifth (V. i-v), the Battle of Philippi, at which occur the defeat and the suicides of Cassius and Brutus.

We have already looked with some care at I. ii, in which the juxtaposition and opposition of the names begins (ll. 138 ff.): "'Brutus' and 'Caesar': what should be in that 'Caesar'?/ . . . Write them together, yours is as fair a name." To recapitulate the conversation will be enough. Cassius' pairing is an invitation to turn both names around, contemplate them from a distance, test what each means for the good of Rome. Rome is the issue, and the Rome that matters is republican Rome, free Rome: "Now is it Rome indeed and room enough,/ When there is in it but one only man." Here it is that Brutus' patriot ancestor, though unnamed, is glanced at, and here it is that Brutus, in speaking of himself in the third person, begins to see himself conceptually as one who will act for freedom: "Brutus had rather be a villager" than a Roman under a tyrant (ll. 172 ff.). At the end of the scene, Cassius in soliloquy informs us of a complicating issue, the friendship between Caesar and Brutus:

> Caesar doth bear me hard, but he loves Brutus.
> If I were Brutus now and he were Cassius,
> He should not humor me.

Cassius sees, however, that the noble Brutus may be "seduc'd," his "honorable mettle . . . wrought/ From that it is dispos'd." Cassius will undertake the seduction. He will appeal to the best in Brutus, his strong sense of patriotic duty; but the indirect method of the appeal, through anonymous messages from supposed citizens, will be the subtlest form of flattery.

In the scene of Brutus' deliberation with himself (II. i. 1-58), it is the general reflection on the remorselessness of power which oversways the particular knowledge he has of Caesar's reasonableness. It is Cassius' forged "writings," inexplicit, but hinting at enormous meanings and issues ("'Brutus, thou sleep'st; awake, and see thyself!/ Shall Rome, etc. Speak, strike, redress!'") which, after he has pieced out the implications, clinch his decision.

> 'Speak, strike, redress!' Am I entreated
> To speak and strike? O Rome, I make thee promise,
> If the redress will follow, thou receivest
> Thy full petition at the hand of Brutus!

He sees himself as he is meant to do—as fulfilling the obligation laid on him by the earlier Brutus, the one who drove Tarquin from Rome "when he was call'd a king." Brutus will speak and strike for Rome. In the conversation with Portia later in the same scene (II. i. 233 ff.), her "Brutus" in the third person shows us the other side of the coin: not Brutus the patriot, but the "gentle Brutus," now seeming to her sick in mind and alienated from his proper self.

At the climax of the action in the Capitol (III. i. 33-77), Caesar and Brutus are for the first time brought face to face— Caesar seated in the chair of state and Brutus kneeling with the other conspirators at his feet, pleading for Publius Cimber. It is Caesar who speaks Brutus' name three times. The first time, he asks a startled, or shocked, question—"What, Brutus?" —when Brutus goes down on his knees beside Metellus Cimber to press the appeal for his brother. The question may be read in the second person, as "What, thou, Brutus?" or in the third, as "What, can Brutus be doing this?" A choice need not be made, for the intent is the same. Shortly afterward, Caesar tries to get rid of the petitioners with his "Doth not Brutus bootless kneel?"—even Brutus, who is dear to Caesar? The naming of Brutus in these brief questions directs our attention to him in the confused action of the stabbing a moment later. The note of intimacy and affection prepares us for the poignancy of Caesar's "*Et tu, Brute?*" Though spoken with different emphases, the three sentences have all the same implication: "*Even* Brutus." Thus, when the blow is struck for Rome, the iteration of Brutus' name in surprise and hurt by Caesar brings us back to the complicating personal issue, which Brutus had suppressed.

From this point until after Caesar's funeral, during the contest between Brutus and Antony for the hearts of the populace, when "Rome" and "Roman" are not spoken without heavily charged meanings, "Brutus" and "Caesar" are constantly paired (in Antony's prudent message to the conspirators, in Brutus' oration, in Antony's), and the good of Rome is the point of reference by which the dead Caesar and the living Brutus are supposed to be judged by the Romans. In fact, the choice is made by passion, not judgment.

The pairing begins in Antony's message after the killing. The conspirators, who as "Caesar's friends" and as "Romans" have bathed their hands in Caesar's blood, and who see themselves as "the men that gave their country liberty," are setting out for the market place when they are interrupted by Antony's servant (at l. 122) bringing a circumspect message. As Cassius had done in his first conversation with Brutus, Antony sets the names of Brutus and of Caesar side by side, in the third person; only this time they are apparently equal in value. The equality is carefully marked by precise balance and repetition:[25]

> Brutus is noble, wise, valiant, and honest;
> Caesar was mighty, bold, royal, and loving.
> Say, I love Brutus, and I honor him;
> Say, I fear'd Caesar, honor'd him, and lov'd him.

If Brutus' wisdom and honesty seem to outweigh in moral virtue Caesar's might and royalty, the balance is restored by Caesar's "loving." But a faintly troubling imbalance between the third and fourth lines is introduced with the addition of a new term, "fear'd," making the fourth line asymmetric. The change of order in honoring and loving, moreover, harks back to Caesar's "loving," and also, perhaps, puts a slight extra weight in Caesar's scale. One can scarcely miss the reproach to Brutus for his own apparent forgetfulness of Caesar's love. The condition of Antony's joining Brutus, that he may "be resolv'd/ How Caesar hath deserv'd to lie in death," is carefully phrased: if he is satisfied with the answer, "Mark Antony shall not love Caesar dead/ So well as Brutus living." The contraries of life and death are unresolved, all appears still in the balance; but there is a sting in "Caesar dead"—"Brutus living" as there was in Caesar's "loving." The "loving" and "living" are even tied together by paranomasia. A shift of Antony's love to Brutus is not committed. Brutus picks up none of these implications in the message. In reply he uses what would be to him the highest praise: "Thy master is a wise and valiant Roman."

In the meeting between Brutus and Antony which follows shortly (at l. 147), Antony plays a bold game. Though he shakes the bloody hands of the assassins, he does not disguise his grief at Caesar's death. Thus he acts out the knife-edge balance of the earlier phrasing. His behavior loses him nothing in the eyes of the generous Brutus, who trustingly gives him the right to speak at Caesar's funeral.

In his speech to the people (III. ii. 13-47), Brutus boldly confronts the issue between him and Caesar in a display of paradox. His thesis is that to the "Romans, countrymen, and lovers" he addresses, Caesar living meant slavery; Caesar dead means freedom: "Had you rather Caesar were living, and die all slaves, than that Caesar were dead, to live all freemen?" It is unimaginable that any Roman will not do what he must to preserve the freedom which is Rome's great gift to her citizens. "Who is here so base that would be a bondman? . . . Who is here so rude that would not be a Roman? . . . Who is here so vile that will not love his country?" This general issue of a free versus an enslaved Rome had always been to Brutus "the cause." But he must explain away the complicating personal issue. He seeks to put it in perspective by stating a hypothetical case and speaking of himself in the third person:

> If there be any in this assembly, any dear friend of Caesar's, to
> him I say, that Brutus' love to Caesar was no less than his. If
> then that friend demand why Brutus rose against Caesar, this is
> my answer: Not that I lov'd Caesar less, but that I lov'd Rome
> more.

At the close he says, more simply, "I slew my best lover for the
good of Rome." He seeks a resolution of contraries: love of
Caesar and the killing of Caesar, contraries which perhaps cannot be resolved except by his own death. One of the saddest
ironies in Brutus' tragedy lies in his attempt and his failure to
resolve these contraries. For he did not really know that
Caesar's death was necessary for the good of Rome. In the
event, tyrannous disorder, not republican freedom, was bought
by Caesar's death.[26] Brutus' costly choice went for nought.

Antony, likewise, makes a point of addressing "Romans"
("You gentle Romans" and "Friends, Romans, countrymen";
III. ii. 72 ff.) and states once, later in his speech (at ll. 189-92),
the consequences to Romans of the assassination:

> great Caesar fell.
> O, what a fall was there, my countrymen!
> Then I, and you, and all of us fell down,
> Whilst bloody treason flourish'd over us.

But the argument of Antony's oration is not on the issue of
freedom and tyranny, indeed not on any issue; it is based on
pathos (the pity and horror of Caesar's death), on the assumed
ethos of Caesar (his nobility and generosity), on the implied
ethos of the conspirators (their dishonesty), and finally on an
"inartificial" argument, the fact of Caesar's will, with its be-
quest to the Romans of his gardens and its gifts of money to
every man. Caesar the person is the theme of Antony's speech,
and his name is sounded every few lines. Brutus' name in certain key places (at the beginning of the oration and at one of
the high points) is spoken nearly as often.

In the opening thirty-five lines (73-107), in a trick to turn
his hearers' sympathies from Brutus to Caesar, Antony pairs
the names in a repetitive scheme of assertion ("Brutus says he
was ambitious" and "Brutus is an honorable man") and ques-

tion ("Was this ambition?"), with one of Caesar's deeds cited
each time as a test case. Through this clever device—loaded
with innuendo and suppressed irony—of taking away with one
hand what he gives with the other, Antony raises a doubt about
Brutus' credibility and integrity—about the other conspirators',
too, but about Brutus's chiefly. As Antony leads into the subject
of the will, with the listeners audibly coming over to his side,
he keeps returning to his refrain of the "honorable men." Brutus' name again appears in a cluster with Caesar's in the first
climax of the speech (ll. 169-92), the part in which Antony is
displaying Caesar's mantle:

> Look, in this place ran Cassius' dagger through;
> See what a rent the envious Casca made;
> Through this the well-beloved Brutus stabbed.

The dishonesty of Brutus' behavior is no longer hinted at but
made explicit; and, moreover, made the worse by being interpreted as a betrayal of friendship. Brutus knocked "unkindly";
he was "Caesar's angel," whom Caesar dearly loved.

> This was the most unkindest cut of all;
> For when the noble Caesar saw him stab,
> Ingratitude, more strong than traitors' arms,
> Quite vanquish'd him. Then burst his mighty heart,
> And in his mantle muffling up his face, . . .
>   great Caesar fell.
> O, what a fall was there, my countrymen!

Brutus tried to resolve the contraries of his love and his killing
of Caesar by an appeal to a greater love, his love of Rome.
Antony simply rules out both loves. Brutus is a betrayer of his
friend and a traitor to the Roman people; by bringing down
Caesar, he has brought down Rome.

With the people now thoroughly roused to burn, fire, kill,
Antony pretends anxiety (ll. 210-16, 235) at their "sudden flood
of mutiny." The doers of the deed are honorable men and will
no doubt reveal the private grief that made them do it. Now
it is himself he sets in opposition to Brutus (ll. 217-30). He,
Antony, is no orator, as Brutus is, but a plain blunt man that

loves his friend. All he can do is to show sweet Caesar's wounds and let them speak for him.

> But were I Brutus,
> And Brutus Antony, there were an Antony
> Would ruffle up your spirits, and put a tongue
> In every wound of Caesar that should move
> The stones of Rome to rise and mutiny.

The expected cry of the people is "We'll mutiny"; "We'll burn the house of Brutus." Antony has yet to hold them while he reads the will (ll. 240 ff.), but Brutus' name is no longer needed: "Here was a Caesar! when comes such another?" As they take the body and rush off to pluck down benches, windows, forms, anything to make the funeral pyre, and brands to fire the "traitors'" houses, Antony has the final word: "Now let it work. Mischief, thou art afoot,/ Take thou what course thou wilt!" Who loves Rome more, Brutus or Antony? and who loved Rome more, Brutus or Caesar?

There follows the grotesque anticlimax (III. iii), when the plebeians tear to pieces Cinna the poet because he has the same name as Cinna the conspirator.

> *Cin.*   I am not Cinna the conspirator.
> *4. Pleb.*   It is no matter, his name's Cinna. Pluck but his name out of his heart, and turn him going.
> *3. Pleb.*   Tear him, tear him!

"What should be in that 'Caesar'?" What should be in that "Cinna"? Caesar had sought to invest his name with some kind of greatness of position or will and to live by the meaning he gave it. Brutus has found in the name he shares with his ancestor the same obligation to patriotism and tyrannicide. And the people tear apart the innocent Cinna merely on account of his name. Is there some fascination in names which makes men endow them with reality, even if that assumed reality may lead to catastrophe? Is what we call people, and even things or deeds, more important than what they are? We remember the purified name by which Brutus distinguished the killing of

Caesar from the killing of Antony: "Let's be sacrificers, but not butchers, Caius."

We have already noticed how Brutus and Caesar are linked in the latter part of the play—in the appearances of Caesar's ghost to Brutus, in Antony's bitter taunt before Philippi, in Brutus' recognition of the nemesis which overtakes him. The theme of Rome and what it stands for also reappears. To be called a Roman is the highest term of praise which can be given to the departing heroes. Before the battle, Cassius is to Brutus "thou noble Roman" (V. i. 110) and after his suicide "the last of all the Romans" (V. iii. 99); to Titinius he is "the sun of Rome" (V. iii. 63). Titinius, when he stabs himself for love of Cassius and fellowship, calls it "a Roman's part" (V. iii. 89). And Brutus, in viewing the dead Titinius and the dead Cassius side by side, asks, "Are yet two Romans living such as these?" Nothing is precisely defined as peculiarly Roman, but in the context of the battle, of the cause they are fighting for, of the renewed friendship and trust between Brutus and Cassius, of the loyalty of Titinius, it is clear that being Roman implies manliness, courage, resolution, loyalty, dedication to Rome and her cause—those virtues associated in every schoolboy's mind, through history and tradition, with republican Rome. Note the speeches which formally dismiss Cassius from the play. Titinius, finding him dead by his own sword, laments:

> So in his red blood Cassius' day is set!
> The sun of Rome is set. Our day is gone,
> Clouds, dews, and dangers come; our deeds are done!

Brutus speaks in the same vein:

> The last of all the Romans, fare thee well!
> It is impossible that ever Rome
> Should breed thy fellow.

These farewells to Cassius leave us with the best impression of him—we are moved to recall his faithful love of Brutus, the concern for liberty that lay beneath the more obvious personal dislike of Caesar,[27] the loyalty his leadership could inspire, his essential patriotism. Granted that Titinius and Brutus speak with the allowed hyperbole of praise for a fallen hero, we are also left with the wider implication that the old Rome is gone, and perhaps also the virtues it stood for.

Something both Roman and Stoic is implied about the suicides. I have already noticed Titinius' "Roman part" in his. In the conversation between Brutus and Cassius about suicide, when they take farewell of one another (V. i. 92-121), there is an overtone of Stoicism in the implied resolution of the man who frees himself from circumstances he cannot control. Although Brutus's Stoic creed of patiently accepting what Providence gives seems to conflict with his decision,[28] it is abhorrence of the loss of freedom which wins:

> Think not, thou noble Roman,
> That ever Brutus will go bound to Rome;
> He bears too great a mind.

Stoic self-mastery was earlier identified as a Roman virtue in the composure with which Brutus received the news of Portia's death:

> *Bru.*   Now as you are a Roman tell me true.
> *Mes.*   Then like a Roman bear the truth I tell:
> For certain she is dead, and by a strange manner.
> *Bru.*   Why, farewell, Portia. We must die, Messala. . . .
> *Mes.*   Even so great men great losses should endure.
>   (IV. iii. 187-93)

And it is the Stoic Brutus, the man in whom all the elements are rightly mixed, whom Antony finds to be "the noblest Roman of them all." For it is Antony, Brutus' chief antagonist, who speaks the refining comment on him at the end of the play, and brings the three names together—Caesar, Brutus, and Roman. In separating Brutus from his fellow conspirators by the purity of his motives—"All the conspirators, save only he,/ Did that they did in envy of great Caesar"—Antony ends the disjunction between Brutus and Caesar which Cassius began in setting their names against one another, and resolves the dilemma of Brutus' divided loyalties. He can call Brutus "the noblest

Roman of them all," for "he, only in a general honest thought/
And common good to all, made one of them." Antony's apology
for Brutus can be accepted, where Brutus' plea, though based
on a similar argument from motive, cannot. For Brutus sought
to justify the deed by the motive; Antony discriminates between them, not condoning the deed but finding some mitiga-
tion in the motive. In this epitaph, precisely and justly spoken
by the victorious enemy, not by a partial friend, we must hear
no hyperbole.

"What should be in that 'Caesar'?" What indeed? " 'Brutus'
and 'Caesar'. . . . Write them together, yours is as fair a name."
Indeed so. And Shakespeare has made it as fairly remembered.

The Language of Hyperbole
in *Antony and Cleopatra*

W HEN SHAKESPEARE opens the play of *Antony and Cleopatra* with an adverse judgment spoken by one of his officers, he sets the former Antony, the famous soldier, beside the present Antony, the lover of Cleopatra; and he puts the infatuation in the most demeaning terms:

> Nay, but this dotage of our general's
> O'erflows the measure. . . .
> . . . his captain's heart,
> Which in the scuffles of great fights hath burst
> The buckles on his breast, reneges all temper,
> And is become the bellows and the fan
> To cool a gipsy's lust.

"The triple pillar of the world," he says, is "transform'd/ Into a strumpet's fool." If that were all the play was about—an aging

Delivered as a public lecture at Queen's University, Kingston, Ontario, in the autumn of 1964; published in *Queen's Quarterly* 72 (Spring 1965), 26-51, and used here by permission of *Queen's Quarterly*. The essay has been slightly revised.

dotard's ruinous infatuation for a scheming strumpet—we should scarcely be moved by it, or return to it again and again as a special play, something with a poetic radiance that tells us Shakespeare wrote it *con amore*—with zest, with love, and a free spirit. It is not unlike him to show a character or a situation in the worst light at first, in order to make the truth which follows all the more impressive. (This he had done, for instance, with Othello.) Shakespeare is nothing if not bold, and so sure is he of his power to win our sympathies for Antony and Cleopatra that he takes the risk of showing the worst of them straight off.

On the heels of Philo's comment, Antony enters with Cleopatra, and Antony himself seems to confirm the adverse judgment by his waving away the messengers with their urgent business from Rome, and then by turning to embrace Cleopatra:

> Let Rome in Tiber melt, and the wide arch
> Of the rang'd empire fall! Here is my space.
> Kingdoms are clay; our dungy earth alike
> Feeds beast as man; the nobleness of life
> Is to do thus [*embracing*]—when such a mutual pair
> And such a twain can do't, in which I bind,
> On pain of punishment, the world to weet
> We stand up peerless.

We are taken in a great leap, in Antony's large and generous imagination, to the issue of the play: the world for love. The terms on both sides are magnificent: "the wide arch of the rang'd empire" for the love of "such a twain," who "stand up peerless."

Although our judgment of Antony's heedlessness is in no way qualified, we are at once charmed by the vitality of the characters and by the experience that has begun to unfold before us; we would not have it otherwise.

Antony's "rang'd empire" speech immediately sets the tone of the play—the greatness of the issue, the sweep of the scene, the spendor of the imagery. The action moves freely back and forth between the two poles of Antony's conflicting lures—

Rome, the world of Octavius Caesar, and Alexandria, the world
of Cleopatra; the world of power and the world of love. The
imagery enlarges "Rome" to mean the whole world. The kings
of the earth assemble for war:

> Bocchus, the king of Libya; Archelaus
> Of Cappadocia; Philadelphos, King
> Of Paphlagonia; the Thracian king, Adallas;
> King Manchus of Arabia; King of Pont;
> Herod of Jewry; Mithridates, King
> Of Comagena; Polemon and Amyntas,
> The Kings of Mede and Lycaonia,
> With a more larger list of sceptres.
>
> (III. vi. 68-76)

The triumvirs are the triple pillars of the world, Antony—weak
Lepidus not thought of—is "the demi-Atlas of this earth," Caesar
at the end is "the universal landlord." He and Antony cannot
"stall together/ In the whole world." On the other side, Cleopatra is "Egypt." She o'erpictures Venus, and her person beggars all description. Antony is "the sun," "the star" which falls;
Cleopatra the "terrene moon." In setting and image alike, hyperbole may be said to be the dominant trope of the play.

In a sense, Shakespeare is simply using with special richness
and intensity the trope for which the taste was so strong in the
literature of his time. I believe we must look to more than
school training in rhetoric to explain or understand the taste.
The school training is a symptom as well as a cause. At the
basis of the taste is probably something deeply grounded,
something that I shall not try to explain but merely note the
signs of. The pressure in much Elizabethan literature is towards the ideal, the excellent, the distinguished, the quintes-
sential. Theories of society, of poetry, and of history alike put
value on what might be called the ideal of excellence—not on
the little known, the mean, the ordinary in event or character,
but on the famous, the great, the distinguished.

I shall digress a little on this topic before returning to *Antony and Cleopatra,* for a right understanding of the characteristic attitude may help us to avoid critical pitfalls in the interpretation of the play. I need not develop the point as it applies

to society, so familiar is the Renaissance doctrine of degree. Sidney, in the *Defense of Poesy* (1595), best states the ideal of excellence as it applies to poetry: "Only the poet . . . lifted up with the vigor of his own invention, doth grow in effect into another nature, in making things either better than Nature bringeth forth or quite anew, . . . Nature never set forth the earth in so rich tapestry as divers poets have done—neither with so pleasant rivers, fruitful trees, sweet-smelling flowers, nor whatsoever else may make the too much loved earth more lovely. Her world is brazen, the poets only deliver a golden. . . . Know whether she have brought forth so true a lover as Theagenes, so constant a friend as Pylades, so valiant a man as Orlando, so right a prince as Zenophon's Cyrus, so excellent a man every way as Virgil's Aeneas."[1] There are, of course, at least two sorts of excellence implied here: one, the transcendence of the perfect idea over the imperfect fact, the other, moral excellence, always strongly emphasized by Sidney. But there may be absolutes as well in villainy as in goodness— witness More's and Shakespeare's Richard III, that "excellent grand tyrant of the earth." And the excellence need not be put in moral terms, but thought of simply as the perfection of a quality. The quality may be beauty. Is it, asks Sidney, "better to have it set down as it should be, or as it was?" Cicero's story of the painter Zeuxis (in *De inventione* II. i), who was said to have chosen the best features of the five most beautiful women in the city of Croton and combined them to form his portrait of Helen, becomes, with Renaissance literary critics, an axiomatic assumption about the way painters and poets alike go about their imitation. Or the quality might be ugliness. One thinks of Leonardo's sketches of the grotesque faces of old men, in which the features of age are intensified and concentrated. Leonardo himself justifies such intensifying in his account of how an artist should depict emotions, for he says that "a figure is not worthy of praise unless such action appears in it as serves to express the passion of the soul: . . ." As an example he chooses the figure of an angry man:

> An angry figure should be represented seizing someone by the hair and twisting his head down to the ground, with one knee on his ribs, and with the right arm and fist raised high up;

let him have his hair dishevelled, his eyebrows low and knit
together, his teeth clenched, the two corners of his mouth
arched, and the neck which is all swollen and extended as he
bends over the foe, should be full of furrows.[2]

This way of conceiving of character, event, place—whatever
one's topic—and of marking it by superlatives—the "most," the
"best," the "highest," the "greatest," the "noblest"; or their opposites, the "least," the "worst," and so on—is everywhere met
with in Elizabethan literature. The trees beside the purest
crystal spring where amorous Corydon sits versing to Phyllida
are the finest of the several kinds—of elm, beech, and oak; of
pine, palm, and laurel. The ladies of the sonneteers reach in their
beauty the type ancient poets only thought they saw in Helen:

> Then in the blazon of sweet beauty's best,
> Of hand, of foot, of lip, of eye, of brow,
> I see their antique pen would have express'd
> Even such a beauty as you master now.
> So all their praises are but prophecies
> Of this our time, all you prefiguring.

In Shakespeare's *Timon of Athens*, the Poet remarks on the
Painter's portrait of Timon that

> It tutors nature. Artificial strife
> Lives in these touches, livelier than life.

We shall remember the phrase, "livelier than life."

Clearly this attitude does not preclude the most vivid realism in the observation of detail. And there is besides a strong
current of objective realism in Elizabethan literature that appears to be outside the thing I am talking about. Even here, I
think, the important thing is that mere ordinariness, mediocrity,
or commonplaceness, is not glorified as such—or if so, only
tentatively and sentimentally, and with an apology. The drab,
the flat, the colorless, the futile are not thought interesting.
Deloney's and Dekker's Simon Eyre was worthy of putting
into a novel and a play not because he was ordinary, but because he was not: he became Lord Mayor of London.

The idea of excellence expressed in poetic theory was matched in the commonly held view of history that it was interesting and instructive for the examples it furnished of great men and great events. History was seen as highly personal and dramatic, composed not of "trends" and "movements," but of distinguishable events and distinguishable people. Thomas North, Englishing (in 1579) Jacques Amyot's preface to his French translation of Plutarch, notes that "the proper ground" of history "is to treate of the greatest and highest thinges that are done in the world: . . . It is a picture, which (as it were in a table) setteth before our eies the things worthy of remembrance that have bene done in olde time by mighty nations, noble kings & Princes, wise governors, valiant Captaines, & persons renowmed for some notable qualitie, . . . and their demeaning [i.e., behavior] of them selves when they were comen to the highest, or throwen down to the lowest degre of state."[3] It was among the great men of history that tragedy sought its subjects, its falls of princes. The post-classical grammarians had taught that tragedy was concerned with the falling of the great into adversity; its subjects were heroes, nobles, kings; its actions were conflicts, exiles, and violent deaths.[4] "Let us sit upon the ground/ And tell sad stories of the death of kings," Shakespeare makes his Richard II say. Sidney observed that tragedy should be "high and excellent." The rhetorical mode of *de casibus* tragedy, moving as it does from the throne to the grave, is naturally hyperbolic. Richard would give his "large kingdom for a little grave,/ A little, little grave . . ."

In the fifteenth century, in his *Fall of Princes*, Lydgate contemplates, from the slippery top, the depth of the descent. In the late sixteenth, Marlowe looks up to the glorious height, when he makes Tamburlaine speak of the "thirst of reign and sweetness of a crown":

Nature . . .
Doth teach us all to have aspiring minds:
Our souls, . . .
Still climbing after knowledge infinite,
And always moving as the restless spheres,
Wills us to wear ourselves and never rest,

> Until we reach the ripest fruit of all,
> That perfect bliss and sole felicity,
> The sweet fruition of an earthly crown.

No brief period in history furnished more examples of famous falls, or was better chronicled, than the period of the Roman revolution, from Marius and Sulla to the establishment of the empire by Octavius Caesar, and the achievement of the Peace of Augustus. In this sequence of reversals and falls—of Marius, Sulla, Pompey, Julius Caesar, Brutus, Cassius, and Mark Antony—none save Caesar's tragedy was more fascinating than Antony's. For Antony, a generously gifted man, famous for his "absolute soldiership," threw all he had won away in a moment, when in the midst of the Battle of Actium, his chances as good as his enemy's, he sailed after Cleopatra's retreating galleys. Antony's kissing away kingdoms and provinces would have been known to Shakespeare not only through Plutarch and the Roman historians, but also through the medieval Falls of Princes tradition, as a great and unique event in history.[5]

Moreover, the two lovers had another kind of long association, with a different and more sympathetic tragic emphasis. In those gatherings-up of famous names, those Houses of Fame medieval writers were fond of making, Antony and Cleopatra were usually to be found beside Helen and Paris, Dido and Aeneas, Pyramus and Thisbe, Hero and Leander, Tristram and Iseult—those notable victims of the cruel and resistless God of Love.[6] In *The Assembly of Ladies,* an anonymous poem that found its way into the sixteenth-century editions of Chaucer, a lady is led in a dream into a great hall, on the walls of which were

> . . . graven of storyes many one
> Fyrst howe Phyllis/ of womanly pyte
> Dyed pyteously for love of Demophone
> Nexte after was the story of Tysbe
> Howe she slewe her selfe under a tree
> Yet sawe I more/ howe in a right pytous caas
> For Antony was slayne Cleopatras.[7]

Shakespeare knew this tradition well enough, for he makes Antony say, thinking Cleopatra dead:

> Where souls do couch on flowers, we'll hand in hand,
> And with our sprightly port make the ghosts gaze.
> Dido and her Aeneas shall want troops,
> And all the haunt be ours.

(IV. xiv. 51-54)

This is not quite the Virgilian note. Medieval love poetry has contaminated it.

The two traditions of the story—the falls of princes and the woes of famous lovers—had been brought together by Boccaccio in *L'Amorosa Fiammetta*. The book was translated into English by Bartholomew Young and published in 1587. The heroine, in comparing her misfortunes in love with the renowned ladies of the past, singles out Cleopatra, of "so high a mynde, and so prowde a conceit," as "the most unfortunat and sorrowful Lady . . . that might be." For in one hour, by one unfortunate battle, she suffered the double loss of her dear and brave husband and of her hope of being crowned Roman empress, "sole and soveraigne Ladie and Queene of the whole circuite of the earth."[8]

For such a high event as the tragedy of Antony and Cleopatra high statement was appropriate. There is nothing surprising about Shakespeare's choosing to be hyperbolic in a treatment that should be worthy of the event and of the tradition. But of course he is not simply hyperbolic. His sensitive and sympathetic knowledge of men and women as they are, his sure sense of moral values, his profound sense of irony, make completely sustained or unqualified hyperbole impossible for him. He found in Plutarch's life of Marcus Antonius a full, thoughtful, quite unidealized, largely detached, but mainly sympathetic account of Antony—this man formed of very mingled stuff, of large virtues and large vices. Of Cleopatra in Plutarch Shakespeare found both explicit disapproval and implicit wonder, for Plutarch, blame her as he might for Antony's ruin, was yet fascinated by this great and extraordinary woman. Having caught from Plutarch a sense of vital, interesting people, living at a place and time in history, Shakespeare went far beyond his source in giving their personalities wholeness within his dramatic action. What we have in the play, therefore, is something of extraordinary subtlety. We have a story of a complex, unsentimental relationship between two richly endowed but very imperfect people, a story acted out in the thorough worldliness of Egyptian luxury and Roman power politics. At the same time, characters and action are set in a poetic frame which creates an aura of uniqueness and greatness—of "infinite variety," of "nature's piece 'gainst fancy," beyond "the size of dreaming," of high events that make the beholders feel that "time is at his period." The vision, however, is not therefore double; it is fused into one with wit, irony, sympathy, and delight.

Something needs to be said briefly about hyperbole as a trope before turning to Shakespeare's use of it in *Antony and Cleopatra*. This figure is defined by Puttenham (in *The Arte of English Poesie*, 1589) as "the overreacher": "when we speake in the superlative and beyond the limites of credit, that is by the figure which the Greeks called *Hiperbole* . . . I for his immoderate excesse cal him the over reacher . . . & me thinks not amisse: . . ."[9] But the overreaching trope may be used in quite different ways—as Puttenham says, "when either we would greatly advaunce or greatly abase the reputation of any thing or person." It may be used, as the modern temper prefers to read it, as overreaching actuality so as to diminish it and make it appear smaller or less worthy than we usually think it is. It may also be used—and this was the more frequent use in the Renaissance—to heighten or amplify actuality to some ideal perfection, to what it might be in idea, to something beyond the common reach. The distinction may be readily seen in two notable plays on the theme of ambition, *Tamburlaine* and *Sejanus*. Marlowe used hyperbole absolutely in *Tamburlaine*, without ironic implication. Tamburlaine's "high aspiring mind" sweeps us (like Zenocrate) resistlessly with him across Persia, Turkey, and Syria, and, in his mind's eye, around the world—until his ships

> Sailing along the oriental sea,
> Have fetched about the Indian continent,
> Even from Persepolis to Mexico,
> And thence unto the Straits of Jubalter.

In *Tamburlaine* action and trope are one. Jonson, on the other hand, used hyperbole with precise satiric value as the "over-reacher" in *Sejanus*. His hero is a prodigy, who feels his "advanced head/ Knock out a star in heav'n"; his swelling joys prove hollow bubbles.

Shakespeare, however, is no Marlowe, in whose heroes there can be no accommodation between all or nothing, all the world or hell. And he is no Jonson, whose remorseless logic must cut human dreams down to size. The effect of Shakespeare's hyperbole is neither to overwhelm our judgment as in *Tamburlaine*, nor to sharpen our critical faculty to a satiric edge as in *Sejanus*, but to give us a sense of pleasurable participation in a credible, but rare, experience, an experience that we know did indeed happen in some fashion to actual people at a time and place in history, yet one so special that it became a famous tragedy to all the world; and one now carried in Shakespeare's art to the utmost stretch of the possibilities of such an experience and such a choice.

It is easier to describe the effect of this complex vision than to say how it is achieved. But perhaps we can find some clues in the particular ways in which Shakespeare qualifies his hyperbole—qualifies to enrich and complicate, but not to destroy.

A principal method, operative throughout the play, is in the strong yet supple web of the language itself. The golden threads running throughout it are crossed by the plain, tough fibers of direct and simple speech: "Well; is it, is it?" "My being in Egypt, Caesar,/ What was't to you?" "Let the old ruffian know/ I have many other ways to die"; "He words me, girls, he words me." The heightened style and the plain are often set side by side. The combined richness and strength of such juxtaposing is well illustrated in the scene of Antony's death in Cleopatra's monument (IV. xv). Her defense against grief is made in several ways. One way is in employing a fanciful conceit to exclaim against fortune:

No, let me speak, and let me rail so high
That the false huswife Fortune break her wheel,
Provok'd by my offense.

Another is in her habitual coquetry, now in a new key:

Noblest of men, woo't die?
Hast thou no care of me? Shall I abide
In this dull world, which in thy absence is
No better than a sty?

Still another, most movingly, is in lyric cadences:

O sun,
Burn the great sphere thou mov'st in! darkling stand
The varying shore o' th' world! O Antony,
Antony, Antony!

These variations are Shakespeare's new way with the old rhetorical copiousness "in exclaims"[10] recommended for the augmentation of passion. But the undertone in the scene is Antony's simple repetition, "I am dying, Egypt, dying." Farther along in the scene, when Antony is dead, Cleopatra in her grief sees herself as

No more but e'en a woman, and commanded
By such poor passion as the maid that milks
And does the meanest chares.

Far from reducing the greatness of her sorrow, the comparison gives it rather the strength of common human experience.

Another such contrast of the hyperbolic and the literal statement, at a farther remove, but at paired dramatic points, comes in two of the crucial speeches marking Antony's choice. The first is the "rang'd empire" speech, with its expansive splendor —"Let Rome in Tiber melt, and the wide arch/ Of the rang'd empire fall! Here is my space." The choice here is imaginary, one that he hardly thinks of as a real choice. At the moment both the world and Cleopatra are his, and he can afford to scorn the "dungy earth." The action of the play shows him trying to hold both the world and Cleopatra, until his defeat at Actium seals his eventual fate. Then, with the world lost indeed, and more than the world, the world's esteem—

> Hark, the land bids me tread no more upon't, . . .
> I am so lated in the world that I
> Have lost my way for ever
>
> (III. xi. 1-4)

—he embraces Cleopatra with words that sadly echo that first confident embrace:

> Fall not a tear, I say; one of them rates
> All that is won and lost. Give me a kiss.
> Even this repays me.
>
> (ll. 69-71)

The speech is all the more poignantly ironic for its sad simplicity.

I have been speaking of a general method in the management of the language. We shall note now, more particularly, how the alternatives of Antony's choice, the world of power and the world of love, are described and how hyperbole is used and qualified. In the discussion, I shall also consider the conceptions of the two central characters themselves.

First for Rome and power, and Antony's part in these. The reach and greatness of Rome and the urgency of its business are of course implicit in the action and suggested in the constant references to events and geography. One has the sense of something going on at every moment everywhere within the empire: "Italy shines o'er with civil swords," in the borders maritime "flush youth revolt" to Pompey, Fulvia's garboils are uncurbable, Labienus shakes his conquering banner from Lydia to Syria and Ionia, Ventidius jades "the ne'er-yet-beaten horse of Parthia" out of the field, in Alexandria Antony proclaims his sons the kings of kings. The magnificence of the power wielded by the Roman rulers is suggested, as I have already noted, by the running images of them as owners or upholders of the whole world: world-sharers, triple pillars, demi-Atlases. Octavius finally becomes, in Cleopatra's ironic compliment, "sole

sir o' th' world." In proposing a stronger union between himself
and Antony, after their first quarrel, Octavius says,

> Yet if I knew
> What hoop should hold us staunch from edge to edge
> O' th' world,[11] I would pursue it.
> > (II. ii. 114-16)

When they fall out a second time, they are the world's jaws,
a pair of chaps,

> And throw between them all the food thou hast,
> They'll grind th' one the other.
> > (III. v. 14-15)

Wars between them would be

> As if the world should cleave, and that slain men
> Should solder up the rift.
> > (III. iv. 31-32)

But these images of greatness may be variously qualified,
comically, sardonically, or playfully. The world-sharers' image
is reduced to comic bathos when Lepidus, the weakest of the
three, is carried drunk off Pompey's galley at the end of the
peace-celebrating feast (II. vii). The servant who is carrying
him is "a strong fellow," because, as Enobarbus says, " 'a bears
the third part of the world, man; seest not?" "The third part
then," replies Menas, "is drunk." The same world-sharers'
image is varied rather sarcastically by Pompey, at the meeting
to sign the terms of peace (II. vi), when he addresses the
triumvirs as

> The senators alone of this great world,
> Chief factors for the gods.

The implication of overreaching becomes clear when he goes
on to ask:

> > What was't
> That mov'd pale Cassius to conspire? and what
> Made all-honor'd, honest, Roman Brutus,[12]
> With the arm'd rest, courtiers of beauteous freedom,

> To drench the Capitol, but that they would
> Have one man but a man?

There is a whole set of images that magnifies the power by reducing the objects of its control, the subject kings and kingdoms. There was a time, before Actium, we hear, when Antony had "superfluous kings" for messengers; when, if he called for a servant, "kings would start forth/ And cry, 'Your will?'" There is a fine carelessness about these phrases. Caesar says, in disapproval, that Antony gives "a kingdom for a mirth." And Cleopatra tells us, not in disapproval, that

> In his livery
> Walk'd crowns and crownets; realms and islands were
> As plates dropp'd from his pocket.
> (V. ii. 90-92)

This double effect of hyperbole (heightening) and meiosis (diminishing) is most delightfully seen in a speech of Antony's to Alexas, who is to carry back to Cleopatra the gift of an orient pearl:

> 'Say the firm Roman to great Egypt sends
> This treasure of an oyster; at whose foot,
> To mend the petty present, I will piece
> Her opulent throne with kingdoms. . . .'
> (I. v. 43-46)

If these images magnify Antony's Gargantuan prodigality, together with the means Rome furnishes him to be prodigal, they also, in their lighthearted extravagance, prevent us from being altogether solemn about the power and the glory.

For the Roman world we see in operation is, after all, only the world, the very realistic world Shakespeare found in Plutarch. It is no better than the men in it, and no one of them is touched with any idealism about the business of war and politics they are engaged in. No one, that is, but Pompey, in the rather nostalgic speech about Cassius and Brutus as "courtiers of beauteous freedom." All the same, we are asked to judge the decline of Antony against a standard from which he has fallen. It is the standard of what one might call the Roman

republican virtues of spare living, courage, fortitude in the
face of hardship, devotion to duty, and responsibility and prudence in the performing of it. These are first of all a soldier's
virtues, but also, in part, a ruler's. They are everywhere implied or expressed as something opposed to the effeminacy and
voluptuousness of Egypt, to which Antony the soldier has surrendered. Our judgment assents to the truth of most that is
said in reproof of Antony, such as that

> his captain's heart,
> Which in the scuffles of great fights hath burst
> The buckles on his breast, reneges all temper.
> (I. i. 6-8)

We assent even to Caesar's diagnosis, which, in spite of his
temperamental prejudice, is just:

> 'tis to be chid—
> As we rate boys who, being mature in knowledge,
> Pawn their experience to their present pleasure
> And so rebel to judgment.
> (I. iv. 30-33)

We assent, above all, to what is said by Enobarbus, whose
clearly choric comments mark the stages of Antony's decline.
In a scene (III. xiii) soon after Actium, he makes three
speeches of acute analysis. First he tells Cleopatra that Antony
was responsible for the defeat because he "would make his
will/ Lord of his reason." When Antony challenges Octavius
to single combat, Enobarbus comments in soliloquy that
Caesar has subdued his judgment, for

> men's judgments are
> A parcel of their fortunes, and things outward
> Do draw the inward quality after them
> To suffer all alike.

And finally, when overconfident Antony boasts of the deeds he
will perform in the battle before Alexandria, Enobarbus tells
us that "a diminution in our captain's brain/ Restores his
heart," for "when valor preys on reason,/ It eats the sword it
fights with": Antony will "outstare the lightning." We assent.

At the same time Antony's generosity, his liberality, his large imagination, even his impulsiveness and his enthusiasm for gaudy nights, win our liking and our sympathy in a way that Caesar's cold prudence never does. Caesar will win the world right enough, and deserves to; but there is more charm in Antony's splendid carelessness. As so often happens in Shakespeare, we find him taking our judgment one way, our sympathy another. After Antony is dead, his former friends resolve the dilemma:

> *Maec.*   His taints and honors
> Wag'd equal with him.
>   *Agr.*   A rarer spirit never
> Did steer humanity; but you gods will give us
> Some faults to make us men.
>
>   (V. i. 30-33)

But we have also seen Antony through Cleopatra's eyes as her "man of men," her "lord of lords," "the arm and burgonet of men," and when he is dead, her words are all choric lament and praise. To these I shall return. After his death, we hear no more of Antony's weaknesses; he is "good, being gone," as Fulvia had seemed to Antony. Not long before her own end, Cleopatra tells Dolabella her dream of Antony. In this bravura piece, we have what must surely be the boldest heaping up of superlatives in the play:

> I dreamt there was an Emperor Antony—
>
>   .   .   .   .   .
>
> His face was as the heav'ns, and therein stuck
> A sun and moon, which kept their course, and lighted
> The little O, th' earth.
>
>   .   .   .   .   .
>
> His legs bestrid the ocean, his rear'd arm
> Crested the world, his voice was propertied
> As all the tuned spheres, and that to friends;
> But when he meant to quail and shake the orb,
> He was as rattling thunder. For his bounty,
> There was no winter in 't; an autumn 'twas
> That grew the more by reaping. His delights

Were dolphin-like, they show'd his back above
The element they liv'd in. In his livery
Walk'd crowns and crownets; realms and islands were
As plates dropp'd from his pocket.
(V. ii. 76-92)

What we have is the "idea" of Antony, Cleopatra's vision of what was essential in him—the nobility, the bounty, the largeness of spirit, above all, the full participation in life raised to the highest power. Yet it is all done wittily, for the fun of saying it, as well as seriously. The sheer virtuosity of this astonishing "portrait" takes us. In this way it is true to the tremendous vitality of the character Shakespeare has created. It tutors nature; its "artificial strife" is "livelier than life." Significantly, this splendid piece comes late in the play. "Strumpet's fool" was the epithet with which Antony was introduced to us; but it is not the word of dismissal.

In the same way, the worst that can be said of Cleopatra is said at the beginning, when she is called a "strumpet" and a "gipsy," connoting, as well as Egyptian, a trickster, a cheat, a worker of spells to no one's good. The terms are repeated during the play with variations—"witch," "spell," "charm," "trull," "whore"—as when Antony himself, thinking she has betrayed him, abuses her in the ugliest language (III. xiii and IV. xii). But the sordidness of the epithets simply cannot prevail against the vitality and invention in Shakespeare's conception of her. His method of handling the varying points of view towards her is, however, somewhat different from the way he manages those towards Antony. For as Antony declines in greatness, Cleopatra rises. Since she achieves her greatness, there is no need, as with Antony, to use hyperbole to restore the "idea" of her. The great hyperbolic set-piece about her—Enobarbus' description of her in her barge at Cydnus—comes early; the mystery and the power therein suggested are something to be realized as the play progresses, and are fully reached only at the end.

We come, then, to the world of Egypt, of which Cleopatra, Antony's "serpent of old Nile," is the most essential part. If Rome is the epitome of power, Egypt is the epitome of pleas-

ure. But it is to be observed that we hear far more of this riot-
ous living than we see of it. As the splendor of Rome was
largely in the poetry, so is the luxury of Egypt. This is important. Hollywood supposes that it is to be laid out grossly, in full
color, for reel after reel in a way which quite misses its point
and its function. To translate poetic superlatives of opulence
and of sensuality into visual fact can result only in vulgarity
or ridiculousness. Display without reservation ends for us all
the fascination that exotic Egypt—with its "pyramises," its overflowing Nile, its foison and famine, not to mention its Cleopatra—have for us. Too much representation ends the fun, too.
"Y' have strange serpents there," says Lepidus; "your serpent
of Egypt is bred now of your mud by the operation of your
sun. So is your crocodile" (II. vii. 26-27). The beast is even
stranger by the time Antony has finished telling him that it is
shaped like itself, is as broad as it hath breadth, is just so high
as it is, moves with its own organs, lives by that which nour-
isheth it, and is "of it own color too." True it is that in the language of Octavius Caesar, Antony's life in Egypt is described
sarcastically and with disgust:

> Let us grant it is not
> Amiss to tumble on the bed of Ptolemy,
> To give a kingdom for a mirth, to sit
> And keep the turn of tippling with a slave,
> To reel the streets at noon, and stand the buffet
> With knaves that smell[13] of sweat.
> (I. iv. 16-21)

But the speech is supposed to tell us something about Caesar
as well as about Antony. We also hear of Alexandrian high
living in the gossip of Enobarbus and his Roman friends,
whose half-joking, half-envious curiosity Enobarbus loves to
satisfy in full measure:

> *Maec.* . . . You stay'd well by't in Egypt.
> *Eno.* Ay, sir, we did sleep day out of countenance, and
> made the night light with drinking.
> *Maec.* Eight wild boars roasted whole at a breakfast, and
> but twelve persons there; is this true?

>   *Eno.*   This was but as a fly by an eagle; we had much
> more monstrous matter of feast, which worthily deserv'd
> noting.
>   *Maec.*   She's a most triumphant lady, if report be square to
> her.

                              (II. ii. 176-85)

We catch in Maecenas the note of fascination with something
exotic and perhaps wonderful. This dialogue is indeed the beginning of the conversation in which Enobarbus gives his
Roman friends the account of how Cleopatra first "purs'd up"
the heart of Antony "upon the river of Cydnus." In that show-
piece of description, he far transcends mere gossip. The discussion of it must wait still a moment longer.

When we move from comment to representation, what do
we see? When Antony and Cleopatra are shown together in
Egypt, where we know that the beds are soft, we hear more
talk of gaudy nights, of wine peeping through the scars of
Antony's officers, of Cleopatra drinking Antony to bed ere the
ninth hour in the morning. But we see no lascivious wassails
acted out. During the play we see even very few of the many
thousand kisses Antony tells us of as he is dying.

What we do see, when Antony and Cleopatra are together,
is not love-making of the ordinary sort, but Cleopatra teasing,
quarreling, coquetting, having fits of the sullens, entangling
him in her wit, being endlessly exasperating and changeable.
Her deep and unaffected love of Antony appears most when
her "man of men" is not present, or at nearly wordless moments of reconciliation. The point of all this is that the superlatives about Egyptian ease as about Roman splendor are chiefly
in the mind.

Cleopatra is in the mind, too, as well as in the action. Nothing better illustrates than the Cydnus scene (II. ii) Shakespeare's management of the hyperbolic and the actual so that
the value of neither is destroyed. I have spoken of the gossip
between Enobarbus and his Roman friends with which the
conversation opens. The subtle change of tone in Maecenas'
comment, "She's a most triumphant lady, if report be square
to her," prompts Enobarbus to begin (l. 190):

> I will tell you.
> The barge she sat in, like a burnish'd throne,
> Burnt on the water. The poop was beaten gold,
> Purple the sails, and so perfumed that
> The winds were love-sick with them; the oars were silver,
> Which to the tune of flutes kept stroke, and made
> The water which they beat to follow faster,
> As amorous of their strokes.

Every detail taken from Plutarch is heightened in the direction of amorousness and artifice. Plutarch has only the physical objects and their materials, not the personifications and the gestures. Cleopatra is the very type of the earthly Venus (except that she even outdoes the type), the Venus who knows every art of seduction, and who does not, therefore, appear in the nakedness of simple truth, but most artfully clothed.

> For her own person,
> It beggar'd all description: she did lie
> In her pavilion—cloth-of-gold, of tissue—
> O'er-picturing that Venus where we see
> The fancy outwork nature. On each side her
> Stood pretty dimpled boys, like smiling Cupids,
> With divers-color'd fans, whose wind did seem
> To glow the delicate cheeks which they did cool,
> And what they undid did.

"O, rare for Antony!" interposes the enthusiastic Agrippa. Enobarbus continues:

> Her gentlewomen, like the Nereides,
> So many mermaids, tended her i' th' eyes,
> And made their bends adornings. At the helm
> A seeming mermaid steers; the silken tackle
> Swell with the touches of those flower-soft hands,
> That yarely frame the office.

That this barge was never meant for wind and waves is wittily pointed up in the delightful anomaly of the flower-soft hands and the nautical adverb "yarely" to characterize their work in the rigging. Here in this scene the whole description creates a moment of perfection caught in the mind's eye through the eloquence of Enobarbus.

Notice that Antony does not come aboard and break the illusion. Instead we are eased back to actuality by a different route, the same route of comedy by which we moved out of it. We are told that in excited curiosity everybody in town rushed to the river to see the great sight:

> The city cast
> Her people out upon her; and Antony
> Enthron'd i' th' market-place, did sit alone,
> Whistling to th' air.

Invited to supper by Cleopatra,

> Our courteous Antony,
> Whom ne'er the word of 'No' woman heard speak,
> Being barber'd ten times o'er, goes to the feast;
> And for his ordinary pays his heart
> For what his eyes eat only.

The tone has changed, and Agrippa, reminded of another of her conquests, puts it coarsely:

> Royal wench!
> She made great Caesar lay his sword to bed;
> He plough'd her, and she cropp'd.

Enobarbus continues in the earthy vein, but only to catch up in his anecdote the paradox of her quality:

> I saw her once
> Hop forty paces through the public street;
> And having lost her breath, she spoke, and panted,
> That she did make defect perfection
> And, breathless, pow'r breathe forth.

To Maecenas' comment, "Now Antony/ Must leave her utterly," Enobarbus replies:

> Never, he will not.
> Age cannot wither her, nor custom stale
> Her infinite variety. Other women cloy
> The appetites they feed, but she makes hungry
> Where most she satisfies; for vilest things
> Become themselves in her, that the holy priests
> Bless her when she is riggish.

He has composed the contraries of the scene and the character, of the "most triumphant lady" and the "royal wench." He has, besides, suggested someone both convincingly "real" and yet beyond description. The final contrast is full of anticipatory irony. Maecenas remarks on the coming wedding of Antony to Octavia:

> If beauty, wisdom, modesty, can settle
> The heart of Antony, Octavia is
> A blessed lottery to him.

Enobarbus has already said all that is necessary; he lets this speculation pass without comment.

As with Antony, but even more than with him, what we feel about Cleopatra is the energy of the dramatist's conception. Both characters sound and act like living people, yet both have an "excellence"—in the artistic sense in which I have been using the word—beyond actuality.

The reach for this excellence, this quintessence, the very idea of their story, is made especially as the play draws towards its close. As we have seen, Antony declines with his fortunes. The "grand captain" falls farther and farther from the image of that heroic ancestor of his, the Hercules he would like to be. He has, in a way, disintegrated, lost what he feels to be his essential self. After Actium he was "unqualitied with very shame." Now, just before his attempted suicide (in IV. xiv), he uses the analogy of the towering thunderheads one sees towards evening, the clouds that at one moment have a form—like "a tower'd citadel" or "a pendant rock"—and at the next lose it:

> That which is now a horse, even with a thought
> The rack dislimns, and makes it indistinct
> As water is in water.

He tells Eros that he is

> Even such a body. Here I am Antony,
> Yet cannot hold this visible shape, . . .

Perhaps he means no more than that he must die, but the overtones, in the light of all that we have seen happen, are

far wider for us. He does hold to the best of himself in the act
of suicide. As Dercetas puts it later to Octavius:

> He is dead, Caesar,
> Not by a public minister of justice,
> Nor by a hired knife, but that self hand
> Which writ his honor in the acts it did
> Hath, with the courage which the heart did lend it,
> Splitted the heart.
>
>   (V. i. 19-24)

When Mardian brings the false word that Cleopatra is dead,
Antony's tortured jealousy and rage at her simply fall away:

> Unarm, Eros, the long day's task is done,
> And we must sleep. . . .
> I will o'ertake thee, Cleopatra, and
> Weep for my pardon.
>
>   (IV. xiv. 35-45)

His last words, in Cleopatra's arms, are all the more poignant
for the note of Stoic acceptance of his fate in so un-Stoic a
man, and for the holding to the one dignity left to him—the
fact that he made his own choice of death.

> The miserable change now at my end
> Lament nor sorrow at; but please your thoughts
> In feeding them with those my former fortunes
> Wherein I liv'd, the greatest prince o' th' world,
> The noblest; and do now not basely die,
> Not cowardly put off my helmet to
> My countryman—a Roman by a Roman
> Valiantly vanquish'd.
>
>   (IV. xv. 51-58)

But the meaning of the death has already become greater in
our minds than Antony himself. The guards who found him,
mortally wounded but not dead, after he had fallen on his
sword, spoke lyrically and chorically:

> 2. *Guard.*   The star is fall'n.
> 1. *Guard.*   And time is at his period.
> *All.*   Alas, and woe!
>
>   (IV. xiv. 106-7)

The scene of the death itself (IV. xv) is enclosed by the choric lament of Cleopatra. Her words are, at the beginning:

> O sun,
> Burn the great sphere thou mov'st in! darkling stand
> The varying shore o' th' world! O Antony,
> Antony, Antony!

And when he is dead:

> The crown o' th' earth doth melt. My lord!
> O, wither'd is the garland of the war,
> The soldier's pole is fall'n! Young boys and girls
> Are level now with men; the odds is gone,
> And there is nothing left remarkable
> Beneath the visiting moon.

All here is tragic elevation. The dross has fallen away. There is left only the *idea* of Antony the absolute soldier, whose arm "crested the world," and whose death leaves the world a meaner, poorer place. All the widening meaning of such a death, of the fall of such a prince, is borne in the imagery. It is a great event in history, after which nothing will be the same as if it had not happened. His death "is not a single doom." This is the very essence of historical tragedy, of the meaning the old medieval Falls of Princes theme might hold when brought to noble fruition in a great play.

It is to the "idea" of Antony that Cleopatra rises—an idea she helps create, both here in the death scene and in the dream speech to Dolabella ("I dreamt there was an Emperor Antony,/ ... His face was as the heav'ns, ..."). To her women she says:

> Our lamp is spent, it's out. Good sirs, take heart,
> We'll bury him; and then, what's brave, what's noble,
> Let's do 't after the high Roman fashion,
> And make death proud to take us.
>   (IV. xv. 85-88)

In her resolution and in the manner of her death, the conflict between the idea of Egypt and the idea of Rome is finally resolved. For she is ready to put off her femininity for masculine courage, and for the Stoic ideal of the free and constant mind, superior to accident and unterrified by death.[14]

> My resolution's plac'd, and I have nothing
> Of woman in me; now from head to foot
> I am marble-constant, now the fleeting moon
> No planet is of mine.
>
> (V. ii. 238-41)

She is ready to take herself beyond the world of time and circumstance:

> To do that thing that ends all other deeds,
> Which shackles accidents and bolts up change.
>
> (V. ii. 5-6)

But in the doing of it she triumphs over Caesar, and in a woman's way.

The end takes us back to the beginning. For the ranged empire Antony had used the metaphor of the Roman triumphal arch. In the image of the "triumph" or victory procession, the great formal "pomp" of the Roman conqueror, Shakespeare gathers up all the conflicts, the victories and defeats, the multiple ironies of the play. Caesar, "sole sir o' th' world," winner of the kingdoms and provinces that Antony had kissed away, is most concerned to keep Cleopatra alive and in health, "for her life in Rome/ Would be eternal in our triumph." But Cleopatra designs her own triumph:

> Show me, my women, like a queen; go fetch
> My best attires. I am again for Cydnus
> To meet Mark Antony.

There once before, we remember, she had been "a most triumphant lady." Little is left, in this triumph of Cleopatra's, of hyperbole. There is now no need for it, for the thing and the idea are one. She has assumed her greatness:

> Give me my robe, put on my crown, I have
> Immortal longings in me. Now no more
> The juice of Egypt's grape shall moist this lip.
> Yare, yare, good Iras; quick. Methinks I hear

> Antony call; I see him rouse himself
> To praise my noble act. I hear him mock
> The luck of Caesar, which the gods give men
> To excuse their after wrath. Husband, I come!
> Now to that name my courage prove my title!

There is room for coquetry. "If she first meet the curled Antony," she says of Iras, who has fallen first,

> If she first meet the curled Antony,
> He'll make demand of her, and spend that kiss
> Which is my heaven to have.

And there is room for a triumphant joke. She addresses the asp she has applied to her breast:

>   O, couldst thou speak,
> That I might hear thee call great Caesar ass
> Unpolicied!

The brief dialogue at the end between Charmian and Cleopatra is lyric and in low key:

> *Char.*   O eastern star!
> *Cleo.*   Peace, peace!
> Dost thou not see my baby at my breast,
> That sucks the nurse asleep?
> *Char.*   O, break! O, break!
> *Cleo.*   As sweet as balm, as soft as air, as gentle—
> O Antony!

Only Shakespeare, bold in his assurance of what he had done, would dare Charmian's final epithet for Cleopatra:

> Now boast thee, death, in thy possession lies
> A lass unparallel'd.

Is the world well lost for love, as Dryden phrased it? The question is not asked. It is impertinent. The loss, the love, simply are. To Antony, Cleopatra's bosom was his crownet, his chief end. For Cleopatra, her courage proved her title to call him husband. They reach the end they make. *Finis coronat opus.*

Caesar, after all, has the last word—rather, the last two words. The first is a tribute to the triumphant lady, spoken without rancor or personal grievance. He is captured, like all the rest, by the wonder of Cleopatra:

> she looks like sleep,
> As she would catch another Antony
> In her strong toil of grace.

The second is the dismissal and final judgment, spoken as always in Shakespearian tragedy, directly, plainly, and formally:

> Take up her bed,
> And bear her women from the monument.
> She shall be buried by her Antony;
> No grave upon the earth shall clip in it
> A pair so famous. High events as these
> Strike those that make them; and their story is
> No less in pity than his glory which
> Brought them to be lamented. Our army shall
> In solemn show attend this funeral,
> And then to Rome. Come, Dolabella, see
> High order in this great solemnity.

But I have an epilogue of my own. If this play strikes you as fancy's piece 'gainst nature, I recommend to you Cleopatra's words to the incredulous Dolabella, after her extravagant characterization of the Antony of her dream—the Antony whose legs bestrid the ocean, whose reared arm crested the world. She asked him, "Think you there was or might be such a man/ As this I dreamt of?" And he replied, "Gentle madam, no." Then she said:

> You lie, up to the hearing of the gods!
> But if there be, or[15] ever were one such,
> It's past the size of dreaming. Nature wants stuff
> To vie strange forms with fancy; yet, t' imagine
> An Antony were nature's piece 'gainst fancy,
> Condemning shadows quite.

This is Pelion on Ossa, hyperbole upon hyperbole—or so it seems. Is it not, rather, hyperbole confronted, outfaced in an assertion that the truth is beyond anything hyperbole can reach? It would not be uncharacteristic of Shakespeare to suggest that the true wonder, something always beyond statement, lay, after all, in human beings themselves—in these two and in their story.

The Language of Contention
in *Coriolanus*

IF WE COME to *Coriolanus* straight from *Antony and Cleopatra*, the preceding play, we are brought up short. That play is loose and expansive in time, place, action, and feeling, seemingly (but deceptively) careless in the putting together. This play is tight and restricted, its parts neatly mortised in a simple, strong design. We have exchanged the Roman *imperium*, with its ranging dependencies, its armies and fleets, its powers and splendors, its ripeness and cynicism, for early republican Rome, with its poverty and its patriotism, its clashing patricians and plebeians, its savage war against its Volscian neighbors. For "the wide arch of the rang'd empire" we have the Tarpeian Rock; for Cydnus and Actium, the gates of Corioli; for the gaudy nights of Alexandria, the noise and tears of Coriolanus' passage; for Antony's "serpent of old Nile," Coriolanus' mother, "worth of consuls, senators, patricians, a city full"; for Antony, whose bounty had "no winter in't," Coriolanus, the "lonely dragon" going to his fen with hatred stored in his heart.

The style of each play clearly answers to plot, character, and setting, and largely defines its distinctive feeling, or tone: the magnificence, sensuousness, openness of *Antony and Cleopatra*, the closeness, hardness, and harshness of *Coriolanus*. Diction and grammar in *Antony and Cleopatra* are treated with great boldness and freedom; syntax as well—sometimes knotty, more often relaxed and supple, expressive of many shades of feeling and attitude. The imagery spreads out in widening circles and eddies of evocation. The verse is immensely varied in its harmonies and dissonances, its lyric cadences. The style of *Coriolanus* is not less masterly, and no less subtly managed in the effects aimed at, but these are fewer, more concentrated, less ambiguous. The meaning is less often oblique. The images are harder of surface. The verse less often sings. Mars alone, not entangled with Venus, requires harsher music. It is difficult to open our hearts to a hero who works so hard not to be loved. Yet I think *Coriolanus* is not a lesser work of art than *Antony and Cleopatra*. It takes us boldly, by means of new riches of language, into an altogether different realm of experience—a less sympathetic realm, indeed, but one which it penetrates no less profoundly.

In the distinctive styles of these two late tragedies, Shakespeare was responding imaginatively to what might be called the genius of each story as it was recounted in Plutarch. For *Antony and Cleopatra*, with the scene the stretch and ripeness of Rome on the verge of becoming an empire, and with the action Antony's loss of that world for the love of the most fascinating and enigmatic woman in it, hyperbole is the natural trope and figure of thought. We might think it would be so for the following tragedy as well, dominated as it is by a single heroic figure, one famous for his military deeds and one charged by both his friends and his enemies with overweening pride. And certainly hyperbole does play an important part in *Coriolanus*. It is used, however, in a narrower, more sharply focussed way than in *Antony and Cleopatra*, and in a very special way in connection with its opposite figure of extenuation. The combination functions as an adjunct to the dominant figures of opposition or contrariety, and will be discussed together with them. In the earlier play, hyperbole is the lan-

guage of a wonderful spendthrift impudence and freedom—
the language of largesse, not of inflation. It is applied to life,
not death—not truly to death, for in death the two lovers will
"make the ghosts gaze." But of Coriolanus it is said: "Death,
that dark spirit, in 's nervy arm doth lie,/ Which, being advanc'd, declines, and then men die." In his play, hyperbole is
largely restricted to the hero himself, in his own asseverations
or in what is said of him by others. The constant theme of it is
his excellence in physical courage and in dealing death: "His
sword, death's stamp,/ Where it did mark, it took"; he "struck/
Corioles like a planet. Now all's his." The counter-theme of it
is his egotistical pride: "Such a nature/ . . . disdains the
shadow/ Which he treads on at noon"; "City,/ 'Tis I that made
thy widows."

For the tragedy of the Roman patriot who was banished as
a traitor by the Romans he had saved and who then, by joining
their enemies, became one in fact, and who for sparing Rome
when he had the city at his mercy broke faith with his enemies,
the obvious figures are those of contrariety and contradiction:
antithesis, paradox, and dilemma.[1] These figures, and others
associated with them, do indeed seem to me to be the dominant ones in the play. Opposition is constantly present in the
thought and in the language; at key points or at moments of
heightening, it is sharpened in formal features of diction and
schematic syntax.

Before we come to the analysis of thought and style in detail, with attention to some of the most crucial passages, it will
be useful to review the structure of the plot. It is built upon a
scheme of conflicts. The external conflict, the framework of the
action, is the military struggle between the Romans and the
Volscians. Much of the first act is given over to the defeat of
the Volscians and to Caius Martius' part in the victory by the
taking of Corioli; for this part he is awarded his honorific name
of Coriolanus. After the turning point of the play in the third
act, Coriolanus in the fourth defects to the Volscians. In the
fifth act, the initial situation is reversed, with Rome at the
mercy of its former hero, now at the head of a Volscian army.

Coriolanus' decision to withdraw leads to his death and to an uneasy peace between the erstwhile enemies.

This large conflict is sharpened in focus and heightened in interest by being narrowed to a personal antagonism between Caius Martius and Tullus Aufidius, the respective heroes of the two peoples. Aufidius, mentioned in Plutarch only after Martius seeks asylum in Antium, is introduced by Shakespeare early, before the battle for Corioli; during it he fights hand to hand with Martius and after the fall of the city he is shown vowing relentless hate to the Roman hero. In this way he becomes the formal antagonist of the tragedy. Although, for his own interest, he befriends Coriolanus briefly during the latter's exile, he returns after the truce with Rome to his old envious hatred and schemes successfully for the assassination of his former enemy. Shakespeare also puts Aufidius to choric use by giving him an objective analysis of the character of the hero.

Internal conflict in Rome, social and political, between the patricians and the plebeians, is introduced at the outset, in the very first scene, and provides the action and the complication in the second and third acts leading up to the climactic point of Coriolanus' banishment from the city. This conflict—first in the matter of the dearth of corn, then in the matter of Coriolanus' suit for the consulship—is, like the external conflict, narrowed and sharpened in the antagonism between particular characters: for the patricians, Coriolanus—wrathful, overweening, and intransigent; for the plebeians, the tribunes Brutus and Sicinius—self-seeking, dishonest, scheming. All attempts at moderation on the part of Cominius, Menenius, and Volumnia, through appeals to both parties, fail, as they are bound to. After the climax, the political conflict between the patricians and the people lingers in the fourth and fifth acts as mutual distrust and paralysis in the face of the new Volscian invasion, and is ended, formally at least, only with the news that Rome is to be spared after all.

The expected conflict in a tragedy, that within the hero, is in this one less a sustained inner questioning of motives or standards than a brief resistance or a reluctant yielding to pressure. And indeed the resistance seems to come more from the hero's inability to imagine another position than from an inner conflict between equally unpalatable alternatives. This inflexibility is phrased in Aufidius' suggestion that Coriolanus' nature is "not to be other than one thing," "not moving from th' casque to th' cushion." The yielding is owing not to a rational choice between two evils, but to an inability to withstand pressure from his mother. The deeper, subtler conflict, unrecognized for what it is by Coriolanus himself, is between the two sides of his own pride—the driving ambition to win honor and the rude unsociability which loses him the fruits of it.[2]

Coriolanus faces two points of stress. The first is in the obligation put upon him to sue for the consulship; the second, in the appeal of his mother that he spare Rome. Both choices present themselves to him in the form of dilemmas of action. In both crises his integrity is at issue. The consequences of his "choices" (if they are, properly, choices)—in each case one horn of the dilemma—put him in paradoxically ironic situations, that is, in the loss of the very integrity he so much prizes. The first time, at his banishment on the false charge of being a traitor to Rome, he puts himself in the position of becoming one; the second time, in sparing Rome and making the humane and generous choice, he becomes a breaker of faith to the Volscians. At this point, to right one betrayal he can only commit another. A right choice is a wrong choice. Of such paradoxes may great tragedy be made.

The movement of the action is accompanied by a theatrical device that makes contentiousness part of our physical sensations, and that is a direct assault on our ears with noise, the noise of beating drums, blaring trumpets and horns, shouting voices. In the martial music of a victory celebration the noise may symbolize a temporary, limited, and imperfect social harmony; in the discordant shouts of the mob for blood, whether Roman or Volscian, it clearly symbolizes social disorder. At the sound of the trumpets announcing Martius' arrival in Rome after the victory at Corioli, Shakespeare puts into Volumnia's mouth a bold image: "Before him he carries noise, and behind him he leaves tears" (II. i. 158-59). In the many scenes devoted to the matter of the consulship in the second and third acts, the "voices" of the people, which at first mean only "votes" (the word is North's),[3] given hesitantly but generously, take on, with Coriolanus' increasingly sarcastic iteration of "voices" and the tribunes' engineered reversal of popular sentiment, the sense of noise. The people's altered vote is now given in the terrible cry, "To th' rock, to th' rock with him!" (III. iii. 75), and after the sentence of banishment, in their joyful shout, "Our enemy is banish'd, he is gone! Hoo! hoo!" (III. iii. 137).

There is a temporary lull during Coriolanus' absence in Actium, but the news of his and Aufidius' advance on Rome brings back the "voices" and the sounds. Menenius and Cominius charge that the people have hooted him out of the city and will roar him in again (IV. vi. 121-24). The double sense of "voices" returns and is made explicit in the bitter reproaches of Cominius and Menenius to the citizens: "Y' are goodly things, you voices!" "You have made/ Good work, you and your cry!" (IV. vi. 146-47). With the good news in Rome that Coriolanus has yielded to the pleas of the women and withdrawn from the gates, the martial music of victory sounds again, but with no Coriolanus to follow it:

> The trumpets, sackbuts, psalteries, and fifes,
> Tabors and cymbals, and the shouting Romans,
> Make the sun dance.
>
> (V. iv. 49-51)

They cannot "unshout the noise that banish'd Martius" (V. v. 4). Coriolanus himself, on the other hand, in a strangely ominous echo of his former entry into Rome after Corioli, is being welcomed in the Volscians' city with the sound of drums and trumpets and "great shouts of the people," "splitting the air with noise" (V. vi. 49-51), an ironic prefiguring of the final dreadful uproar in the cries of the people and of the conspirators as they kill him.

So much for a general view of the structure of the play and of the stage effects which re-enforce it.

What we are especially concerned with are the ways in

which Shakespeare uses the language of contention to give life to his contentious plot. The principal rhetorical figures of opposition are antithesis, synoeciosis, paradox, and dialysis (the figure for a dilemma). *Antithesis* (in Latin *contra positum* or *contentio;* Puttenham's "Quarreller") is the direct opposition of contraries (peace:war) in words or sentences, sometimes with two terms cross-paired: "In pace bellum quaeritas, in bello pacem desideras" ("In peace you seek war; in war you long for peace"); "Inimicis te placabilem, amicis inexorabilem" ("To enemies you are conciliatory, to friends inexorable").[4] *Synoeciosis* (Puttenham's "Crosse-couple") is the composition of contraries in the form of an oxymoron (warring peace, peaceful war) or in a more extended form: "Seeking honor by dishonoring and building safety upon ruin."[5] *Paradox* (Puttenham's "Wonderer") is logically a statement which is self-contradictory, or apparently so, but it was generally used more loosely of a surprising conjunction of opposites. "For what the waves could never wash away,/ This proper youth has wasted in a day" is Puttenham's version of Cato's observation on the young unthrift who had sold his patrimony of salt marshes on the Capuan shore.[6] Or the word might be used of some incredible attitude or event, contrary to common sense. In these looser senses there is sometimes an element of paradox in interwoven antitheses or in the composition of contraries. *Dilemma* (*duplex conclusio*) is strictly a form of argument in which one is refuted whichever alternative one chooses:

> Now gentill Sirs let this young maide alone,
> For either she hath grace or els she hath none:
> If she have grace, she may in time repent,
> If she have none what bootes her punishment?[7]

But, more loosely, dilemma is an argument in which one is presented with alternative courses of action of which one must be accepted, but of which neither is acceptable. A word may be added about *irony*. Although it is in itself a trope or figure of contrariety, in which the intended meaning of the word or statement is the opposite of the literal meaning, some degree

of irony in attitude or circumstance may be felt in any of the
other figures of opposition.

A steady use of the formal schemes of contrariety and contradiction, strictly framed, would make for a style too stiff to
tolerate for very long; it would not enliven the action but kill
it. For these figures invite balance of members, parallel grammatical structure or parison, and various forms of repetition
and alliteration, in short, the Gorgianic figures, of which Lyly
was a master. In *Coriolanus* Shakespeare eschews such stul-
tifying formality. The whole tissue of *Coriolanus* is antithetical,
yet the contraries are managed with such variety and freedom
that they never freeze or grow stale. In the interests of naturalness and energy a great deal of the normally contentious
dialogue is not in the form of precise antithetical figures. At a
key moment, however, a terse antithesis points up opposing
attitudes or crystallizes the issues in conflict: "If any think
brave death outweighs bad life . . ."; "With a proud heart he
wore his humble weeds"; "My birthplace hate I, and my love's
upon/ This enemy town." Such pointed antitheses serve for
heightened emphasis on the action.

Even in those more formal speeches which are built on antithetical argument the schemes are rarely carried out at length
in perfectly balanced syntax.[8] These speeches are few and they
are of two sorts. They are the public ones which serve as orations (i.e., Coriolanus' argument to the senators, during the
turmoil over the consulship, against the tribunicial powers, and
Volumnia's appeals to her son to spare Rome). And they are
the speeches of analysis or direction-giving (i.e., Coriolanus'
taking stock, in soliloquy, of his situation before presenting
himself to his enemy, Aufidius, and Aufidius' detached analysis, after that event, of Coriolanus' strengths and weaknesses).
The most consistently balanced of these four is the soliloquy,
and it is also the most static; the analysis by Aufidius is less
balanced and somewhat less static, but neither one of these
speeches (to be returned to later) is required to be dynamic,
as are the two orations. In both of the latter the central issue
is at some point formulated in a precise antithesis or dilemma,
and is more than once rephrased, but perfect syntactical bal-

ance is not sustained throughout the argument and the alliteration of contrary terms, used sparingly, is not allowed to become tedious to the ear. The effect is to keep the antithetical structure firm beneath, but the surface in lively motion.

We shall look at Volumnia's speeches to Coriolanus at the proper time. But we may illustrate the point from Coriolanus' impassioned argument to the senators that they should abolish the newly created office of tribune. The kernel of the argument is caught in a series of antithetically phrased alternatives:

> If he [Sicinius] have power,
> Then vail your ignorance; if none, awake
> Your dangerous lenity. If you are learn'd,
> Be not as common fools; if you are not,
> Let them [the tribunes] have cushions by you. You are
> plebeians,
> If they be senators; and they are no less,
> When, both your voices blended, the great'st taste
> Most palates theirs.
>
> (III. i. 97-104)

The argument, opening in the form of two hypothetical dilemmas and densely phrased, is that the senators' folly in allowing the election of tribunes as representatives of the people will lead to the loss of their own power—a paradoxical consequence, since they will have changed places with the tribunes. Coriolanus continues at length, recurring in varying forms to the antipathies on which his argument is based, to develop the theme that this division of power, in effect a surrender, will mean putting the ultimate power into the hands of the people, the many-headed monster, Hydra, and that such an event will destroy the integrity of the state and end in the ruin of Rome.

In the passage quoted notice that the antithetical pairs (after the first one) are kept from perfect matching by the uneven members, by a shift of metaphor (from "vail" to "awake," from "voices" to "palates"), and by a shift of construction from an unmetaphoric comparison ("Be not as common fools") to a metaphoric action ("Let them have cushions by you"). In his antithetical figures, wherever they occur, Shakespeare uses subtle ways to tease us by substituting for the expected opposite term one in a different form, such as a metonymy of the adjunct, or a sign, for a simple epithet: call "him vile, that was your garland"; or such as a particular term for a general one in a form of synecdoche: "Before him he carries noise, and behind him he leaves tears." Or he may not use literal opposites in the balancing pairs of a chiasmus: "O, he's a limb that has but a disease:/ Mortal, to cut it off; to cure it, easy." The effect of these evasions of perfect symmetry is to keep the style always dynamic, rarely static. Another effect is the enlargement of our perceptions. There are no closed doors; one is always opening into another room.

There are also other modes of expressing contrariety which are not antithetical figures in the strict sense (that is, opposites of the same class), but which nevertheless imply some form of adversative relationship. Cicero treats these in his *Topics* under the topic of contraries. One form of contrary is comparison, such as double and single, many and few, greater and less, better and worse.[9] These are also, of course, relative terms. Comparisons of this kind, both quantitative and qualitative, are to be found everywhere in *Coriolanus*. Here are some examples: "Now put your shields before your hearts, and fight/ With hearts more proof than shields" (I. iv. 24-25), a comparison of quality intensified by the chiasmus and the syllepsis of the sense in "proof." Martius "is himself alone,/ To answer all the city" (I. iv. 51-52); the quantitative comparison is heightened by being not relative, few against many, but absolute, one against all.[10] Titus Lartius praises Martius in a comparison of greater and less, in which the less is made the greater: "A carbuncle entire, as big as thou art,/ Were not so rich a jewel" (I. iv. 55-56). Coriolanus vows revenge on Rome "as spacious as between/ The young'st and oldest thing" (IV. vi. 68-69), a quantitative comparison in relative terms. Coriolanus speaks of his mother bowing to him, "as if Olympus to a molehill should/ In supplication nod" (V. iii. 30-31); the comparison is both qualitative and quantitative, since better and worse as well as greater and less are implied. Comparison is one of Quintilian's recommended means of amplification,[11] and in the examples quoted Shakespeare has achieved this intensifying by the comparison of things at opposite ends of a scale.

The theme to which this form of amplifying is most commonly applied is the distance, and the antipathy, between the hero and the people. The comparisons are exaggerated in both directions—in augmenting, on the one hand, and in diminishing, on the other.[12] For example, after Coriolanus has been banished, Volumnia turns on the tribunes: "As far as doth the Capitol exceed/ The meanest house in Rome, so far my son/ . . . does exceed you all" (IV. ii. 39-42). The effect of such a comparison is to emphasize extremes of difference, and hence to intensify the sense of unbridgeable gaps in attitude. One frequent form of meiosis (what Puttenham calls "the Disabler")[13] is in the debasing metaphoric comparisons of the common people to despised animals—sheep, mice, rats, geese, mules—metaphors effective in the implication that the people are hardly men at all: "You souls of geese,/ That bear the shapes of men . . ." (I. iv. 34-35).[14] In such metaphors, based on the natural antipathies between certain animals, the patricians are of course the superior kind. Coriolanus charges that the senators, in giving the people power through their tribunes, "bring in/ The crows to peck the eagles" (III. i. 138-39). Coriolanus is the eagle that flutters the Volscians in their dove-cote (V. vi. 114-15). Aufidius thinks that Coriolanus will be to Rome, "as is the osprey to the fish, who takes it/ By sovereignty of nature" (IV. vii. 34-35).

In the analysis which follows I propose to point out how certain themes and opposing attitudes which are persistent throughout the play are established by various stylistic forms of contrariety and contradiction; next, to assess the effect of hyperbole and meiosis in the scenes celebrating Martius' victory over Corioli; and then to look more closely at the two points of crisis: the events and speeches just preceding the banishment and those leading to the catastrophe.

As in beginning a braid, three strands are separated and laid out in the first three scenes of the play: the first or left-hand strand, the conflict between the plebeians and the patricians; the middle strand, the war with the Volscians; the right-hand strand, the influence on Coriolanus of his mother. In each of these sections of exposition and introduction, contraries in attitude or value are expressed in formal ways which will reappear later.

To take the middle strand first, the war and the antagonism between Aufidius and Coriolanus. When Martius is told that the Volscians are in arms, he replies:

> They have a leader,
> Tullus Aufidius, that will put you to't.
> I sin in envying his nobility;
> And were I any thing but what I am,
> I would wish me only he.
>
> .   .   .   .   .
>
> He is a lion
> That I am proud to hunt.
>
> (I. i. 228-36)

Aufidius, on his side, when told that Martius, his old hated enemy, will be one of the leaders, promises

> If we and Caius Martius chance to meet,
> 'Tis sworn between us we shall ever strike
> Till one can do no more.
>
> (I. ii. 34-36)

There are no figures of antithesis here. None is needed, because the opponents share the same attitude. The repeated reminders which run up to the climax of the play, of the personal enmity between the two, are focussed on the hoped-for clash of equals: "beard to beard," "true sword to sword." At a meeting during the street-fighting in Corioli, Martius says, "I'll fight with none but thee, for I do hate thee/ Worse than a promise-breaker," and Aufidius replies, "We hate alike:/ Not Afric owns a serpent I abhor/ More than thy fame and envy" (I. viii. 1-4). When Coriolanus goes over to the Volscians, there is a temporary reversal, on Aufidius' part, from hatred to affection, and not long afterwards a return to hatred, but with a difference. Finally, Coriolanus becomes to Aufidius a "boy of

tears," the opposite of all that is manly. These new complexi-
ties, ending the old simple relationship of equality between
admiring, if hating, adversaries, invite antithetical figures. We
shall look at these at the proper time.

Now for the first strand in the braid, the strand with which
the play opens. The citizens, "resolv'd rather to die than to
famish," voice their angry complaint against the patricians in
simple antithetical form: "The leanness that afflicts us, the
object of our misery, is as an inventory to particularize their
abundance; our sufferance is a gain to them. Let us revenge
this with our pikes, ere we become rakes; for the gods know
I speak this in hunger for bread, not in thirst for revenge."
The First Citizen has already picked up the Second Citizen's
"One word, good citizens" with sarcastic emphasis: "We are
accounted poor citizens, the patricians good." With the implied
double sense of "poor," he has given a double focus to the
antithesis, "poor" and "good" as well as "poor" and "rich."
Martius, when he enters (at l. 164), sustains by his arrogance
and by his debasing metaphors the citizen's way of phrasing
the antithesis, but without irony:

> What would you have, you curs,
> That like nor peace nor war? The one affrights you,
> The other makes you proud. He that trusts to you,
> Where he should find you lions, finds you hares;
> Where foxes, geese.

Before commenting more particularly on the antitheses in
the speech, I want to point out the form of arrogant meiosis
I have already mentioned as a way to emphasize the distance
between himself and the people. To Martius the people are
always "rats," "curs," barbarians only littered in Rome, "calved
i' th' porch o' th' Capitol," "measles." And although he makes
a point of belittling his own achievements, the tribunes say
of him later in this scene that "being mov'd, he will not spare
to gird the gods" and "bemock the modest moon" (ll. 256-57).
In any case, the implied conceit in his tone here is enough to
mark the complete disjunction he feels from the people. As one
of the officers of the Senate is later to remark, "he seeks their
hate with greater devotion than they can render it him, and

leaves nothing undone that may fully discover him their opposite" (II. ii. 18-20). The tribunes are to see in his "soaring
insolence" an opportunity to stir up the people against him:

> We must suggest the people . . .
>   that to 's power he would
> Have made them mules, silenc'd their pleaders; and
> Dispropertied their freedoms, holding them,
> In human action and capacity,
> Of no more soul nor fitness for the world
> Than camels in their war, who have their provand
> Only for bearing burthens, and sore blows
> For sinking under them.
>   (II. i. 245-53)

To return to the antitheses in Coriolanus' speech to the citizens:

>   What would you have, you curs,
> That like nor peace nor war? The one affrights you,
> The other makes you proud. He that trusts to you,
> Where he should find you lions, finds you hares;
> Where foxes, geese.

The attitudes and behavior of the people, both in their lack of
judgment and in their inconstancy, are sufficient reason to
Martius to prove them unfit to have any voice in the government. Their behavior is directly contrary to what it ought to
be; therefore it is seen not only as perversity, but also as behavior improper to soldiers and citizens. And he expresses the
unfitness in various antithetical ways:

>   You are no surer, no,
> Than is the coal of fire upon the ice,
> Or hailstone in the sun. Your virtue is
> To make him worthy whose offence subdues him,
> And curse that justice did it. Who deserves greatness
> Deserves your hate; . . .
>   Hang ye! Trust ye?
> With every minute you do change a mind,
> And call him noble that was now your hate;
> Him vile that was your garland.
>   (I. i. 172-84)

These are their perversities in peace. The idea of their unfitness in war he particularizes in the first of the battle scenes,
when he curses the soldiers for running away:

> You souls of geese,
> That bear the shapes of men, how have you run
> From slaves that apes would beat! Pluto and hell!
> All hurt behind! backs red, and faces pale
> With flight and agued fear!
>   (I. iv. 34-38)

The transposed epithets in the penultimate line emphasize the
impropriety of the people's behavior as soldiers; it is the faces
which should be red with blood.

Menenius, at the close of the fable of the belly, his political
moral delivered in the opening scene to the discontented people, sees another kind of impropriety in their behavior:

> What do you think,
> You, the great toe of this assembly?
> [*1.*] *Cit.*   I the great toe? Why the great toe?
> *Men.*   For that, being one o' th' lowest, basest, poorest
> Of this most wise rebellion, thou goest foremost;
> Thou rascal, that art worst in blood to run,
> Lead'st first to win some vantage.
>   (I. i. 154-60)

The impropriety Menenius sees is in the citizen's assumed position at the opposite extreme from his capabilities. The difference in tone, rough but humorous, appears not to give
offense in the way Martius' insults do, and Menenius begins
here the rôle he plays throughout, along with Cominius, as
the voice of moderation, reason, and accommodation.

The tribunes, who, though their representatives, think no
better of the people's capabilities than Menenius does, are soon
to be subject to charges of impropriety in their own actions—
much graver charges, because they have power and responsibility. Menenius, in a humorous, but sarcastic, portrait of them
(II. i. 67 ff.), says that when they are called to decide any
controversy between citizens they make it worse: "All the
peace you make in their cause is calling both the parties
knaves." Later, in the crisis over the consulship, he brings a

more serious charge against them. After they have succeeded
in stirring up the citizens to rescind their favorable vote for
Coriolanus as consul, have pronounced him traitor, and have
started a riot, Menenius, appealing for more considered action,
protests the shocking impropriety of their conduct in two situations he sees as paradoxical. The first:

> Now the gods forbid
> That our renowned Rome, whose gratitude
> Towards her deserved children is enroll'd
> In Jove's own book, like an unnatural dam
> Should now eat up her own!
>   (III. i. 288-92)

The second:

> What has he done to Rome that's worthy death?
> Killing our enemies, the blood he hath lost . . .
>   he dropp'd it for his country;
> And what is left, to lose it by his country
> Were to us all that do't and suffer it
> A brand to th' end o' th' world.
>   (ll. 296-302)

He urges them to

>   Proceed by process,
> Lest parties (as he is belov'd) break out,
> And sack great Rome with Romans
>   (ll. 312-14)

—the unthinkable paradox.

The impropriety in behavior that Coriolanus himself is principally subject to is that charged by the tribune Brutus, justly
enough:

>   You speak o' th' people
> As if you were a god, to punish; not
> A man of their infirmity.
>   (III. i. 80-82)

This is a later statement, but it echoes their comments in this
first scene on his insolent pride: "Being mov'd, he will not
spare to gird the gods" and "bemock the modest moon."

The bone of contention in this scene between Martius and the citizens is the distribution of corn. We are prepared by the language of this first skirmish for a more critical confrontation yet to come.

We are slow in coming to the third scene and third strand in the braid, the introduction to the family of Coriolanus—his mother, wife, and child—and, through their talk, to the upbringing he has had. By devices of comparison and antithesis we get a sense of something contrary to natural or expected emotions and values. The first thing we hear Volumnia say, after urging her daughter-in-law to be more cheerful during her husband's absence in war, is this:

> If my son were my husband, I should freelier rejoice in that absence wherein he won honor than in the embracements of his bed where he would show most love.[15]

Volumnia augments the value of one thing by comparing it with something else of great value, but contrary to it; the contraries are clearly understood—absence in the field and presence in bed. The perfectly balanced phrasing, moreover, makes us take the honor and the love as contraries as well. Another preference Volumnia expresses takes the form of a comparison of the many and the few in an antithetical relation: "Had I a dozen sons, each in my love alike, . . . I had rather had eleven die nobly for their country than one voluptuously surfeit out of action." Still another comparison is given as a rebuke to Virgilia, who protests against Volumnia's gory vision of Martius going forth to slaughter—"His bloody brow? O Jupiter, no blood!" "Away, you fool!" replies Volumnia:

> it more becomes a man
> Than gilt his trophy. The breasts of Hecuba,
> When she did suckle Hector, look'd not lovelier
> Than Hector's forehead when it spit forth blood
> At Grecian sword, contemning.

Although there is no precise antithesis here, we accept the signs (the suckling breasts, the bloody forehead) as signifying contrary values and are jolted by the perversity of the prefer-

ence. We also hear from Volumnia that the little son of Coriolanus prefers swords and drum to his schoolmaster and from a
lady caller who has just come in the tale of his mammocking
the butterfly—"One on 's father's moods." During the whole
scene these opposing habits and views of life—the domestic
and the martial—are visibly represented in the figures of the
modest, quiet wife, Virgilia, and the aggressive mother, Volumnia.

Think for a moment of a later scene in which the two
women are side by side. You may remember in the noise of
Coriolanus' triumphal return from Corioli, the entry prefaced
by Volumnia's "Before him he carries noise, and behind him
he leaves tears," the moment of stillness in which Coriolanus
greets his wife:

> My gracious silence, hail!
> Wouldst thou have laugh'd had I come coffin'd home,
> That weep'st to see me triumph? Ah, my dear,
> Such eyes the widows in Corioles wear,
> And mothers that lack sons.
>   (II. i. 175-79)

A perfect antithesis. Another impropriety? It is phrased so;
but it is one sounding depths of unspoken irony. A moment
later, Menenius mediates between the weeping and the laugh-
ing by wanting to do both: "A hundred thousand welcomes! I
could weep,/ And I could laugh; I am light, and heavy." I
should call this a composition of contraries.

The play begins, then, by setting forth the relations between conflicting parties and the attitudes towards the issues
in various antithetical or related forms. In such stylistic ways
we are kept aware throughout the play of these hard lines of
opposition, these strained attitudes, these topsy-turvy impro-
prieties of behavior, actual or imagined, which have an almost
paradoxical quality about them. The style amplifies the sense
that the action gives us of a turbulent community, at odds
with itself.

Attempts at composition are to fail every time. Cominius
and Menenius try it by appealing to reason, common sense,

and the law rather than to violence. The people, showing good
will, move hesitantly towards it, but Martius and the tribunes,
each through his own kind of selfishness, will not allow it.

We come now to the epitasis, the increase in intensity, of
the action. Two scenes—of Martius' victory after Corioli and
of the formal honors done him in Rome—are crucial in prepar-
ing for the trouble to come and are a brilliant exercise in combined hyperbole and meiosis, of fulsome praise and surly
reticence.

In the impromptu celebration after the battle (I. ix), Cominius expresses directly to Martius ("his arm in a scarf") the
surprise and relief at the victory by making it seem incredible,
a paradox of wonder:

> If I should tell thee o'er this thy day's work,
> Thou't not believe thy deeds: but I'll report it
> Where senators shall mingle tears with smiles;
> Where great patricians shall attend and shrug,
> I' th' end admire; where ladies shall be frighted,
> And gladly quak'd, hear more; where the dull tribunes,
> That with the fusty plebeians hate thine honors,
> Shall say against their hearts, 'We thank the gods
> Our Rome hath such a soldier.'
>   (ll. 1-9)

This extended composition of contraries is both a way to amplify praise of Martius' victory and an attempt to associate all
of Roman society, even the grudging tribunes and plebeians,
in the general rejoicing. But Martius brushes aside the praise
by levelling the distinctions between himself and the others
who have fought:

> I have done
> As you have done—that's what I can; induc'd
> As you have been—that's for my country:
> He that has but effected his good will
> Hath overta'en my act.

It seems a modest speech. But his continued diminution of
his achievements—"I have some wounds upon me, and they
smart/ To hear themselves rememb'red"—and his ungracious

refusal of the gifts he is offered because he "cannot make [his] heart consent to take/ A bribe to pay [his] sword," suggest an inverted pride. Rewards seem to him cheapening. Then comes his outrageous outburst at the flourish of trumpets and the shouts of acclaim:

> May these same instruments, which you profane,
> Never sound more! When drums and trumpets shall
> I' th' field prove flatterers, let courts and cities be
> Made all of false-fac'd soothing!
> When steel grows soft as the parasite's silk,
> Let him be made a coverture[16] for the wars!
> No more, I say! For that I have not wash'd
> My nose that bled, or foil'd some debile wretch— . . .
> You shout me forth
> In acclamations hyperbolical,
> As if I lov'd my little should be dieted
> In praises sauc'd with lies.
>
> (ll. 41-53)

Martius presents in a paradox of incredible extremes what he regards as the improper use of the instruments of war, but does not see that his own behavior is grossly and insultingly improper. The hyperbole, not very great, has been the expression of honest enthusiasm and admiration, not flattery or falsehood. Cominius politely corrects his manners,

> Too modest are you;
> More cruel to your good report than grateful
> To us that give you truly,

before offering him the "war's garland," his own noble battle-horse, and the addition of "Coriolanus" to his name. Martius' disallowance of the common rejoicing and celebration of his honors opens the gulf Cominius had tried to close, and prepares us for events to come. The tribunes do not say, against their hearts, "We thank the gods our Rome hath such a soldier."

At the rejoicing in Rome these two stand apart (II. i. 205 ff.) describing the curious holiday crowd which has turned out for Martius' entry into the city, and predicting that Martius will soon give the fickle commoners cause, "upon their ancient malice," to forget his new honors. His "soaring insolence" will be the "fire to kindle their dry stubble."

In the following scene, at the Capitol (II. ii), in which Coriolanus' friends petition the Senate to grant him the honor of a consulship, Cominius has his chance to make a full ceremonial speech of praise (ll. 82-122). He recounts Martius' military exploits from the time when, at sixteen, he fought in his first battle until his taking of Corioli. The oration is built on the text that "valor is the chiefest virtue, and/ Most dignifies the haver," and on the hypothesis that if this opinion be true, then "the man I speak of cannot in the world/ Be singly counterpois'd." The praise of Martius' valor, episode by episode, is made in a series of implied comparisons which emphasize differences, all to Martius' credit: "with his Amazonian chin he drove/ The bristled lips before him"; "Tarquin's self he met,/ And struck him on his knee"; "when he might," because of his youth, "act the woman in the scene,/ He prov'd best man i' th' field"; he "stopp'd the fliers,/ And by his rare example made the coward/ Turn terror into sport." Beneath this sequence of comparisons, which, though amplifying, are not hyperbolic, lies a hyperbolic substratum of absoluteness, of one against all: he "cannot in the world be singly counterpois'd"; in seventeen battles "he lurch'd all swords of the garland"; "alone he enter'd" Corioli, "aidless came off," "now all's his."

Martius is not by to contradict this speech; he left before it began because he could not "idly sit/ To hear [his] nothings monster'd." He is called in at the close to receive the Senate's approval of his being made consul, and to be told he cannot avoid the custom of showing his wounds to the people to receive their approval. The tribunes are ready for the fire which will light the stubble.

In these two scenes, we have had a dramatic exhibition of Coriolanus' strength and weakness, his valor and his selfishness, set side by side in the hyperbole of honest and warm praise given him on the part of others and in the meiosis of self-belittling on his own part—suspect because it goes with an ungenerous rejection of what is generously offered. We have been given a glimpse into the nature of this tight, self-centered man, whose pride must be expressed in withdrawal, and we are prepared for the still more ungenerous rejection of the plebeians' good will in the ordeal which is to follow.

In the intensifying irritation between Coriolanus and the people that his standing for the consulship brings about, and in the eruption, through the agency of the tribunes, of open conflict between the nobles and the people which leads to the climax of the play, the style is rich with all the antithetical forms.

I shall comment only on the issue of Coriolanus' integrity, since his understanding of it is what poses the ruinous dilemma by which he is trapped. The question of his integrity arises when, in his suit for the consulship (II. iii. 60 ff.), he must wear the white gown, display his wounds, and act the humble part in asking the people for their "voices." As Sicinius, one of the tribunes, has predicted, he "will require them/ As if he did contemn what he requested" (II. ii. 156-57); and Menenius will tell us later that Coriolanus "would not flatter Neptune for his trident" (III. i. 255). Uneasy in his false part, he plays up the falsity in heavy sarcasm: "And since the wisdom of their choice [the people's] is rather to have my hat than my heart, I will practice the insinuating nod and be off to them [i.e., take his hat off] most counterfeitly" (II. iii. 98-100). Half way through the solicitation of votes he exclaims, "Rather than fool it so,/ Let the high office and the honor go/ To one that would do thus." Yet he sticks it out, with the note of insulting irony rising in his voice:

> Your voices![17] For your voices have I fought;
> Watch'd for your voices; for your voices bear
> Of wounds two dozen odd; . . .

and so on: "Your voices!/ Indeed I would be consul." The people, trying to do what is right, are more generous than he—"He has done nobly, and cannot go without any honest man's voice"—and they hesitantly give him their votes. He has no sooner left, however, than the tribunes go to work on the people for not perceiving "with what contempt he wore the humble weed" (l. 221). Sicinius rebukes them sharply for what he phrases as contrariness:

> Have you
> Ere now denied the asker? and now again,
> Of him that did not ask but mock, bestow
> Your su'd-for tongues?
>
> (ll. 205-8)

He and Brutus have no difficulty in persuading the people to revoke their assent. The scene ends with Sicinius' forehanded move:

> To th' Capitol, come.
> We will be there before the stream o' th' people;
> And this shall seem, as partly 'tis, their own,
> Which we have goaded onward.

A confrontation is not long in coming. Coriolanus' response to the tribunes' word that his petition has been denied after all is to address a long and angry speech to the senators urging the abolition of the office of tribune (III. i. 90 ff.). The paradoxical crux of this speech—"You are plebeians,/ If they be senators; and they are no less"—I have already quoted. Coriolanus' argument is,

> when two authorities are up,
> Neither supreme, how soon confusion
> May enter 'twixt the gap of both, and take
> The one by th' other.
>
> (ll. 109-12)

The effect of this double authority, in which the tribunes, because they have the backing of the ignorant many, have greater power, is to ruin the purpose of government, which is to serve the general good, wisely determined; for "gentry, title, wisdom"

> must omit
> Real necessities, and give way the while
> To unstable slightness. Purpose so barr'd, it follows
> Nothing is done to purpose.
>
> (ll. 146-49)

"The multitudinous tongue . . . lick/ The sweet which is their poison." The senators' dishonor

> Mangles true judgment, and bereaves the state
> Of that integrity which should becom't;
> Not having the power to do the good it would,
> For th' ill which doth control't.
>
> (ll. 158-61)

The frame of the whole speech is constructed on the contraries of nobles vs. people, wisdom vs. ignorance, purpose vs. whim, valor vs. cowardice, singleness vs. doubleness, integrity vs. multitudinousness. If Coriolanus does not help the inflammatory situation, neither do the tribunes. They take a way "to kindle, not to quench," a way which Cominius says

> is the way to lay the city flat,
> To bring the roof to the foundation,
> And bury all, which yet distinctly ranges,
> In heaps and piles of ruin.
>
> (ll. 203-6)

They pronounce a sentence of death on Coriolanus and order him cast from the Tarpeian Rock. Note that the image of bringing the roof to the foundation may be thought of as a contrary of position and function; the image of burying that which yet distinctly ranges in heaps and piles of ruin, a conversion of something into its opposite in the sense of changing its form into formlessness. To Menenius, "confusion's near." He finally wins for Coriolanus a chance to be questioned in a lawful form by frightening the tribunes with the danger of civil war, put in the form of the ironic paradox I have noted earlier: "Lest parties (as he is belov'd) break out/ And sack great Rome with Romans" (ll. 313-14).

Coriolanus, outraged by the people's reversal of their vote and by the summons to him, has to be prepared in the next scene (III. ii) for the questioning; he must be disciplined "to answer mildly." Puzzled at his mother's criticism of his behavior, he asks of her a crucial question:

Why did you wish me milder? Would you have me
False to my nature? Rather say, I play
The man I am.

(ll. 14-16)

The issue is his integrity. Volumnia replies, at first wisely
enough, "You might have been enough the man you are/
With striving less to be so." But her argument for him to
be less "absolute," that if "honor and policy, like unsever'd
friends,/ I' th' war do grow together," then why not in peace?
is put in terms which are abhorrent to him. She does not suggest that the policy he needs at this moment may be compat-
ible with a larger view of his honor, but treats it frankly as an
expedient lie:

it lies you on to speak
To th' people; not by your own instruction,
Nor by th' matter which your heart prompts you,
But with such words that are but roted[18] in
Your tongue, though but bastards, and syllables
Of no allowance, to your bosom's truth.
Now, this no more dishonors you at all
Than to take in a town with gentle words,
Which else would put you to your fortune and
The hazard of much blood,

with more in the same vein (ll. 52 ff.). Words and deeds, it
may be noted, are to Coriolanus normally antithetical in a different way: "When blows have made me stay, I fled from
words." She gives him elaborate instructions on how to act out
the lie, with his bonnet in his hand, his knee bussing the
stones, his waving head correcting his stout heart, "now humble as the ripest mulberry/ That will not hold the handling."
He is to say that he is their soldier, that he will frame himself
"hereafter theirs." She is proposing what will look like a composition of the contraries of head and heart, but what will in
fact be a concealment of the contrariness. It will be a fine act
of false-seeming.

Coriolanus' inner struggle between the repugnance he feels
for such a part and his disposition to do what his mother asks

of him is shown in a this-way that-way wavering between
assent and refusal: "Must I/ With my base tongue give to my
noble heart/ A lie that it must bear? Well, I will do't"; "Well,
I must do't"; "I will not do't"; "Pray be content." The speech
of refusal shows an acute perception of the moral consequences of acting a false part:

> I will not do't,
> Lest I surcease to honor mine own truth,
> And by my body's action teach my mind
> A most inherent baseness.
>
> (ll. 120-23)

The dilemma is clearly implied, though he nowhere phrases it
precisely: To win the consulship he must show humility and
be false to himself, or else be true to himself by refusing to
show humility and thereby lose the office. He yields, nevertheless, to his mother's final taunt:

> Do as thou list;
> Thy valiantness was mine, thou suck'st it from me;
> But owe thy pride thyself.
>
> (ll. 128-30)

To do Coriolanus credit, when he goes again to the market-
place (III. iii), he does try to be calm, even patient ("The
word is 'mildly'"), but, also to his credit, he tells no lies.
In a characteristic way of treating some of his flawed characters, Shakespeare takes the onus of failure from him by
putting it on the tribunes. They charge him with treason and
the fat is in the fire. His explosion brings the people's cry,
"To th' rock, to th' rock with him!" (l. 74). The tribunes pronounce the lesser sentence of banishment (ll. 93-105).

Coriolanus has not been able to be other than the man he is,
and we cannot blame him for not being. It is not his honesty
that is at fault, but his manner of exercising it. He does not
know that honesty need not be clothed in arrogant pride. The
problem with Coriolanus' integrity is that it is too narrowly
based, too rigid, without any play in it; therefore it is a trap
for him, not a power.

Shakespeare does not in *Coriolanus* use the word "integrity"
for moral soundness; the word for that is "honesty" or sometimes "honor." But he does use the word in its primary sense
of something's being complete, whole, undivided, when he
makes Coriolanus argue that the integrity of the Roman government will be lost if the senators divide their power with the
tribunes (III. i. 142-61). The interesting thing is that Coriolanus, in his philosophy of government, equates its integrity
with its literal "oneness" or singleness, with its not being divided. He does not entertain the idea that wholeness might be
achieved by co-operation of the social parts; to him the whole
must be single.

We might follow the idea of "oneness" or singleness as it is
implied of Coriolanus himself in another way; it has a bearing
on the man he is, the man whose nature is, as Aufidius tells us,
"not to be other than one thing." Aufidius intends this of his
inability to be anything other than a soldier, but this same
inflexibility also has a bearing on other things about him—on
his understanding and exercise of his moral integrity, and on
his unsociability. Another facet of his being one thing is to be
alone. "Alone," often used of him and by him, has more than
one implication. The sense of his being single and alone in his
great achievement at Corioli is a note that is sounded throughout the play. It is said in praise of him by his fellow officers—
"Know, Rome, that all alone Martius did fight/ Within Corioles
gates"; "Alone he enter'd/ The mortal gate of the city." And
it is said by himself more than once as a source of sustaining
pride—"Alone I fought in your Corioles walls"; "Alone I did it."
We are not allowed to miss in these "alone's" the implied adversative sense of one against all: "he is himself alone,/ To
answer all the city."

"Alone," however, apart from the bold, rash entry into the
enemy city, takes on a wider implication of singleness, that is,
of separation from society.[19] At the moment of Coriolanus'
farewell to his family and friends, the separateness is caught in
different moods in two great, haunting images, the one by
Coriolanus:

> I go alone,
> Like to a lonely dragon, that his fen
> Makes fear'd and talk'd of more than seen;
>
> (IV. i. 29-31)

the other by Cominius, asking Coriolanus to let them hear
from him in exile,

> so if the time thrust forth
> A cause for thy repeal, we shall not send
> O'er the vast world to seek a single man.
>
> (ll. 40-42)

Shakespeare marks the reversal in the action by giving
Coriolanus a soliloquy (IV. iv. 12-25) which seems less a
speech in character than a bridging one to prepare the audience for a radical change. The speech is phrased in a sustained, highly schematic, though not wholly symmetrical, antithesis. I shall not lay it out. When, disguised, Coriolanus is
about to present himself to Aufidius, for better or worse, he
reflects on the world's "slippery turns," which come about by
the merest chance—on friends fast sworn breaking out to bitterest enmity, and fellest foes growing dear friends—and applies the general situation to his own case: "So with me,/ My
birthplace hate I, and my love's upon/ This enemy town." This
cynical view of the reversals of fortune leads to his gambler's
decision to take a chance of asylum with Aufidius: "I'll enter.
If he slay me,/ He does fair justice; if he give me way,/ I'll do
his country service."

When in the next scene (IV. v) he is brought before Aufidius, these are precisely the alternatives he offers him. In effect
he says, "Help me to take my revenge on Rome and benefit
yourself, or cut my throat." But then he adds a consequence to
force the choice. If Aufidius does neither, he will be a fool,
letting his country's enemy live to shame him. Aufidius does
agree to join with Coriolanus against Rome, but for his own
unexpected reason. Moved at having in his hands his hated
and admired enemy, he shifts the old contest between them to
one of love:

> Let me twine
Mine arms about that body, . . .
>   Here I clip
The anvil of my sword, and do contest
As hotly and as nobly with thy love
As ever in ambitious strength I did
Contend against thy valor.
>   (ll. 106-13)

"Here I clip/ The anvil of my sword" is a bold and compressed synoeciosis, or composition of contraries. And in an intensifying hyperbole of comparison, Aufidius swears that he feels more joy in seeing Coriolanus, "thou noble thing," "than when I first my wedded mistress saw/ Bestride my threshold." But the composition that is made between the former enemies is marked with hints of its fragility: reminders on Coriolanus' part of how many tuns of blood he has drawn out of Volscian breasts, and on Aufidius' part a story of his nightly dreams of encounters with the Roman, when they have been down together, "unbuckling helms, fisting each other's throat."

On the comic level, the servants talk about which is better, peace or war. The definitive reason given as preference for war is the paradoxical one that peace makes men hate one another. We have been well prepared for more slippery turns in friendship and in war. The scenes which follow to the end act out the paradoxical turn of the soliloquy, but in reverse order: the "fellest foes" "grow dear friends and interjoin their issues," and these friends, "fast sworn," "break out to bitterest enmity."

When the strain in the new alliance between Aufidius and Coriolanus is beginning to be felt, Aufidius, in conversation with one of his officers, makes a shrewd analysis (IV. vii. 28-57) of what caused Coriolanus to be "fear'd,/ So hated, and so banish'd." He suggests three things: pride, defect of judgment, and nature—"Not to be other than one thing, not moving/ From th' casque to th' cushion, but commanding peace/ Even with the same austerity and garb/ As he controll'd the war," an emphasis on the "oneness" and the rigidity of Coriolanus. He makes no choice among these three possibilities, and sets against them a simple adversative: "but he has a merit/ To choke it in the utt'rance." This leads him into a general reflection in the form of a paradox:

> So our virtues
> Lie in th' interpretation of the time;
> And power, unto itself most commendable,
> Hath not a tomb so evident as a chair
> T' extol what it hath done.

I take the lines to mean that power (that is, as manifested in a person) has no place of burial so certain as the public rostrum in which it (or he) is praised.[20] This may be read as a reflection on the fickleness of public opinion, a theme of which Shakespeare is fond.[21] But "interpretation of the time" may suggest also, in a profounder sense, what changing occasion may favor or may not. Aufidius goes on to conclude, in a commonplace maxim, that "one fire drives out one fire; one nail, one nail," and he adds a rime to round out the couplet: "Rights by rights founder;[22] strengths by strengths do fail." The second line may be read as equivalent to the first, that is, the replacement of one person in power by another; or it may mean that rights and strengths have in themselves the seeds of their own failure. But in any case, the sense of the whole passage seems to be the paradox that to win is to lose.

> When, Caius, Rome is thine,
> Thou art poor'st of all; then shortly art thou mine.

We come now to the crisis which leads directly to the catastrophe. Coriolanus must face his second and final dilemma, in which Volumnia again is the poser, this time more explicitly. Coriolanus, at the head of the Volscian army, sits at the gates of Rome. He has repelled all embassies of appeal to him, the priests, the general Cominius, and his old friend Menenius. He has said to Menenius, in a shocking reversal of feelings, obligations, and values,

> Wife, mother, child, I know not. My affairs
> Are servanted to others; . . .

> That we have been familiar,
> Ingrate forgetfulness shall poison rather
> Than pity note how much.
>   (V. ii. 82-87)

When his wife, mother, and child appear as the next deputa-
tion (V. iii. 20 ff.), he "melts." "Great Nature" cries to him,
"Deny not!" and he must stiffen himself to "stand/ As if a man
were author of himself,/ And knew no other kin." ("Alone I
did it!" in a fearful change of key.) When, at his kneeling to
her (l. 50), his mother makes him get up while she goes down
on the flint, he expresses the appalling impropriety of this reversed relation in one of the great figures of extremes, both of
things and of distances:

> What's this?
> Your knees to me? to your corrected son?
> Then let the pebbles on the hungry beach
> Fillip the stars; then let the mutinous winds
> Strike the proud cedars 'gainst the fiery sun,
> Murd'ring impossibility, to make
> What cannot be, slight work.

He sees the world itself in a vast, paradoxical upheaval, turning all things topsy-turvy, and making the impossible possible.
Although Coriolanus tries to prevent the women's petition and
so to end the intolerable situation, Volumnia of course persists.

She prefaces her formal argument with a statement, phrased
in balanced antitheses, which puts the onus of a dreadful
impropriety on Coriolanus himself:

> Think with thyself
> How more unfortunate than all living women
> Are we come hither; since that thy sight, which should
> Make our eyes flow with joy, hearts dance with comforts,
> Constrains them weep and shake with fear and sorrow,
> Making the mother, wife, and child to see
> The son, the husband, and the father tearing
> His country's bowels out.

She then presents Coriolanus with a series of dilemmas. Two
are introductory to the principal one. The first is the one his

action has placed the women of his family in if they try to
pray to the gods. These elegant lines are for the ear—in the
isocolon (equal numbers of syllables) in each of the two
phrasings of the dilemma, yet the slight departures from structural balance; in the iteration, the repetition of word and
phrase, the chiming endings of "country," "victory," and "ca-
lamity."

> For how can we,
> Alas! how can we, for our country pray,
> Whereto we are bound, together with thy victory,
> Whereto we are bound? Alack, or we must lose
> The country, our dear nurse, or else thy person,
> Our comfort in the country. We must find
> An evident calamity, though we had
> Our wish which side should win.

Either way they must lose. Now follows a second dilemma; or
perhaps it may be seen as the same one put from the point of
view of the consequences to himself of his choice of action.
Either he must be led as "a foreign recreant" through the
streets or he must "triumphantly tread on" his country's ruin,
bearing the palm for having shed his wife's and children's
blood. This one is phrased, for variety and movement, with
less parison and repetition, but it is still a dilemma. She promises him that as for herself, no sooner shall he march to assault
his country than he will tread on his mother's womb. But she
sees a way out of these unthinkable alternatives.

The third dilemma, the crucial one he faces, she states only
hypothetically, for she does not recognize it as a real one.

> If it were so that our request did tend
> To save the Romans, thereby to destroy
> The Volsces whom you serve, you might condemn us
> As poisonous of your honor. No, our suit
> Is that you reconcile them: while the Volsces
> May say, 'This mercy we have show'd', the Romans,
> 'This we receiv'd'; and each in either side
> Give the all-hail to thee and cry, 'Be blest
> For making up this peace!'

Notice the phrasing: antithetical in the hypothetical dilemma; perfectly balancing in the reconcilement, and repetitive except for the complementary action of "show'd" and "receiv'd"; all differences composed in "each in either side . . ." Beautiful rhetoric! But it has little to do with the realities of the situation. We know what she does not, that Aufidius is lurking in the wings.

Volumnia is not through, however. She turns again to the frightening prospect of what will happen if he does not take her way out. If he conquers Rome, his name will be cursed. Victory will mean dishonor. The truth is, Coriolanus faces dishonor either way. She makes an appeal to true honor: "Think'st thou it honorable for a noble man/ Still to remember wrongs?" But when he persists in silence and turns away, she goes down on her knees again (l. 171), taking the other women and the child with her:

> let us shame him with our knees.
> To his surname Coriolanus 'longs more pride
> Than pity to our prayers.

The final taunt, that "this fellow had a Volscian to his mother," is a way to emphasize his unnatural behavior. Coriolanus, the Folio stage direction reads, "holds her by the hand, silent." When he speaks, it is with pitiable realization of his helplessness in an intolerable situation:

> O mother, mother!
> What have you done? Behold, the heavens do ope,
> The gods look down, and this unnatural scene
> They laugh at. O my mother, mother! O!
> You have won a happy victory to Rome;
> But, for your son, believe it—O, believe it—
> Most dangerously with him you have prevail'd,
> If not most mortal to him. But let it come.
>   (ll. 182-89)

He was the rock, the oak not to be wind-shaken; the one who would stand as if a man were author of himself and knew no other kin. The ground is gone from under him. What is left of

Coriolanus, the man himself? The right yielding and the wrong
yielding are one.

How complete is his flash of recognition intended to be? We
lose the full poignancy of it if we argue it away because it
seems to lapse in the last surprised speeches before his death.
The slight changes in the phrasing of the four lines from
North's Plutarch are significant: "Oh mother, sayed he, you
have wonne a happy victorie for your countrie, but mortall and
unhappy for your sonne: for I see myself vanquished by you
alone."[23] It is true that Shakespeare's Martius discriminates
between certain danger and hypothetical death. But omitting
the acknowledgment of his mother's victory and replacing it
with a different conclusion changes the emphasis of the source
somewhat. The finality of "Let it come" can only mean, it
seems to me, that the hero is meant to foresee his end. Shakespeare may be doing what he not infrequently does, that is,
sacrifice perfect consistency to other strong effects which seem
more important. And the effect in the death scene is strong
indeed.

Aufidius, who has stood by watching Coriolanus give way,
reminds us in an aside that he has not escaped the dilemma:

> I am glad thou hast set thy mercy and thy honor
> At difference in thee. Out of that I'll work
> Myself a former fortune.
>
> (ll. 200-202)

Ironically, Volumnia had just told her son that his honor was
not honor unless it was joined with mercy. "Rights by rights
founder; strengths by strengths do fail."

In an antithetic and ironic parallel to his entry into Rome
after the victory over the Volscians, Coriolanus enters their
city—without a victory over the Romans, but to the sound of
drums and the joyous shouts of the people in a celebration of
the peace. The parallel continues, but in compressed time.
Harmony quickly changes to discord, as it did in Rome. He is
plotted against by a malicious enemy; he is charged with treason, this time with cause; he stands at bay, enraged; he is
brought down, this time in death.

Let us go back. After the formal entry into the city, Coriolanus announces to the lords of Corioli that he has made peace
(V. vi. 78-83). But before he can read the treaty to them,
Aufidius stands up and denounces him as a traitor. In a few
swift lines Aufidius strips him of all the things which had
made him himself: his name—

> Ay, Martius, Caius Martius! Dost thou think
> I'll grace thee with that robbery, thy stol'n name
> Coriolanus, in Corioles?

his honor—

> You lords and heads o' th' state, perfidiously
> He has betray'd your business, and given up,
> For certain drops of salt, your city Rome,
> I say 'your city', to his wife and mother,
> Breaking his oath and resolution like
> A twist of rotten silk, . . .

his manhood—

>   at his nurse's tears
> He whin'd and roar'd away your victory.

Most intolerably of all, Aufidius calls this devotee of Mars
"thou boy of tears!" Coriolanus' last defiant words fall back to
his center, his pride, and its sustaining memory:

> Cut me to pieces, Volsces, men and lads,
> Stain all your edges on me. 'Boy', false hound!
> If you have writ your annals true, 'tis there
> That, like an eagle in a dove-cote, I
> Flutter'd your Volscians in Corioles.
> Alone I did it. 'Boy'!

"Alone I did it" is a resonant echo.

In the final lines we are to catch another echo. A recurrent
image has been that of hardness—of steel, rock, oak; another
has been the complementary one of fracture—of being cast
down from "the steep Tarpeian death," of Rome cleaving in
the midst, of an ashen staff breaking against Coriolanus' body
and scarring the moon with splinters. These images of hard-

ness and fracture taken together imply opposing forces. They are kinetic, augmenting character and story in a feeling or sensing way, a way in which we sense below the rational, reflective level the ruin of Coriolanus as a jolting fracture.

Now at the end, these images are joined with the other sensational image of conflict, noise—the dreadful noise of all the people crying, "Tear him to pieces! Do it presently!—He kill'd my son!—My daughter!—He kill'd my cousin Marcus!—He kill'd my father!" Do we hear the paranomasia with "pieces" in the lords' crying in vain above the uproar, "Peace ho! . . . peace!" It is the second conjunction of "pieces" and "peace" within a few lines. Then the fear and the pity of that final, terrible cry, as the conspirators fall upon Coriolanus, shouting, "Kill, kill, kill, kill, kill him!" Before him he carries noise, and behind him he leaves tears.

In his customary way, Shakespeare gives the last words, the words of composition, to the antagonist, his rage now gone. The word Aufidius uses of Coriolanus is "noble," the epithet most frequently applied to him throughout the play. Like "alone," it is a word by now rich in overtones:

> Beat thou the drum, that it speak mournfully;
> Trail your steel pikes. Though in this city he
> Hath widowed and unchilded many a one,
> Which to this hour bewail the injury,
> Yet he shall have a noble memory.

Like Hamlet, Coriolanus is to have a soldier's burial, and is carried out to the sound of the drum, speaking mournfully.

APPENDIX & NOTES

Imagery in *Richard II* and in *1 Henry IV*

It IS a commonplace that the development of Shakespeare's style is away from verbal ingenuity and exuberance for their own sake and towards concentrated expression under control for dramatic ends. What I shall have to say here is nothing very new in itself but it may be said in such a way as to give new significance to an old subject. I shall be concerned only with imagery, and with that only in two plays which come at crucial stages in Shakespeare's poetic and dramatic growth: *Richard II* about 1595, at the end of his "experimental" years, and *1 Henry IV* a year or two later, when he has unmistakably attained his majority. Most of the work on Shakespeare's imagery has had to do with its content and its

---

Reprinted from the *Modern Language Review* 37 (April 1942), 114-21, by permission of the Modern Humanities Research Association. Errors have now been corrected, the notes renumbered (since they were originally distributed by pages), and modifying comments added in brackets to some of the notes. Shakespeare quotations have been brought into conformity with *The Riverside Shakespeare,* with exceptions as for the other quotations throughout the book.

distribution. But the quality of an image—its fabric and structure and relation to its immediate context—is also interesting and may, as is recognized, be important in revealing something of the poetic process. Much may yet be done in the way of examining Shakespeare's images from this intensive point of view.

On reading the First Part of *Henry IV* immediately after *Richard II* one is struck, along with evidences of greater maturity in other matters, by the difference in the handling of the images. I shall begin with a general statement which will obviously need qualification and if pushed too far will distort the picture, but which, for convenience, has nevertheless to be made at the outset. It may be said that the images in *Richard II* tend to be direct or explicit, complete, correspondent, point by point, to the idea symbolized, and separate one from another; whereas the images in *1 Henry IV* tend to be richer in implicit suggestion and in ambiguity, not fully developed, fluid in outline and fused with one another.

These qualities will be evident in the following illustrations:

> *Rich.*   I have been studying how I may compare
> This prison where I live unto the world;
> And for because the world is populous,
> And here is not a creature but myself,
> I cannot do it; yet I'll hammer it out.
> My brain I'll prove the female to my soul,
> My soul the father, and these two beget
> A generation of still-breeding thoughts;
> And these same thoughts people this little world,
> In humors like the people of this world:
> For no thought is contented. The better sort,
> As thoughts of things divine, are intermix'd
> With scruples and do set the word itself
> Against the word,
> As thus: 'Come, little ones,' and then again,
> 'It is as hard to come as for a camel
> To thread the postern of a small needle's eye.'
> Thoughts tending to ambition, they do plot
> Unlikely wonders: how these vain weak nails
> May tear a passage through the flinty ribs

Of this hard world, my ragged prison walls;
And, for they cannot, die in their own pride.
Thoughts tending to content flatter themselves
That they are not the first of fortune's slaves,
Nor shall not be the last—like seely beggars
Who sitting on the stocks refuge their shame,
That many have and others must sit there;
And in this thought they find a kind of ease,
Bearing their own misfortunes on the back
Of such as have before endur'd the like.
Thus play I in one person many people,
And none contented.

                    (*Richard II*, V. v. 1-32)

Except for the compact and allusive "do set the word itself/ Against the word," etc. (ll. 13-17), which at once strikes one because it is so unlike the style of the rest of the play, the passage is explicit throughout. Notice the completeness of the image on the peopling of the world with thoughts, and the equation of terms—brain to mother, soul to father, thoughts to children with all varieties of temperament who will in turn grow up to breed more of their kind, equally discontented. And then the discontented thoughts are enumerated one by one, each equated with an image more or less fully worked out. In the remainder of the speech, not quoted, it will be recalled how extensively treated is Richard's conceit of himself as a clock. With such a subject, requiring a listing of ideas, the separation of the images is perhaps not as indicative as in some other places. All of Richard's long speeches tend to show this succession of separate images[1] and it may be objected that from the speeches of a character so specially conceived as is Richard we have no right to draw too general conclusions about Shakespeare's style. To this point I shall return later. But it may be noted here that the qualities I have been remarking on in the passage quoted occur generally in the speeches of other characters throughout the play, though Richard's long speeches afford the best examples to illustrate the presence of all of them in any one place.[2]

Now consider this passage from *1 Henry IV*:

> The skipping King, he ambled up and down
> With shallow jesters and rash bavin wits,
> Soon kindled and soon burnt, carded his state,
> Mingled his royalty with cap'ring fools,
> Had his great name profaned with their scorns,
> And gave his countenance, against his name,
> To laugh at gibing boys, and stand the push
> Of every beardless vain comparative;
> Grew a companion to the common streets,
> Enfeoff'd himself to popularity,
> That, being daily swallowed by men's eyes,
> They surfeited with honey and began
> To loathe the taste of sweetness, whereof a little
> More than a little is by much too much.
> So when he had occasion to be seen,
> He was but as the cuckoo is in June,
> Heard, not regarded; seen, but with such eyes
> As, sick and blunted with community,
> Afford no extraordinary gaze,
> Such as is bent on sunlike majesty
> When it shines seldom in admiring eyes;
> But rather drows'd and hung their eyelids down,
> Slept in his face and rend'red such aspect
> As cloudy men use to their adversaries,
> Being with his presence glutted, gorg'd, and full.
>   (III. ii. 60-84)

Notice the rapid succession of images, the quick suggestion rather than elaboration in such compact and elliptical lines as "To laugh at gibing boys . . ." (ll. 66-67) and "Enfeoff'd himself to popularity" (l. 69), the fusion of one image with another: the skipping and capering with the quick burning of faggots ("rash bavin") and with the adulteration suggested by carding; the enfeoffment with the idea of surfeit (itself boldly linked with eyes), it in turn with the common sight of the cuckoo in June and with the drowsiness of men in constant sunshine, and this latter image shifting ground with "cloudy men." In contrast to the way in which the firm outlines of the images in Richard's speech hold the mind within certain limits set by the close equation of idea and image, the rapidity, complexity, and fluidity of the images in Henry's speech help (as well as their substance) to increase their obliquity. Fewer doors are closed.

It is obvious that the interweaving of images such as one finds in the following speech of the Duchess of Gloucester is not the same thing as the fusion in the speech from *Henry IV* just quoted:

> Edward's seven sons, whereof thyself art one,
> Were as seven vials of his sacred blood,
> Or seven fair branches springing from one root.
> Some of those seven are dried by nature's course,
> Some of those branches by the Destinies cut;
> But Thomas, my dear lord, my life, my Gloucester,
> One vial full of Edward's sacred blood,
> One flourishing branch of his most royal root,
> Is crack'd, and all the precious liquor spilt,
> Is hack'd down, and his summer leaves all faded,
> By envy's hand and murder's bloody axe.
>   (*Richard II*, I. ii. 11-21)

The vials and the branches retain their distinctness, and their relation to the idea is rather tediously explored. Again, take a genuinely complex figure from *Richard II:*

>   for within the hollow crown
> That rounds the mortal temples of a king
> Keeps Death his court; and there the antic sits,
> Scoffing his state and grinning at his pomp,
> Allowing him a breath, a little scene,
> To monarchize, be fear'd, and kill with looks,
> Infusing him with self and vain conceit,
> As if this flesh which walls about our life
> Were brass impregnable; and humor'd thus,
> Comes at the last and with a little pin
> Bores through his castle wall, and farewell king!
>   (III. ii. 160-70)

"Death" hesitates ambiguously in "Keeps Death his court" between Death as a ruler holding court and Death as a jester holding the real power in the king's court, then shifts certainly to Death "the antic" (still *within* the hollow crown), and then shifts again to a borer from without. Set this passage against one from *Henry IV:*

> Those opposed eyes,
> Which, like the meteors of a troubled heaven,
> All of one nature, of one substance bred,
> Did lately meet in the intestine shock
> And furious close of civil butchery,
> Shall now, in mutual well-beseeming ranks,
> March all one way and be no more oppos'd
> Against acquaintance, kindred, and allies.
>
> (I. i. 9-16)

Here the fusion of images results in a syntactical boldness seldom found in *Richard II*. Moreover, for all the complexity of structure in the passage on Death, the images are fully explicatory; whereas in the passage from *Henry IV* the meanings of "opposed eyes" and "meteors of a troubled heaven" are almost wholly implicit.

The differences observed in the passages already quoted are exhibited in certain other ways, namely, in respect to similes, allegorically handled metaphor, and words retaining both a literal and a figurative meaning.

My first impression was that similes were more common in *Richard II* than in *Henry IV*. In a simile, stated as an equation, there is, at least formally, no fusion of idea and image. A closer examination of the two plays does not, in point of fact, bear out my first impression of greater frequency of similes in *Richard II*. But numerical difference is not so important as the character of the similes themselves, and it is true that in *Henry IV* there are fewer fully extended similes of the type here illustrated from *Richard II:*

> See, see, King Richard doth himself appear,
> As doth the blushing discontented sun
> From out the fiery portal of the east,
> When he perceives the envious clouds are bent
> To dim his glory and to stain the track
> Of his bright passage to the occident.
>
> (III. iii. 62-67)[3]

Two examples of a similar kind in *Henry IV* occur in set speeches, and two occur in a passage where a scene is being vividly described.[4] But most of the similes in *Henry IV* are brief and colloquial: they are the "unsavory similes" applied by Hal and Falstaff to one another; the homely comparisons in the talk of Falstaff and his companions (skin like an old lady's loose gown, withered like an old apple John, roaring like a bullcalf, ragged as Lazarus, vigilant as a cat to steal cream, dank as a dog, stung like a tench); the quick, vivid figures in Hotspur's overflowing speech (fresh as a bridegroom, perfumed like a milliner, tedious as a tired horse or a railing wife, worse than a smoky house). It is characteristic of the style of the play that Hotspur's objection to Kate's swearing (III. i. 250-59), which begins with a simile, "Heart! you swear like a comfit-maker's wife" (itself by no means a simple statement), leads into an image that embodies a whole nest of subsidiary images, complex and fused:

> And givest such sarcenet surety for thy oaths
> As if thou never walk'st further than Finsbury.
> Swear me, Kate, like a lady as thou art,
> A good mouth-filling oath, and leave 'in sooth'
> And such protest of pepper-gingerbread
> To velvet-guards and Sunday-citizens.

It is surely not insignificant that one finds allegorical use of metaphor only in *Richard II*, not in *1 Henry IV*. Allegory is sustained metaphor.[5] One expects it to have a definite core of statement, of clear correspondence between figure and idea, with however much peripheral suggestion it may be enriched. The little allegory of the garden scene (III. iv), in its exact correspondence of figure and idea, point by point, is explicit and little else. The only places where it achieves obliquity are in the implicit allusion in "our sea-walled garden" (l. 43) to John of Gaunt's speech, and in the allusion to Eden and the fall of man in the Queen's address to the Gardener as Adam (ll. 73-80). In the latter allusion a profounder meaning is suggested than is stated.

In *Henry IV* there are a number of single words which, to-

gether with a figurative meaning, retain their literal meaning
and greatly enrich the context by this ambiguity. A good example is *balk'd* in Henry's statement that

> Ten thousand bold Scots, two and twenty knights,
> Balk'd in their own blood, did Sir Walter see
> On Holmedon's plains.
>
> (I. i. 68-70)

Professor Kittredge (in his notes to the play) defines a *balk* as
"the ridge between two furrows." Hence, the statement means
literally that the bodies are "piled up in ridges and soaked in
blood"; but it also means that the Scots have been thwarted
and defeated. The nowadays more immediately apprehended
figurative meaning is deepened and modified by the force of
the literal meaning. Other words in the play which get a
similar re-enforcement from two layers of meaning are *ma-
levolent* (I. i. 97), *countenance* (I. ii. 29), *baffle* (I. ii. 101),
frontier (I. iii. 19), *nettled* (I. iii. 240), *bombast* (II. iv. 327),
teeming (III. i. 27), *bootless* (III. i. 66), *common-hackney'd*
(III. ii. 40), *"stain'd* nobility" (V. iv. 13). This use of words is
not the same thing as the play on John of Gaunt's name in
Richard II (II. i. 73-84, 115), although it springs, of course,
from the same alertness to the suggestive power of words. In
the passage in *Richard II*, the meanings are all made explicit;
in *Henry IV*, they are left implicit, without statement, and
often without special emphasis. Moreover, the use in question
is not the same thing as an implied pun, for in the former the
meanings are overlaid and mutually enriching, in the latter
generally disparate and incongruous. In a really good pun, of
course, the obvious incongruity may cover a deeper congruity,
as in Falstaff's remark to Prince Hal, who finds a bottle of sack
in Falstaff's pistol case, "There's that will sack a city." But in
the use under discussion in the words from *Henry IV*, there is
no incongruity.

Words used with this special re-enforcement of meaning are
rarer in *Richard II*. An example is *down* in Richard's great
climactic speech when he surrenders to Bolingbroke:

> Down, down I come, like glist'ring Phaëton,
> Wanting the manage of unruly jades.
> In the base court? Base court, where kings grow base,
> To come at traitors' calls and do them grace.
> In the base court, come down? Down court! down king!
> For night-owls shriek where mounting larks should sing.
>   (III. iii. 178-83)

But even here, the secondary meaning of *down* is made explicit, and *base* is played upon as Gaunt's name is played upon.[6]

Bearing in mind Coleridge's distinction between *fancy* as "the aggregative and associative power" and *imagination* as "the shaping and modifying power" or "the fusing power," one is tempted to call the images from *Richard II* so far given fanciful, and those from *Henry IV* imaginative. One need not commit oneself to Coleridge's theory of faculty psychology to find the terms useful in describing differences of effect, by whatever mental operation produced. But the matter is too complex to allow of such a simple distinction. A speech such as the Queen's at the sight of Richard coming on his way to the Tower (V. i. 7-15) is an aggregate of separate images, yet at least two of them, "my fair rose" and "the model where old Troy did stand," are imaginative in their evocation of meanings not stated. Moreover, Richard *is* the rose; the two terms have coalesced and mutually modify one another, *Richard* contributing all that we have seen throughout the play of his fresh coloring, youth, and charm, the *rose* bringing in a whole aura of associations from experience and literature—color, freshness, fragrance, beauty, youth, sensuous pleasure, love, evanescence, the *carpe diem* theme. A passage of similar structure is Gaunt's speech on England (II. i. especially ll. 40-60), where, though the rapidly succeeding images (throne, scepter'd isle, seat of Mars, Eden, fortress, little world, precious stone, nurse, teeming womb) are not fused, they are individually more or less rich in suggestion and the whole speech is intense with feeling. However, I do not wish to raise an issue over terms or make the discussion as complex as their just application would entail. I have approached the matter from a somewhat different point of view and have found a different set of terms to be helpful: distinct and fused, explicit and implicit, extended and quickly suggested, and so on. Briefly, the differences in the handling of the images so far exhibited are the differences between enunciation and suggestion.[7]

The examples have been carefully selected, of course, to make the point, and, although they are typical, there are many exceptions. Not all the images in *Richard II* are extended, separate, and enunciatory, and not all in *Henry IV* are brief, fused, and more implicit than explicit. It seems to me significant, however, that there are more exceptions in *Richard II* than in *Henry IV*. This is what one would expect if the difference is a sign, not just of the differences between subject-matter and characters, but of the maturing powers of the writer. The later manner is likely to appear long before it becomes predominant, and *Richard II* is at most only two years earlier than *Henry IV;* but once the later manner has been fully achieved, the earlier manner will almost certainly disappear except when it is consciously adopted for some specific purpose: Gertrude's pretty and formalized description of the death of Ophelia comes to mind. (As a parallel case of stylistic development compare Yeats.) There are, for instance, almost no conceits that can be strictly so called in *Henry IV;* the most striking exception is Hotspur's description of the fight between Mortimer and Glendower on the banks of the frightened Severn (I. iii. 95-107), and the effect of rhetorical exaggeration is intended. The king's response is, "Thou dost belie him, Percy, thou dost belie him."

It is interesting that the exceptions to the type in *Richard II* occur almost always in passages describing what the effect of war will be on English soil:

> For that our kingdom's earth should not be soil'd
> With that dear blood which it hath fostered;
> And for our eyes do hate the dire aspect
> Of civil wounds plough'd up with neighbours' sword;
> And for we think the eagle-winged pride
> Of sky-aspiring and ambitious thoughts,

With rival-hating envy, set on you
To wake our peace, which in our country's cradle
Draws the sweet infant breath of gentle sleep;
Which so rous'd up with boist'rous untun'd drums,
With harsh-resounding trumpets' dreadful bray,
And grating shock of wrathful iron arms,
Might from our quiet confines fright fair peace
And make us wade even in our kinred's blood:
Therefore we banish you our territories.

(I. iii. 125-39)

Here the fusion of images is combined with the same sort of
syntactical boldness we have observed in the passage from
Henry IV on opposed eyes.[8] The oblique allusion contained
in the imagery of the opening lines of *Henry IV* to these fine
passages in *Richard II* re-enforces with powerful effect the
sense of continuity established by the explicit allusion to
events in the earlier play:

No more the thirsty entrance of this soil
Shall daub her lips with her own children's blood,
No more shall trenching war channel her fields,
Nor bruise her flow'rets with the armed hoofs
Of hostile paces.

(I. i. 5-9)

The idea of war on English soil was evidently one which
called forth from Shakespeare an intense imaginative response.

I said I should return to the objection that the imagery in
Richard II is what it is because of the kind of character Richard is and therefore should not be pressed for another significance. It is true enough that its appropriateness is so great
that anything better to exhibit his character can hardly be
imagined. But I should like to raise the question whether or
not Shakespeare would have been tempted by just such a
figure at any time very much later in his career. The question
is not idle. Although I have not carefully examined the
imagery of all the early plays with respect to the qualities
here considered, I suspect that it will be found to be generally
of the same kind as in *Richard II;* certainly it is in *Romeo and*

Juliet. King John, though perhaps exceptional in the abundance of imaginative images, is strongly marked, nevertheless, by the elaborate type so frequent in *Richard II.*[9] But in the case of *Richard II,* these characteristics of the imagery are especially striking because they are so beautifully adapted to exhibit the central character. The perfection of the play, within its limits, is the perfection of union between character and a style that Shakespeare had mastered at this stage of his career. He had it at his fingers' ends and he found a character for whom it was dramatically right.

But *1 Henry IV* is a stage beyond *Richard II* in the welding of poetic imagination to dramatic need. This is best illustrated in the case of Hotspur. Dr. Tillyard says that there is no profound obliquity in Richard's character and that a good deal of the play is the poetry of statement.[10] Richard's character is exhibited directly. He is a poet and he speaks poetically. But Hotspur is a hater of poetry who speaks some of the most vivid and the most beautiful poetry in the play. In all of Richard's poetical speeches, he has nothing like Hotspur's speech on honor, so loaded with unexpressed meaning.[11] Yet Hotspur's animadversions on poets and poetry remain convincing. It will not do to say that we do not take him at his word. That is a very superficial view of his character and of Shakespeare's art. We do take him at his word if we pay attention to the play. He is an entire man of action, as he says he is, without artistic habits or interests. He is intensely imaginative, certainly, but imagination is not enough to make a poet. Whereas Richard's speeches are the poems that Shakespeare puts into his mouth as his own compositions, Hotspur's speeches are Shakespeare's poetry to express the mind of a character who could not himself compose a poem at all. This is a very high degree of obliquity in the use of artistic means. It is accomplishment of an altogether different order from the minor perfection of *Richard II.*

It might prove fruitful to examine the imagery of the rest of the plays from the point of view I have suggested in this paper. Miss Spurgeon and Professor G. Wilson Knight have already shown, in different ways, how the "modifying and shaping power" of the imagination has in the great tragedies produced a kind of running imagery contributory to the tone of each play. One would expect this same power to produce, along with greater boldness in syntax and greater condensation in statement, greater concentration, greater fluidity of outline, and greater suggestiveness in the imagery. The highest achievement of the "fusing power" of the imagination one feels to be, however, not complexity, but something beyond—utter simplicity of form to express multiplicity of meaning. One thinks of *Antony and Cleopatra,* part of whose great obliquity surely arises from its imagery. "Rich" is not an adequate word to describe it. At its greatest, it is evocative of things that can have no statement:

> there is nothing left remarkable
> Beneath the visiting moon.

Notes

The edition of Shakespeare for quotations and references throughout these essays is *The Riverside Shakespeare,* edited by G. Blakemore Evans and others, Boston: Houghton Mifflin, 1974. All significant variations from it are noted. Not noted are (1) occasional changes in punctuation or elision in which the meaning is not affected but the reading is eased; and (2) modern spellings of ordinary words in which the Riverside textual editor has followed his copy-text in common, but insignificant, sixteenth-century spellings.

Shakespeare's Dramatic Language

1 Cf. *Thyestes,* 391-403: "Stet quicumque volet potens/ aulae culmine lubrico;/ me dulcis saturet quies;/ obscuro positus loco/ leni perfruar otio, . . ." ("Let him stand who will, in pride of power, on empire's slippery height; let me be filled with sweet repose; in humble station fixed, let me enjoy untroubled ease, . . . ," trans. Frank Justus Miller, Loeb Classical Library, revised edition, 1929); also ll. 446-70.

2 Edward Hall, *The Union of the two noble and illustrate famelies*

of Lancastre and Yorke (1548), sig. [Ggvii]; Geoffrey Bullough, *Narrative and Dramatic Sources of Shakespeare* (London: Routledge and Kegan Paul; New York: Columbia University Press), III: *Earlier English History Plays* (1960), 183.

3 Hall, sig. AAj^v; Raphael Holinshed, *The Third Volume of Chronicles* (1587), p. 712; Bullough, III, 253. Sir Thomas More's history of King Richard III appeared in Grafton's *Continuation* of Hardyng's *Chronicle* (1543) and in Hall (1548) before it was included in Wm. Rastell's edition of his *Works* (1557); consult Bullough, III, 9-12, 224-26.

4 Hall, sig. EEiiii; Holinshed, p. 735; not in Bullough.

5 *The Mirror for Magistrates,* ed. Lily B. Campbell (Cambridge, 1938), p. 359.

6 *children* (Qq), easier scansion; Evans, *two sons* (F1).

7 For a full account of the history of the Romeo and Juliet story and the versions Shakespeare knew, consult Olin H. Moore, *The Legend of Romeo and Juliet,* The Ohio State University Graduate School Monographs: Contributions in Language and Literature No. 13, Columbus, 1950.

8 See my full discussion of the setting in "Titania's Wood," in *Renaissance Studies in Honor of Carroll Camden,* ed. J. A. Ward, Rice University Studies, Vol. 60, no. 2 (Houston, 1974), pp. 55-70.

9 *Metamorphoses* iv. 55-166. For an account of some medieval and Renaissance versions of this story, see my "Pyramus and Thisbe Once More," in *Essays on Shakespeare and Elizabethan Drama in Honor of Hardin Craig,* ed. Richard Hosley (Columbia, Mo., 1962), pp. 149-61.

10 Holinshed, p. 503; Bullough, III, 406.

11 The character and function of the styles of these three plays have, of course, been much written about, as have their place in Shakespeare's growing mastery of his medium. For a recent sensitive essay on Shakespeare's "poetic-dramatic" development, in which she speaks of *Richard II* as a milestone, see Inga-Stina Ewbank, "Shakespeare's Poetry," in *A New Companion to Shakespeare Studies,* ed. Kenneth Muir and S. Schoenbaum (Cambridge, 1971), pp. 99-115; also Brian Vickers, "Shakespeare's Use of Rhetoric," in the same volume, pp. 83-98.

12 Coleridge, in his notes on *Antony and Cleopatra,* remarks that "*Feliciter audax* is the motto for its style, comparatively with his other works. . . . Be it remembered, too, that this happy

valiancy of style is but the representative and result of all the material excellencies so exprest" (*Coleridge's Shakespearean Criticism*, ed. Thomas Middleton Raysor [Cambridge, Mass., 1930], I, 86).

13 In his *Characters of Shakespear's Plays*, in the *Complete Works*, ed. P. P. Howe (London, 1930), IV, 191-92 (on the principle of contrast and the "violent antitheses of the style" in *Macbeth*), 232-33 (on the naturalness and vitality in the style of *Hamlet*).

14 In "Leading Motives in the Imagery of Shakespeare's Tragedies," Shakespeare Association Lecture, 1930, "Shakespeare's Iterative Imagery," British Academy Lecture, 1931, and *Shakespeare's Imagery and What It Tells Us*, Cambridge, 1935. For thoughtful reviews of studies of imagery, see Muriel Bradbrook, "Fifty Years of the Criticism of Shakespeare's Style: A Retrospect," *Shakespeare Survey* 7 (Cambridge, 1954), 1-11; Kenneth Muir, "Shakespeare's Imagery—Then and Now," *Shakespeare Survey* 18 (1965), 46-57.

15 E.g., Wolfgang Clemen, *Shakespeares Bilder*, Bonn. 1935; translated and revised as *The Development of Shakespeare's Imagery*, Cambridge, Mass., 1951; Maurice Charney, *Shakespeare's Roman Plays*, Cambridge, Mass., 1961; Kenneth Muir, "Image and Symbol in *Macbeth*," *Shakespeare Survey* 19 (1966), 45-54.

16 "Imagery in *Richard II* and *Henry IV*," *Modern Language Review* 37 (April 1942), 113-22; reprinted, with corrections and editorial revisions, as an appendix to this volume. On Shakespeare's movement from formal to more complex imagery, cf. Clemen, *The Development of Shakespeare's Imagery*, Chaps. 7, 8, 9.

17 In his *Table Talk* for 15 March 1834 (ed. T. Ashe for Bohn's Standard Library edition [London, 1888], p. 277), Coleridge makes an arresting statement: "The construction of Shakspere's sentences, whether in verse or prose, is the necessary and homogeneous vehicle of his peculiar manner of thinking. His is not the style of the age." Although he is not making my point, because he is thinking of Shakespeare's difference in style from other writers of his time, his "necessary and homogeneous vehicle" is just the phrase for what I am trying to say about the syntax of each of these two plays, provided that one takes "homogeneous" in as loose a sense as Coleridge does.

"No art at all":
Language in Hamlet

1 Folio reading, supported by Q1 ("O wormewood, worme-wood!"); Evans, following Q2, reads "That's wormwood!"
2 *heraldry* (Q1, F1); Evans, *heraldy* (Q2).
3 To write an *ethopoeia,* a speech in the "passive," or passionate mode, for the grieving Hecuba at the fall of Troy was a regular schoolbook exercise prescribed in the commonly used *Progymnasmata* of Aphthonius (as revised by Reinhard Lorich, 1542, 1546, etc.); also in Richard Rainolde's English adaptation, *The Foundacion of Rhetorike,* 1563 (ed. Francis R. Johnson in Scholars' Facsimiles and Reprints, New York, 1945), sigs. Nj-Niij (note the vocabulary of dolefulness and death).
4 See "Imagery in *Richard II* and in *1 Henry IV,*" in the Appendix, p. 232.
5 For a sensitive and stimulating essay on the language of *Hamlet,* see Arthur R. Humphreys, "Style and Expression in *Hamlet,*" in *Shakespeare's Art: Seven Essays,* ed. Milton Crane (Chicago, 1973), pp. 29-52.
6 Cf. John Hoskins, *Directions for Speech and Style* (1599), ed. Hoyt H. Hudson (Princeton, 1935), pp. 36-37: "This is a fine course to stir admiration in the hearer and make them think it a strange harmony which must be expressed in such discords. . . . This is an easy figure now in fashion, not like ever to be so usual."
7 *Institutio oratoria* VIII. iii. 88, 89 (trans. H. E. Butler, Loeb Classical Library); Quintilian treats *energeia* as one of several related means to attain force (*virium*); his is a less specific use of the term than Aristotle's use of it only to characterize metaphor which makes us "see things" by representing them "in a state of activity" (*Rhetoric* 1411^{b}22-1412^{a}15; W. Rhys Roberts' translation, in *Works,* ed. W. D. Ross, Vol. XI [Oxford, 1924]). Hamlet's style qualifies as "energetic" as well in its easy use of vivid metaphors as in all the other features, verbal and syntactical, of a forceful style. Sidney says in the *Defense of Poesy* that to be persuasive love poetry should betray the passions by "that same forcibleness or *energia* (as the Greeks call it) of the writer" (*Miscellaneous Prose of Sir Philip Sidney,* ed. Katherine Duncan-Jones and Jan van Dorsten [Oxford, 1973], pp. 116-17).

8 J. Dover Wilson, *What Happens in Hamlet* (Cambridge, 1936), pp. 41-42.

9 "Heaven's . . . act," Evans, following Q2; Kittredge, following F1: "Heaven's . . . glow;/ Yea, this . . . mass/ With tristful visage, . . . doom,/ Is . . . act"—one of the many difficult cruxes in *Hamlet*.

10 ἐνάργεια, distinctness, clarity, visibility; Quintilian (*Inst. orat.* IV. ii. 63-65; VIII. iii. 61-62) calls it *evidentia* (vivid illustration) or *repraesentatio* (representation), "which is something more than mere clearness (*perspicuitas*), since the latter merely lets itself be seen, whereas the former trusts itself upon our notice."

11 *brave*, generally glossed in this passage as "fine," "noble"; but the word perhaps carries as well the common sixteenth-century sense of "showy," "splendid," as in "this brave o'erhanging firmament."

12 *scullion* (F1); Evans, *stallion* (male whore), following Q2.

13 *time*, Evans (Qq); *tune*, Kittredge and others (F1).

14 Another Hamlet crux: "as an Ape doth nuttes" (Q1), "like an apple" (Q2), "like an Ape" (F1).

15 "but as . . . conceive, friend," Evans (Q2); "but not as . . . conceive. Friend," Folio reading, followed by Kittredge and most editors.

16 Quoted from the Geneva Bible, 1560.

17 Cf. Holbein's set of woodcuts of the Dance of Death in an edition of the Old Testament printed in Lyons in 1538; reproduced in *Holbein's Dance of Death and Bible Woodcuts*, New York, 1947 (see especially VII The Emperor, X The Queen, XIX The Advocate, XXIV The Nun, XXXVI The Duchess).

18 "of . . . be," Evans (Q2); "ha's ought of what he leaves. What is't to leave betimes?" (F1); "knows aught of what he leaves, what is't to leave betimes? Let be," Kittredge, following Dr. Johnson.

19 On Hamlet's resolution, and much besides, read Maynard Mack's fine essay, "The World of Hamlet," *The Yale Review* 41 (1952), 502-23; reprinted in *Shakespeare: Modern Essays in Criticism*, ed. Leonard F. Dean (New York, 1957), 237-57.

Iago's "If—":
Conditional and Subjunctive in Othello

1 In what I say of Othello, I am not attempting character interpretation for its own sake; my position is that of E. E. Stoll
   (*Art and Artifice in Shakespeare* [Cambridge, 1933], Chap. II)
   in putting dramatic necessity before completeness of motivation. What Shakespeare does is to create within the dramatic
   framework an illusion of credible action, convincing so long as
   one abides by his terms. My study of the movement of the syntax is meant to account in part for this credibility.
2 For the commonplaces in this homily and their history consult
   John Price, "Shakespeare's Mythological Invention" (unpub-
   lished doctoral dissertation, University of Wisconsin, 1959),
   pp. 38-50.
3 For an excellent example of this form of argument note in
   Roderigo's speech to Brabantio (I. i. 120-27) a logical sequence
   of conditional sentences ending in a false conclusion based on
   the argument from sign; dramatically, at this moment, Iago and
   Roderigo are acting as one. On the use of the enthymeme in
   rhetoric see Aristotle's *Rhetoric* (trans. W. Rhys Roberts in
   Works, ed. W. D. Ross, Vol. XI [Oxford, 1924]): esp. 1355^a6
   ff.; 1356^b1 ff. (definition), 1357^a14 ff. (basis in the contingent),
   1357^b1 ff. (type based on sign), 1394^a26-1394^b (relation to
   maxims), 1397^a7 ff. (examples in conditional form), 1400^b35-
   1402^a (spurious kinds, esp. 1401^b, par. 6, arguments from consequences, and par. 7, causes which are not causes).
4 On Iago's destructive rôle put in other terms (i.e., as slanderer)
   see my "Good Name in *Othello,*" *Studies in English Literature*
   7 (Spring 1967), 195-217.
5 In Evanthius, iv. 5, and Donatus, vii. 1-4 (*Comicorum graecorum fragmenta,* ed. G. Kaibel [Berlin, 1899], Vol. I, fasc. 1,
   pp. 67, 69), familiar through Renaissance editions of Terence
   and commentaries on him, especially through the school editions of Melanchthon (the first perhaps at Wittenberg, 1524;
   many later ones) and of Erasmus (Basel, 1532, 1534). For
   bibliography and the humanists' analyses of Terence in these
   structural terms consult T. W. Baldwin, *Shakspere's Five-Act
   Structure* (Urbana, Ill., 1947), Chap. VIII.
6 *promulgate:* the Folio reading, followed by most editors; Evans
   adopts the First Quarto's *provulgate,* a recognized sixteenth-
   century synonym.

7 Lines 270-72: punctuation as in Kittredge edition, following Folio in period after "censure." In a slight but piquant shift of emphasis, Evans punctuates: ". . . is;/ I . . . censure/ What . . . be. If . . . not,/ I . . . !" Punctuation in both Q1 and F1 is ambiguous.

8 *Indian:* the Quarto reading, followed by Evans and most editors; some editors favor the Folio's *Iudean* (i.e., *Judean,* with apparent reference either to Judas or to Herod the Great).

"Give me the map there!"
Command, Question, and Assertion in King Lear

1 The iterative imagery of *Lear* has been noted and interpreted from Bradley on, by Spurgeon, Clemen, Knight, and others; but studied with special fullness by Robert B. Heilman in *This Great Stage: Image and Structure in "King Lear,"* Baton Rouge, La., 1948.

2 *rash,* Evans (Q1); *stick* (F1), easier grammatically, but commonplace. The Quarto reading is given in the Oxford English Dictionary under sense v.[1] 3 (to dash one thing against, in, or through another), but "boarish" also suggests sense v.[2] 1 (to cut, slash); cf. Spenser's *Faerie Queene* IV. ii. 17; V. iii. 8.

3 *dearn,* Evans (Q1): dark, drear, dire; *stern* (F1).

4 Winifred M. T. Nowottny (in a different way from mine) touches on syntax, along with diction and prosody, in her sensitive and penetrating essay, "Some Aspects of the Style of *King Lear,"* in *Shakespeare Survey* 13 (Cambridge, 1960), 49-57.

5 *Know* (Q1); Evans, *Know that* (F1).

6 "the last, not least" (Q1); Evans reads "our last and least" (F1).

7 *can* (Q1); Evans, *will* (F1).

8 Another example is at IV. i. 66-71.

9 "Kent banish'd thus? and France in choler parted? . . ." (I. ii. 23-26); and note the rest of the dialogue between Gloucester and Edmund in this scene.

10 E.g., Edgar's "O gods! Who is't can say 'I am at the worst'?/ I am worse than e'er I was" (IV. i. 25-26), and Cordelia's "Was this a face/ To be oppos'd against the warring winds?" intro-

ducing a series of shocked questions on her sisters' treatment of
Lear (IV. vii. 30-39).

11 Illustrated below, p. 113.

12 See below, pp. 104-5.

13 E.g., Edgar in his two reflective soliloquies (III. vi. 102 ff.; IV.
i. 1 ff.) and in his response to the sight of his blinded father
(IV. i. 27-28); Albany in dialogue with Goneril (IV. ii. 29 ff.);
Kent in response to Lear (I. i. 148-49, 153-54); in reflections
on his and Lear's state (II. ii. 160-62, 165-66) and on the stars
(IV. iii. 32-33). For emphatic assertion, not sententious, note
Kent's unflattering portrait of Oswald (II. ii. 15 ff.) and of
Oswald's kind (II. ii. 72 ff.).

14 For the full history of the story consult Wilfrid Perrett, *The
Story of King Lear from Geoffrey of Monmouth to Shakespeare*,
Berlin, 1904 (*Palaestra* 35); summary of the case for the versions Shakespeare appears to have known, including Geoffrey,
pp. 272-89.

15 *The Countess of Pembroke's Arcadia*, 1590, II. 10 (ed. Albert
Feuillerat, Cambridge, 1912).

16 "Etenim quantum habes, tantum vales, tantumque te diligo."
As Perrett long ago pointed out (*The Story of King Lear*, pp.
14-15, 228-40), only Geoffrey, the first teller of the story as we
know it, motivated Cordelia's double-edged riddling reply to
her father in her acuteness and wit as well as in her honesty.
Aware that her father has been taken in by the exaggerated
protestations of her sisters, Geoffrey's "Cordeilla" wishes to try
him herself ("tentare illum cupiens"), and she frames an answer
which both glances at their speeches and is a test of his understanding. She cannot believe that any daughter would dare to
admit she loved her father more than a father, unless she were
striving to conceal the truth in jesting words ("nisi jocosis verbis
veritatem celare nitatur"). As for herself she has always loved
him as a father and always will. Although he persists in wring-
ing more from her ("a me magis extorquere"), let him hear the
truth of her love and put an end to his questions: "In truth, as
much as thou hast, so much art thou worth, and so much I love
thee." Lear, believing she spoke from the fullness of her heart,
became vehemently angry and disinherited her forthwith. (Passage quoted in full in Perrett, p. 14, n. 1 and p. 228.) Omissions
(especially of the "nisi . . . nitatur" and "pater ratus eam ex
abundantia cordis dixisse" phrases) and changes of emphasis in

the later versions of the tale, including Holinshed's, show that the tellers all missed the point as much as Geoffrey's Lear; the "quantum habes" riddle became shocking if not unintelligible. Although Shakespeare altered the riddle significantly, his Cordelia is closest to Geoffrey's in acuteness and spirit.

17 An exception which proves the rule is Goneril's veiled threat to her father that he had better reduce his train or face the consequences: "Sir,/ I had thought, by making this well known unto you," etc. (I. iv. 204 ff.); it is a masterpiece of syntactical indirection in the conditional subjunctive.

18 Note especially the two in his first curse on Goneril (I. iv. 275-89), the "Hear, Nature, hear!" speech. Since the intent of the curse is to make Goneril sterile, the normal possibility that she have a child he prays Nature not to fulfill: "Suspend thy purpose, if thou didst intend/ To make this creature fruitful. . . ." The restatement of the condition to cover this possibility, "If she must teem,/ Create her child of spleen, . . ." is as much an extension of the horror of his curse as it is a recognition of a deity with intentions he cannot be certain of; it is a second thought inviting a more precise and fitting retribution on his own ungrateful child.

19 E.g., in addition to those quoted, "Nuncle, give me an egg, and I'll give thee two crowns" (I. iv. 155 ff.), "Canst tell how an oyster makes his shell? . . ." (I. v. 25-31), etc.

20 *wilt thou* (Q1); Evans, *will you* (F1).

21 *tine*, Evans (Q1); *tyne* (F1), a monosyllabic word meaning "very small," older and more common than "tiny."

22 *For* (Q1); Evans, *Though* (F1).

23 *Didst* (Q1); Evans, *Wouldst* (F1).

24 Evans, following F1, omits fourth "howl."

25 Evans, following F1 (om. Q1), reads "Look her lips."

26 Evans, following F1, gives the speech to Edgar; I have kept the Quarto's assignment to "Duke" (Albany), an assignment characteristic of Shakespeare's habit of giving the final speech in a tragedy to the person of highest authority.

27 *have* (Q1); Evans, *hath* (F1); although singular verbs with plural subjects are not uncommon in Shakespeare, the plural here makes the statement apply unambiguously to Gloucester as well as Lear.

"What should be in that 'Caesar'?"
Proper Names in Julius Caesar

1 See Marvin Spevack, *A Complete and Systematic Concordance
  to the Works of Shakespeare* (Hildesheim, 1968-70), Vol. III:
  Caesar's name (for Julius Caesar and including "Julius" alone)
  occurs 216 times; Brutus' name (for Marcus Brutus), 137 times;
  I have adjusted Spevack's figures to leave out doublings ("Julius
  Caesar" under both "Caesar" and "Julius") and references to
  others with the same name (Octavius Caesar, Decius Brutus,
  [Junius] Brutus). Since this concordance gives only references
  without quotations, Spevack's new *Harvard Concordance* (Cam-
  bridge, Mass., 1973) or the old Bartlett's Concordance are helpful in making such adjustments; also useful for quick visual
  comparisons by columns of names in other plays, especially to
  "Antony" (Spevack, 136), and "Caesar" (i.e., Octavius, 145) in
  Antony and Cleopatra—the highest frequencies next to those in
  Julius Caesar; Hamlet (80), Iago (60), etc.
      In a penetrating essay ("An Approach to *Julius Caesar,"*
  Shakespeare Quarterly 5 [1954], 259-70), R. A. Foakes has observed the importance of names in themselves in *Julius Caesar,*
  the great frequency of some names (Caesar, Brutus, Cassius,
  Antony, Rome, Roman), and the use of the third person by
  speakers of themselves; he sees the dramatic significance of
  their frequency and use chiefly as a means to draw a contrast,
  crucial to the play, between ideals and actions. For other critics
  who have commented on the names (usually only Caesar's in
  the third person), see note 13, below.

2 Cassius' name (including "Caius Cassius" and "Caius") occurs
  76 times, just over half as often as Brutus's 137.

3 III. i. 84; III. ii. 8, 9, 123, 268; III. iii. 41; IV. i. 41.

4 "Monk's Tale" (F. N. Robinson's *Poetical Works of Chaucer,*
  2nd ed., Boston, 1957), 1. 2697 and note (on occurrence of
  the doublet in other works); *Fall of Princes,* vi. 2871 ff., 2927-
  28 (ed. Henry Bergen, Washington, D.C., 1923).

5 See especially the analysis of the play by Adrien Bonjour, *The
  Structure of "Julius Caesar"* (Liverpool, 1958).

6 "Rome" and "Roman" (including "Roman's," "Romans") occur
  73 times. The 76 times for "Cassius" are less striking because his
  name is primarily used as ordinary direct address in dialogue.

7 Shakespeare may have taken a hint from North's Plutarch on the

special significance of the names; he speaks of how Caesar's "name only was dreadfull unto everie man" (in "The Comparison of Dion with Brutus," Bullough, V, 134) and of how "the onlie name and great calling of Brutus, did bring on the most of them to geve consent to this conspiracie" ("The Life of Marcus Brutus," Bullough, V, 97. References to North are, for convenience, to Geoffrey Bullough's *Narrative and Dramatic Sources of Shakespeare* [London: Routledge and Kegan Paul; New York: Columbia University Press], Vol. V: *The Roman Plays* [1964]). Plutarch did not, of course, put the names to use in the various significant ways Shakespeare chose to do.

8 *Richard II*, III. ii. 85-86; cf. also Gaunt's nice play on his own name (II. i. 72-87).

9 On the importance of this scene in establishing "the magical use of the name 'Caesar'," see Maurice Charney, *Shakespeare's Roman Plays* (Cambridge, Mass., 1961), pp. 69-73.

10 Evans puts in quotation marks only the third name in the line; the Folio is indeterminate, since in it proper names are in italic throughout.

11 For a brilliant account, different from mine, of Shakespeare's rhetorical skill in controlling these shifts in response, see Kenneth Burke, "Antony in Behalf of the Play" (in *The Philosophy of Literary Form: Studies in Symbolic Action* (Baton Rouge, La., 1941), pp. 329-43.

12 Cf. I. ii. 94-99, 115-17.

13 In his total of forty speeches (occupying 150 lines), he uses his own name nineteen times. For a character in a play to speak of himself, or to himself, by name to call attention to his particular position (as lover, avenger, ruler, victim of fortune, etc.) is a useful and I think not uncommon device; there is, for instance, a good deal of it in Kyd. Shakespeare had already used the device sensitively as a means for a character to dramatize himself with Richard II and Falstaff, and would do so again with Hamlet. The special thing about Julius Caesar is the frequency and insistence with which he is made to speak of himself by name. Whether Shakespeare got the suggestion for this habit in *his* Caesar from one or more of the earlier Caesar plays cannot be settled. Certainly it is a marked feature of the boasting Caesar's speeches in the two extant plays in English preceding his—Kyd's *Cornelia* (1595, from Garnier's *Cornélie*) and the anonymous *Tragedy of Caesar's Revenge* (almost certainly

written in early 90's; printed first in ?1606). A number of
critics (among them Dowden, Granville-Barker, G. Wilson
Knight, L. C. Knights, Bonjour, Stauffer, Charney) have briefly
noted this feature in the speech of Shakespeare's Caesar, with
varying interpretations, stated or implied; for fuller discussions
of its effect and implications, consult Foakes, "An Approach to
Julius Caesar," and M. W. MacCallum, *Shakespeare's Roman
Plays and their Background* (London, 1910), pp. 228-32 and
n. 1.

14 Especially Suetonius, *History of the Twelve Caesars* (excerpts
from Philemon Holland's translation, 1606, in Bullough, V,
149-52), secs. 76-80.

15 *The Governour* (1531), II. v (in Bullough, V, 166); cf. also
III. xvi.

16 Particularly in *Hercules Furens* and *Hercules Oetaeus*. It is also
noteworthy that in both of these the hero uses his own name
(Hercules or Alcides) abundantly and in a variety of ways, not
only to amplify his fame as the peerless doer of heroic deeds,
but also to mark the irony of his being overcome.

17 The continental plays are Muretus' *Julius Caesar*, 1544 (publ.
1552), Grévin's *Jules-César*, 1558 (publ. 1561), Garnier's
Porcie, 1568, and *Cornélie*, 1573 (publ. 1574), Pescetti's *Il
Cesare*, 1594 (parts translated in Bullough, V, 174-94). In addition to the two plays in English Shakespeare might have known
(*Caesar's Revenge* and Kyd's *Cornelia*, whose Caesars are both
swollen with pride; see note 13, above), there were two public
plays now lost, *I* and *II Pompey and Caesar*, played by the
Admiral's men, 8 November 1594 and 18 June 1595, respectively (Alfred Harbage, *Annals of English Drama*, 2nd ed.
revised by S. Schoenbaum [Philadelphia, 1964]).

18 A marked change from Plutarch's life of Caesar (Bullough, V,
83-84), wherein, although Caesar was finally persuaded to at-
tend the fatal Senate meeting, he did not initially insist on
going in defiance of Calphurnia's dream and of the auguries;
in fact, fear of them made him at first decide to stay at home.

19 The theme itself was of course older, as in Seneca. The biased
and much-read Lucan, whose Caesar is always a dangerous
megalomaniac, interprets his whole career as overweening, mad
ambition ("O rabies miseranda ducis!") going before a fall;
he makes Caesar's *hubris* before and at Pharsalia ("Hic furor,
hic rabies, hic sunt tua crimina, Caesar") predictive of his even-

tual downfall at the hands of fortune (*De bello civili* ii. 544-75, vii. 551-96, and elsewhere).

20 The sources needed to reconstruct a history of Caesar's reputation are abundant and bewildering; references and a useful summary may be found in Bullough, V, 1-25. Shakespeare followed Plutarch chiefly, but may have consulted Appian and others, and would have gathered in who knows what bits and pieces from his reading in school and later; on his sources (including ancient, medieval, and Renaissance opinions), consult Bullough, but also Kenneth Muir, *Shakespeare's Sources* (London, 1957), I, 187 ff.; Ernest Schanzer, *Shakespeare's Appian* (Liverpool, 1956); Virgil Whitaker, *Shakespeare's Use of Learning* (San Marino, Calif., 1953), pp. 228-34 (for changes from Plutarch); and J. Leeds Barroll, "Shakespeare and Roman History," *Modern Language Review* 53 (July 1958), 327-43.

21 Both points of view are stated in John Higgins' "Caius Julius Caesar," added to the 1587 edition of *The Mirror for Magistrates* (in part in Bullough, V, 168-73).

22 *Richard II*, III. ii. 155-72; cf. Lucan on Pompey's "little, little grave," viii. 792-822.

23 For association or comparison of the two, see Appian, *Civil Wars*, II. xxi. 149-54 (Elizabethan translation, 1578, *Historie ... of the Romanes warres*, Bk. II, pp. 160 ff.); Lucan, *De bello civili* x. 20 ff.; Chaucer, "Monk's Tale," 2722-23; *Caesar's Revenge*, 841-42; Montaigne, *Essais*, II. 36 (see also II. 33, 34, on Caesar generally). Plutarch, interestingly enough, represents Caesar as emulous of Alexander and reproachful of himself for his slow progress to the same goal of dominion over the world ("Life of Julius Caesar," Bullough, V, 63). In *Caesar's Revenge*, much as in Lucan, when Caesar visits Alexander's tomb, the tomb itself is the subject of a moral: "Where he, whome all the world could not suffice,/ In bare six foote of Earth, intombed lies" (ed. F. S. Boas, Malone Society Reprints, Oxford, 1911).

24 Note I. ii. 172-75, II. i. 56-58, III. ii. 13 ff. (oration).

25 In rhetorical terms, by isocolon, parison, anaphora, epistrophe, and homoioteleuton—the so-called Gorgianic figures.

26 Cicero was particularly conscious of this irony: "O di boni! vivit tyrannis, tyrannus occidit!" ("O good gods! the tyranny lives, the tyrant is dead!" *Ad Atticum* xiv. 9; 17 April 44); the paradox is repeated, differently worded, in a letter to Cassius, 3 May 44 (*Epistolae ad familiares* xii. 1; quoted in Bullough, V, 6).

27 Cf. V. i. 73-75.
28 Plutarch leaves no unexplained contradiction (Bullough, V, 119-20); Brutus says that he stated the first opinion, on Cato's suicide, when he was young and inexperienced, but that now, being in the midst of danger, he is of a contrary mind.

"High events as these":
The Language of Hyperbole in Antony and Cleopatra

1 In *Miscellaneous Prose of Sir Philip Sidney,* ed. Katherine Duncan-Jones and Jan van Dorsten (Oxford, 1973), pp. 78-79.
2 *The Notebooks of Leonardo da Vinci,* trans. and ed. Edward MacCurdy (New York, 1938), II, 266.
3 *The Lives of the Noble Grecians and Romanes, . . .* Translated out of Greeke into French by James Amyot . . . and out of French into Englishe, by Thomas North (London, 1579), sig. * iij^v-iiij (the preface is not in Bullough).
4 Diomedes, *Ars grammatica* III. viii, ix, in *Comicorum graecorum fragmenta,* ed. G. Kaibel (Berlin, 1899), Vol. I, fasc. 1, pp. 57-58.
5 For sources consult Geoffrey Bullough's *Narrative and Dramatic Sources of Shakespeare* (London: Routledge and Kegan Paul; New York: Columbia University Press), Vol. V: *The Roman Plays* (1964), Part 2; also references as for *Julius Caesar,* p. 247, note 20, above.
6 As in Boccaccio's *L'amorosa visione,* lib. x, and *L'amorosa Fiammetta,* lib. vii; Chaucer's *Parliament of Fowls,* 288-92 (with Dido, Pyramus and Thisbe, etc.) and *Legend of Good Women,* Prologue, 259-60, Text F (also including Dido and Thisbe) and Legend I ("was nevere unto hire love a trewer quene"); Gower's *Confessio amantis* viii. 2571-82 (preceded by Dido, followed by Thisbe); Lydgate's *Flower of Courtesy,* 194-95. For further references, a sympathetic interpretation based on this tradition, and suggestions that Shakespeare made conscious use of the Dido legend throughout the play, see Donna B. Hamilton, "*Antony and Cleopatra* and the Tradition of Noble Lovers," *Shakespeare Quarterly* 24 (Summer 1973), 245-51.
7 "The assemble of Ladies," in *The workes of Geffray Chaucer* (ed. Wm. Thynne, 1532), fo. CC.xcvi^v (in *The Complete Works of Geoffrey Chaucer,* ed. Walter W. Skeat [Oxford],

Vol. VII [1897], no. xxi, p. 395); also in all sixteenth-century editions of Chaucer, including Speght's, 1598. Cf. Lydgate's "Floure of Curtesye" (also in Thynne's Chaucer, etc.; Skeat, Vol. VII, no. ix); the lady of the poem, who is being praised by comparison to famous ladies of the past, is like Cleopatra "inconstaunce eke and faythe" (Thynne, fo. CC.lxxxiiii; Skeat, p. 272).

8 *Amorous Fiammetta* . . . now done into English by B. Giouano (1587), sig. Hh1.

9 *The Arte of English Poesie* (1589), ed. Gladys Doidge Willcock and Alice Walker (Cambridge, 1936), pp. 191-92. Since Harry Levin's *The Overreacher: A Study of Christopher Marlowe* (Cambridge, Mass., 1952) no one is unaware of the importance of the trope in late sixteenth-century English poetry.

10 ". . . be copious in exclaims": the Duchess of York to Queen Elizabeth, mourning the deaths of the young princes, *Richard III*, IV. iv. 135.

11 "staunch . . . world, I," Evans (F1); following Pope, most editors read "staunch, . . . world I."

12 Evans, following F1; Cambridge editors, Kittredge, etc., following F2, read "Made the all-honor'd honest Roman, Brutus."

13 *smell* (F2); Evans, *smells* (F1).

14 One thinks of Horace's Cleopatra, who, seeking to die more nobly, was not, womanlike, terrified of the sword: "quae generosius/ perire quaerens nec muliebriter/ expavit ensem" (*Carmina* I. xxxvii); and who, deprived of her throne, scorned to be carried in foreign galleys to Caesar's proud triumph: "saevis Liburnis scilicet invidens/ privata deduci superbo/ non humilis mulier triumpho." No humble woman indeed!

15 *or* (F3); Evans, *nor* (F1).

"All's in anger":
The Language of Contention in Coriolanus

1 Antithesis in thought in Plutarch's Greek is not greatly exploited in the style. North, in English, conspicuously points up in the style the oppositions in thought at two places: one, Volumnia's speeches of appeal to Coriolanus to spare Rome; the other, following the Life, the comparison of Alcibiades and Coriolanus as opposites in their strengths and weaknesses. References to

North's Plutarch (1579) are, for convenience, to the text as reprinted in Geoffrey Bullough's *Narrative and Dramatic Sources of Shakespeare* (London: Routledge and Kegan Paul; New York: Columbia University Press), V: *The Roman Plays* (1964), 505-49; for Shakespeare's use of Plutarch and other sources, consult the introduction, pp. 453-95.

2 As Plutarch put it: "Martius stowtnes, and hawty stomake, did stay him from making much of those, that might advaunce and honour him: and yet his ambition made him gnawe him selfe for spite and anger, when he sawe he was despised" (Bullough, V, 549).

3 From Amyot's "voix"; Latin text, *suffragii;* Plutarch's Greek, ψῆφοι, *psephoi* (the pebbles dropped in the voting urn).

4 The examples are from the pseudo-Ciceronian *Rhetorica ad Herennium,* under *contentio,* I. xv. 21, xlv. 58; with the first cf. *Coriolanus,* I. i. 69; with the second, deliberately altered, II. iii. 91-92. Thomas Wilson's version of the second is "to his frend he is churlish, to his foe he is gentle" (*The Arte of Rhetorique* [1560], facsimile reprint by G. H. Mair [Oxford, 1909], p. 199). See also Quintilian, *Institutio oratoria* IX. iii. 81-86 (*antithesis, antitheton, contra positum*); George Puttenham, *The Arte of English Poesie* (1589), ed. Gladys Doidge Willcock and Alice Walker (Cambridge, 1936), pp. 210-11.

5 Example from John Hoskins, *Directions for Speech and Style,* ed. Hoyt H. Hudson (Princeton, 1935), p. 36; see Puttenham, pp. 206-7.

6 Puttenham, pp. 225-26; Henry Peacham, *The Garden of Eloquence* (1577), sig. Mii^v.

7 Puttenham's example, pp. 221-22; see *Rhet. ad Heren.* II. xxiv. 38 (*duplex conclusio*); Cicero, *De inventione* I. xxix. 44-45 (*complexio*).

8 Contrast King Richard's parallel series of antitheses: "I'll give my jewels for a set of beads," etc. (*Richard II,* III. iii. 147 ff.).

9 *Topica* xi. 47-49; the other forms of contraries given are opposites (*adversa*) of the same class (wisdom, folly), privatives (dignity, indignity), and negatives ("If this is so, that is not"). Comparison is also treated as a separate topic (xviii. 68).

10 Many of this sort in the play; cf. I. iii. 21-25; I. iv. 51-52; II. ii. 79-81, 86-87, 101, 110-11; III. iii. 42-43.

11 Quintilian, *Inst. orat.* VIII. iv. 9-14.

12 Cf. Quintilian (*Inst. orat.* VIII. vi. 67), who says that hyper-

bole serves equally well for either augmentation or attenuation ("ex diverso par augendi atque minuendi").

13 Puttenham, pp. 219-21; Peacham (1577 ed., sig. Niiij) puts uncomplimentary comparisons of men to animals (e.g., to call "a foolish man an Asse: a churle, a Hogge") under "Auxesis" rather than "Meiosis," with the idea that the comparison augments the bad quality.

14 See Maurice Charney, in *Shakespeare's Roman Plays* (Cambridge, Mass., 1961), pp. 163-76, on the dramatic effects of the animal imagery; a number of other images not touched on in my essay are similarly discussed.

15 With this distinction between the things of love and war, cf. I. vi. 29-32 and IV. v. 113-18, in which Coriolanus and Aufidius, respectively, fuse the joys of comradeship in war with those of the bridal night.

16 "a coverture," Tyrwhitt's emendation, followed by many editors; Evans (F1), "an overture." No one has been able to explain the Folio reading satisfactorily, not even in twelve pages of comment in the Furness Variorum; E. K. Chambers, in his comment, calls it the most difficult passage in the play.

17 "voices!"; Evans (F1), here and in passage following, punctuates "voices?"; but this may be only a compositor's substitution, one not infrequent in the Folio.

18 *roted,* Evans (F1 *roated*); *rooted,* Kittredge and most editors, following Boswell's suggestion.

19 Cf. Charney's long discussion of "Marcius' isolating pride," *Shakespeare's Roman Plays,* pp. 176-96. See also Plutarch's comments (Bullough, V, 519, 547) on Coriolanus' self-will, "which Plato called solitarines"; for the wilfully obstinate man remains "without companie, and forsaken of all men."

20 The discussion of the possible meanings of this passage occupies twenty-two pages of the Furness Variorum edition.

21 Cf. *Antony and Cleopatra,* I. iv. 42-47 ("he which is, was wish'd until he were . . .").

22 *founder,* Kittredge and most editors, following Dyce; Evans, *fouler* (F1).

23 Bullough, V, 541; the imaginative genesis of the play may lie here. Volumnia's speeches, also, in substance and style are very close to North's Plutarch, although, of course, with poetic heightening and new subtleties.

Appendix
Imagery in Richard II *and in* 1 Henry IV

1 See III. ii. 144-56; III. iii. 143-70; the speeches in the deposition scene, IV. i.

2 For other noteworthy examples of fully worked out images see the latter half of Bolingbroke's speech in III. iii (ll. 54-67), where he first compares the meeting of himself and Richard to the meeting of fire and water, and then compares Richard's appearance to that of the sun; also the Queen's and Bushy's talk about her premonition of sorrow (II. ii), where Bushy compares her emotionally distorted visions to the view of a "perspective," and where the comparison of her premonitions to a child she is about to be delivered of runs throughout the whole episode.

3 Similar extended similes in *Richard II* occur at II. ii. 16-24; III. ii. 8-11; IV. i. 184-89; V. i. 29-34; V. ii. 23-28.

4 (1) Prince Hal's soliloquy (I. ii. 208-15) and Glendower's courtly promise to Mortimer of a song from his daughter (III. i. 213-19); (2) Vernon's comparison of Prince Hal mounting his horse to Mercury or an angel mounting Pegasus, and Hotspur's comparison of the coming of the king's forces to sacrifices to the maid of war, etc. (IV. i. 104-10, 113-17).

5 See E. M. W. Tillyard's *Poetry Direct and Oblique* (London, 1934), Chap. IV, especially pp. 57-58, 60-62. [The definition is, of course, the standard rhetorical one: see *Rhetorica ad Herennium* IV. xxxiv. 46; Quintilian, *Institutio oratoria* VIII. vi. 44 ff.; Erasmus, *De copia* I. xviii; etc. Simply extended metaphors, or *allegoriae*, though not common in *1 Henry IV*, are not wholly absent: e.g., I. ii. 197-203.]

6 See *verge* and *waste*, examples of effective ambiguity, in II. i. 100-115.

7 Tillyard (*Poetry Direct and Oblique*, p. 124) uses these two terms in discussing Shirley's "The glories of our blood and state."

8 Other vividly imaginative passages in *Richard II* on this subject (only one, however, with the degree of fusion exhibited in the passage quoted) occur at III. iii. 42-48, 93-100, 161-63; IV. i. 137-44.

9 See Constance's speeches, especially the one on death, in III. iv; and Arthur's speech on the irons Hubert is heating, IV. i. 60-70.

10 *Poetry Direct and Oblique*, p. 244. It will be evident in this paper how much I owe to the rather pervasive influence in our time of I. A. Richards and William Empson. But I wish to acknowledge a more specific debt to Tillyard's profoundly stimulating book. Some of the terms I use (*directness, statement, obliquity*) will be recognized as coming from him. Since it is the point of view of the book as a whole that has been important to me, I have given references to particular pages only in a few instances.

11 [An oversimplified and perhaps misleading statement.]

DESIGNED BY ROBERT CHARLES SMITH
COMPOSED BY FOX VALLEY TYPESETTING, MENASHA, WISCONSIN
MANUFACTURED BY GEORGE BANTA COMPANY, INC., MENASHA, WISCONSIN
TEXT AND DISPLAY LINES ARE SET IN CALEDONIA

Library of Congress Cataloging in Publication Data
Doran, Madeleine, 1905-
Shakespeare's dramatic language.
Includes bibliographical references.
1. Shakespeare, William, 1564-1616—Style.
I. Title.
PR3072.D6   822.3′3   75-32072
ISBN 0-299-07010-7